British town planning: the formative years

Themes in Urban History

General editor: Derek Fraser

British town planning: the formative years

edited by ANTHONY SUTCLIFFE

Leicester University Press St Martin's Press 1981

First published in 1981 by Leicester University Press
First published in the United States of America by St Martin's Press Inc.
For information write: St Martin's Press Inc., 175 Fifth Ave, New York, N.Y. 10010

Designed by Arthur Lockwood
Photoset, printed and bound in Great Britain by
REDWOOD BURN LIMITED
Trowbridge, Wiltshire

British Library Cataloguing in Publication Data
British town planning – (Themes in urban history)
  1. Cities and towns – Planning – History
  I. Sutcliffe, Anthony   II. Series
  711′.4′0941   HT169.G7
ISBN 0 7185 1174 3

Library of Congress Card Catalog Number 81–51916
ISBN 0–312–10545–2

FOREWORD

Urban history is an expanding field of study, sustained by a considerable volume of research. The purpose of this series, originally conceived by the late Jim Dyos, is to open a new channel for the dissemination of the findings of a careful selection from that research, providing a conspectus of new knowledge on specific themes.

For each volume in the series, each of the contributors is invited to present the core of his work: the essays, originating in theses but now specially written for this volume, are combined under the control of the editor, who writes an introduction setting out the significance of the material being presented in the light of developments in that or a cognate field.

It is hoped that in this way the fruits of recent work may be made widely available, both to assist further exploration and to contribute to the teaching of urban history.

In this, the first volume in the series, Tony Sutcliffe has gathered together contributions from the academic areas of economic and social history, architecture and town planning. The fusion of historical research deriving from these complementary fields illuminates the inter-disciplinary nature of urban history and elucidates the genesis, character and significance of town planning in Great Britain in the period 1880–1914.

Derek Fraser
University of Bradford

EDITOR'S PREFACE

This book is the product of two years of meetings, correspondence, and writing. When it was first mooted, the idea of combining three or four condensed versions of recent theses in one volume seemed simple enough. This is not the place to go into the problems which it raised in practice, but I would like to take this opportunity of thanking the contributors for their patience, co-operation, and enthusiasm. We have enjoyed the experience, or most of it, and we have learned a great deal from one another about our mutual field of interest, the origins of British town planning. We would recommend this method to others, but they should not expect quick results.

Martin Hawtree wishes to thank the editors of the *Town Planning Review* for their permission to reproduce photographs of plans of Knebworth and Alkrington by Thomas Adams, and of Glyn-Cory by Mawson and Adams. I am grateful to Beryl Moore for her careful typing of parts of the manuscript, and to Derek Fraser for his good-humoured understanding. My main debt, however, is to the late H.J. Dyos for the idea of this series.

A.S.
July 1980

CONTENTS

LIST OF ILLUSTRATIONS

LIST OF TABLES

ABBREVIATIONS

Note Places of publication are given only for works published outside the United Kingdom. In abbreviating less frequently cited periodical titles, commonly accepted abbreviations such as *J.* for *Journal, Rev.* for *Review* have been used; other abbreviations are listed below.

ACR	*Architect and Contract Reporter*
AR	*Architectural Review*
BA	*British Architect*
BN	*Building News*
CN	*Co-operative News*
GC	*The Garden City*
HC	Hitchcock Collection
ILP	Independent Labour Party
IR	*Independent Review*
JRIBA	*Journal of the Royal Institute of British Architects*
LCP	*Labour Co-Partnership*
MCN	*Manchester City News*
MCP	Manchester Council Proceedings
MG	*Manchester Guardian*
MOH	*Annual Reports of Medical Officer of Health*
MPL	Manchester Public Libraries, Central Reference Library
MSS	Manchester Statistical Society
MSSA	Manchester and Salford Sanitary Association
NAPSS	National Association for the Promotion of Social Science
NLS	National Library of Scotland
QR	*Quarterly Review*
RIBA	Royal Institute of British Architects
RPL	Rochdale Public Libraries, Central Reference Library
SC	*Sunday Chronicle*
TPR	*Town Planning Review*

NOTES ON THE CONTRIBUTORS

MICHAEL DAY graduated in Town and Country Planning from the University of Manchester. After completing the M.A. thesis on which his contribution to this volume is based, he worked in private practice before joining the London Borough of Havering, where he is now a Principal Planning Officer. He has published articles on planning history in *Town and Country Planning* and *Northern Architect*.

MARTIN GASKELL read History at Cambridge. His essay here is based on the Ph.D. thesis which he presented in the Department of Economic History, University of Sheffield, in 1974. In 1981 he took up the post of Assistant Principal of the City of Liverpool College of Higher Education. He has published widely on housing and planning history in a variety of journals and collective volumes.

MICHAEL HARRISON was educated at the Universities of Leicester, Leeds and Manchester. He is currently Lecturer in Complementary Studies at Birmingham Polytechnic, and is completing his Ph.D. on T.C. Horsfall and social reform in Manchester.

MARTIN HAWTREE read History and English at the University of East Anglia. He went on to complete a postgraduate degree in Town Planning at Liverpool University, and later submitted there the Ph.D. thesis which is presented here in abbreviated form. Since 1973 he has worked in his long-established family practice as a landscape architect, specializing in the design of golf courses.

Introduction:
British town planning
and the historian

ANTHONY SUTCLIFFE

Introduction:
British town planning
and the historian

ANTHONY SUTCLIFFE

Town planning in Britain: its origins and growth

Town planning is now so firmly rooted in British public administration that it has generated a myth of super-competence. 'Planners' are popularly blamed for a range of urban shortcomings which extends far beyond their actual sphere of activity.[1] To arraign the town planner for unemptied dustbins or poor television reception is doubtless a disguised tribute, but such misconceptions make it all the more important to clarify what town planning really means.

Town planning is the concerted intervention by public authority in the development and subsequent use of urban land. The intervention takes positive and negative forms. Positively, the planning authority draws up a programme of development for publicly-provided facilities such as thoroughfares, sewers, and water supplies. Negatively, it imposes restrictions on the development and use of private land, in such forms as use zoning, density limits, reservations of open space, and wayleaves for privately-provided facilities. Both modes of intervention are based, on the one hand, on a scientific analysis of the urban area's current condition and future prospects, and on the other, on certain standards of environment and amenity which are considered essential or desirable for the effective operation of the area as an economic and social unit. Thus carefully interrelated, both modes are incorporated into a single programme or plan.

Clearly, town planning requires the expenditure of public funds and the restriction of individual freedom. These intrusions on liberty have been successfully justified to the legislative authority which has permitted them on the ground that if the process of town-building were left entirely to the private market, certain facilities would be supplied to a harmfully low standard or not at all, while private land would be so misused that not only the interests of the community, but even those of the individual owners, would suffer.

Town planning, thus defined, is a very recent development. The very expression 'town planning' was coined as late as 1905, apparently by the Birmingham city councillor John Sutton Nettlefold.[2] The planning control of all new building development, which we now accept as normal, was not fully established until the Town and Country Planning Act of 1947. Admittedly, it can be shown that public authority has intervened in urban development to some degree for thousands of years,[3] but it was not until the end of the nineteenth century that the idea emerged of a single, comprehensive strategy of intervention. The question of how and why it emerged at that time – so late in the history of urban development – constitutes a fascinating historical problem.

Although it is possible to view the rise of town planning as an adjunct of general social progress, it is more tempting to regard it as a response to the special problems generated by rapid urban growth and change during industrialization. At the root of these problems lies the competition which is inseparable from urban life. The physical development of towns is the product of a conflict between a variety of interests (principally commerce, industry, transport, administration, and labour). These interests compete, first of all, to secure a place in the town, and subsequently to obtain advantageous positions within it. From this competition there normally results *change,* in the form of the growth (or perhaps the decline) of the town as a whole, and adjustments of its internal physical structure. These changes tend to modify the relationships between the competing interests, generating new conflicts and effacing old ones. The town thus exists in a constant state of tension.

But why is the town so attractive in the first place? The simple answer is that it is easier, as a rule, to make money there, in every form of productive activity except agriculture, forestry and the extractive industries, than it is in the countryside. Public administration too, even of rural areas, is easier to carry out from an urban base. Finally, amusement is often easier to procure in the town than in the country. Towns have always enjoyed these advantages, but until industrialization they were able to support only a small minority of the total population. This limited role was the result of low productivity in manufacturing and agriculture, which held back the towns' capacity to buy food, and that of the countryside to supply it.

Industrialization greatly enhanced the relative advantages of the town. In Britain, urban capital formation started to accelerate from the later eighteenth century and the rural population began to flock into the towns to take up the attractive employments which they increasingly offered.[4] By 1900, four Britons out of five were town-dwellers, compared to one in four two centuries earlier.[5] This growth in urban productivity, and the resulting growth in the size of towns, sharpened the conflict between competing interests, because the economic resources on which they could draw to support their claims for urban space were now so much greater than before industrialization.

In the late eighteenth and early nineteenth centuries it came to be widely acknowledged in Britain that these wealth-creating forces of industrialization had been unleashed by allowing free play to the mechanisms of the market. On this premiss, a case could be made for allowing market forces to shape the towns. After all, how better to order a town than to allow the competing interests to *bid* for space? The market would allow the most productive elements to secure the land that they needed to operate most efficiently, thus maximizing the income of the whole town. Indeed, if some elements failed to compete and were expelled altogether, then so much the better for the town as a whole.

There were three main objections to this argument. First, it was difficult if not impossible to secure the provision of certain facilities, essential to the town's well-being, through the private market. The most important of these facilities were thoroughfares and main drainage. Second, in the constricted space of the town, the market often palpably failed to secure a satisfactory physical arrangement of functions. Noxious or noisy industries and uses incorporating high risks of fire or explosion could, through the market, secure positions in the town where, in social terms, the benefits which they brought their owners were outweighed by the harm which they did to other productive functions. In theory, the market would in time adjust to their presence, but growing experience of the industrial town revealed that the adjustment process was usually a painfully long one, because the heavy initial investment in buildings slowed down changes in land use. Third, the weakest bidder in the urban market, labour, did very badly in terms of the location and quantity of the land it could secure to reside upon. This poor start compounded labour's difficulties in securing an adequate supply of residential buildings, and the resulting poor environment, which was associated with a high incidence of disease and death, came to be seen as detracting from the efficiency of the urban economy and as a threat to the physical well-being, political security and peace of mind of urban owners and the prosperous professional classes who served them.

From around the middle of the eighteenth century there thus sprang up a sometimes explicit, sometimes tacit, debate between the advocates of the free-market development of towns, and those who favoured public intervention to regulate the market or supply its deficiencies. The interventionists tended to gain ground as time went on. Until the 1840s the pace of public intervention was set by the improvement commissions, hundreds of which were established from the mid-eighteenth century to act in various ways to improve the physical environment of towns.[6] After the Municipal Reform Act of 1835, however, the elected municipalities, encouraged by Parliament, began to take over from the more specialized authorities. By the early 1870s municipal responsibility for the urban environment had been confirmed and from then until the First World War that responsibility tended to be exercised in an increasingly ambitious way. By the early 1900s the expression 'municipal socialism' was in wide use as a tribute, albeit sometimes a grudging one, to the scale and range of local government activities in the towns, most of which sought to regulate or improve the physical environment.

As the nineteenth century wore on, the positive and negative modes of intervention outlined earlier in this introduction tended to develop in parallel. By 1900 municipally-provided facilities extended far beyond streets and sewers; in many towns, and especially the larger ones, they included water, gas, electricity and public street transport. All but the smallest towns regulated new construction by an intricate code of building regulations which sought to secure minimum standards of public health and amenity, as well as the fire safety which had been almost the sole concern of building regulations in the eighteenth and early nineteenth centuries.[7] In addition, noxious and dangerous industries were carefully regulated or restricted to certain districts of the towns.

Whether this growing public involvement in the town-building process was principally a response to enhanced expectations or to growing problems, we can see, with the benefit of hindsight, that in due course it was bound to generate an awareness that the positive and negative modes could usefully be combined in a single strategy. Indeed, it is not without significance that this awareness, in the form of the town planning idea, emerged in the early 1900s, the heyday of municipal socialism. However, the precise source (or sources) of inspiration remain a matter of debate, as do the processes by which the idea came to command sufficiently wide acceptance in Britain to justify the creation of statutory town-planning powers in 1909. We shall return to these questions, so suffice it to say here that the Housing, Town Planning, Etc. Act of 1909, though a timid measure, laid the foundations of British town-planning activity by allowing urban authorities to draw up rudimentary building and land-use plans for peripheral areas about to be, or in the process of being, developed.

Though most municipalities at first showed no interest in using the new powers, enough experimental planning schemes had been started by 1914 to show that town planning made sense and could (though with very great difficulty) be put into effect. Meanwhile, a professional organization, the Town Planning Institute, had been set up in 1913. The First World War removed many remaining doubts about the desirability of public intervention in the free market and, with a big programme of public housing required to overcome the wartime building backlog, the Housing, Town Planning, Etc. Act of 1919 made town planning a statutory duty of all urban authorities. Subsequent legislation, most notably the 1932 Town and Country Planning Act, extended the scope of planning to cover established built-up areas. Serious practical and legal problems remained, however, and it was not until a new war had again concentrated the public and official minds on the proper scope of public activity that really effective planning powers were created by the 1947 Act.

The post-war history of British town planning is a mixture of success and failure, but the value of planning has never seriously been questioned. Planning has permitted the execution of a programme of new towns without rival in the world, while the planning authorities have supervised a massive programme of slum clearance and urban renewal which in scale and ambition has also outshone anything achieved elsewhere. Since 1945 a wide range of specialisms have reached maturity within the corps of town planners – transport planning, conservation, development control, and recreation planning are just a few of them. Finally, town planning has generated a growing number of people who are interested in its history.

The historiography of British planning

Until British planning reached its apotheosis in the New Towns Act of 1946 and the Town and Country Planning Act of the following year, its history had aroused little interest. Practising planners were acutely aware of the progress that had been made since the early part of the century, and some of their didactic publications included personal reminiscences or historical surveys.[8] However, most of these contributions had lacked either objectivity or full historical awareness. In terms of historiographical development the 1947 Act was of crucial importance, for it suggested that a long process of evolution towards effective town planning had come to a successful conclusion. The history of planning now began to figure more prominently in the textbooks,[9] while British town planning was allotted a more important place in general histories of urban design and policy.[10] However, the most important result of the 1947 Act was to suggest to a research student at the London School of Economics, William Ashworth, that the evolution of British town planning would provide a stimulating topic for a Ph.D. thesis. That post-war generation of young economic and social historians at the LSE produced a whole library of influential books, but few made a stronger impact than the volume which Ashworth published in 1954 on the basis of his Ph.D. thesis, completed in 1951. *The Genesis of Modern British Town Planning* set the bounds of a debate which has dominated British planning historiography ever since.

Ashworth's argument is too rich to be summarized adequately here. Essentially, he saw town planning as the product of a cumulative public intervention in the British urban environment which had begun in earnest during the public health scare of the 1830s and 1840s. However, he allotted an important exemplary role to private initiatives such as model factory communities and planned suburbs. These practical examples, combined with a growing recognition of the importance of the environment, allowed the last leap to be made towards town planning in the early 1900s. Thereafter, Ashworth's analysis loses some of its bite, but he brings the reader up to 1947 via a series of parliamentary debates and enactments.

Ashworth's interpretation of the rise of planning before 1914 was so convincing that most of the work on nineteenth-century developments, which multiplied from the later 1950s, concentrated on adding detail and depth to his account. The study of public health and that of public administration ('the nineteenth-century revolution in government') developed so strongly that they largely broke away from the history of planning, but the enlightenment secured in these areas increasingly informed the study of urban policy. Meanwhile, city centre reconstruction[11] and the design of residential areas and communities[12] attracted much attention from urban historians. In this latter area much interest was shown, especially by historians of architecture and of ideas, in the creation of artistic or theoretical models of totally planned environments and their associated communal institutions. The study of this idealist or 'utopian' tradition sometimes threatened to swamp the history of more mundane efforts to improve existing towns, but it threw much light on the ideals which inspired many participants in the urban and social reform movements.[13]

Furthermore, the culmination of the 'utopian' tradition in Ebenezer Howard's garden city proposal of 1898 allowed planning historians to establish a direct link between the nineteenth century and the important idealist strand in twentieth-century planning. Amidst a plethora of publications on Howard and the garden city,[14] the crucial inter-century connection was established by Walter Creese's influential *The Search for Environment: the garden city before and after* (1966). Indeed, Creese did even more than this. As a widely-read and perceptive architectural historian, he demonstrated the full potential of the design approach to the history of British planning. Establishing for the first time a clear alternative to the Ashworth tradition, he helped encourage the appearance of a number of similar design-oriented studies from the late 1960s.[15]

Whether or not they saw idealism as the key to planning, the historians of design and ideas naturally placed more emphasis on the individual than did those who worked within the socio-administrative tradition of Ashworth and his school. Publications on various founding fathers of British planning had been appearing since the inter-war years, but from the 1950s their generally hagiographical tone was largely replaced by a more objective assessment and more thorough work in the sources. In terms of quantity Patrick Geddes[16] easily heads the list, but Thomas Adams,[17] T.C. Horsfall,[18] and Raymond Unwin,[19] in addition to Howard, have all stimulated valuable work. Of these, it is perhaps Raymond Unwin's star, first noted by Walter Creese, which shines the most brightly. The weakness of the biographical approach is that the all-important urban context of individual action is sometimes ignored, but the results so far have been extremely enlightening and promise to be even more so in the future as more private papers are uncovered.

The history of planning after 1914 remains under-investigated, partly owing to the inaccessibility of sources, but since about 1970 an important shift towards the twentieth century has occurred in the balance of published work. Much of this new interest has been centred on the expanding practice of statutory planning, and on the growth of the planning profession. Outstanding in these areas has been the work of Gordon Cherry, a qualified and experienced local-government planner, who in the last decade has produced a spate of publications on planning history.[20] Meanwhile, the growth in the number of monitoring exercises has produced much work of historical value.[21] An important series of official histories of planning since the Second World War has been inaugurated.[22] Indeed, this growing interest in the twentieth century helped bring about the foundation, in 1974, of the Planning History Group, a loosely-organized association of scholars and planners interested in the development of modern planning. By the end of the decade the Group was publishing a regular newsletter, the *Planning History Bulletin,* and seeking to encourage both the conservation of planning archives and the launching of new initiatives in research.

The essays in this volume

The four studies presented below focus on the crucial formative period of British town planning, between about 1880 and 1920. They lie well within the historiographical tradition outlined above, but each is representative of one or more distinct tendencies within that tradition.

Martin Gaskell's discussion of the links between town planning and the much older movement of housing reform is much in sympathy with the work of Ashworth, but it is overlain by an interest in design which brings him close to the mode established by Creese and Tarn. An economic and social historian by training, he is particularly interested in planning's roots in the housing and land markets, and in estate administration. As such he is able to draw on the extensive work on the history of working-class and middle-class housing which has appeared in recent years (and to which he has himself contributed).[23]

Martin Hawtree, a qualified architect, approaches the birth of the town-planning profession very much from the standpoint of an architectural historian. Although, like Gordon Cherry, he sees the foundation of the Town Planning Institute as an important step towards the professionalization of planning practice, he is interested primarily in the individual practising planners who had emerged before 1913, and who to a large extent transmitted their own personal ideals to the planning profession. This interest in the lone artist and technician has always been a feature of architectural history.

Michael Day's standpoint has much in common with Hawtree's. A qualified planner who now works in a local authority, Day wrote his thesis as just a part-requirement for a Master's degree in planning. Having selected an apparently precise aspect of the work of the most influential partnership in early British planning, Day found that it was impossible to understand the site planning of Parker and Unwin without situating it in a full analysis of their careers, and particularly that of Unwin. This inquiry soon took him back to Unwin's early socialist years in Manchester, and forward to his period as a respected government housing adviser during and after the First World War. He thus found himself echoing and amplifying the work of Creese, who had lighted on Unwin as the key to the whole course of British planning history. Thus two out of the four studies, though for different reasons, are built around personalities.

In Harrison's contribution, finally, we find an amalgam of the tendencies and motivations identified so far. Like Day, Harrison trained as a planner, but his interests took a more academic turn. He obtained his Master's degree entirely by research and now teaches in a school of planning. His work has some similarity to Gaskell's (indeed, they literally cover some of the same ground). However, in selecting Manchester housing reform for detailed analysis, Harrison soon came across another influential individual, the social reformer, T.C. Horsfall. Horsfall had no contribution to make to urban design, but between the late 1890s and about 1905 he was more aware than anyone else in Britain of the achievements, and potential lessons, of German urban planning. His energy and forcefulness invigorated local urban initiatives in Manchester as effectively as they did the British planning movement as a whole. Nevertheless, Horsfall is only one element of Harrison's analysis, and in his careful studies of a number of planned communities in Manchester we can appreciate the combinations of factors which began to shape the peripheral districts of Britain's towns as the new century advanced. Indeed, this comprehensive quality in Harrison's work brings us back to the Ashworth tradition.

Although these four essays complement, rather than contradict, one another, their juxtaposition brings out very clearly some of the important historiographical issues of the foundation period of British planning. The issues fall into three main groups: the *genesis* of planning, its early *character*, and its long-term *significance*. Let us look at each of these groups in turn.

By no means all the possible interpretations of the genesis of town planning appear in this collection, but we are offered a rich choice nevertheless. At one extreme, we have the suggestion that planning was broadly generated by the urban condition. Martin Gaskell, with his emphasis on the link between planning and housing reform, is the outstanding advocate of this interpretation (though his model incorporates other causative factors). Gaskell stresses that housing reform reflected the nature of housing itself; in other words, town planning emerged from the reality of the physical environment created by the British Industrial Revolution. Indeed, he goes one step further, pointing out that there can be no housing without *land*. Land ownership, land law, land economics, and land policy are therefore fundamental to town planning. Gaskell's emphasis on land and building also contributes to his deliberate decision to investigate the roots of planning in the North, rather than in London. In this he is supported by Harrison, who narrows his focus even more, to Manchester alone, in order to detect the local reality from which planning sprang. Neither of the other two contributors, however, is interested in local influences. For them, planning is a concept, created by outstanding intellectuals, artists or technicians.

All the authors would, nevertheless, agree with Gaskell on the centrality of land development to the formulation of the idea and practice of planning. All, moreover, acknowledge the important contribution of the planned estate developments of the co-operative housing movement, in its turn-of-the-century guise of Co-partnership Tenants. They thus provide an important corrective to the common tendency to attribute a paramount influence to the planned housing schemes of enlightened employers. The importance of the co-partnership housing schemes lies in their incorporation, in microcosm, of many of the fundamental ideals of the early planning movement – low densities, self-help, mixing of social classes, and a strong community spirit. In these essays we see how many of the early planners gained essential experience by working on co-partnership schemes.

If co-partnership housing figures prominently in these essays, then what of that frequently-hailed paradigm of the planned urban environment, Ebenezer Howard's garden city? In a sense, there is not necessarily a contradiction between the two, as co-partnership housing was incorporated into Letchworth from the start. However, that there was a tension between Howard's ideal of completely new 'social cities', and the planned suburban extensions of existing towns which most co-partnership schemes inevitably were, is revealed by the internal debates of the Garden City Association between about 1901 and 1907. Martin Gaskell attributes more importance than any other contributor (except perhaps Michael Day) to the garden city idea, but he recognizes it as an inspiring vision which, outside Letchworth, had in practice to be diluted into development 'on garden city lines'. Michael Day demonstrates the importance to Parker and Unwin of their Letchworth experience, and the outstanding, prophetic quality of the planning they carried out there. Parker, indeed, chose to devote himself to Letchworth, but his career suffered in consequence. It was Unwin, who left Letchworth for Hampstead Garden Suburb and other triumphs, who was able to shape the course of British statutory planning. Thomas Adams, too, as Martin Hawtree shows, had to leave Letchworth and renounce the pure milk of garden city theory in order to maintain his momentum as a burgeoning planner.

Though Ebenezer Howard and his ideas suffer a degree of effacement in these pages, idealism in general remains prominent. Michael Day does most to keep it alive by his presentation of Raymond Unwin as an influential visionary. More than just a versatile architect and housing expert, Unwin emerges as an ambitious reformer for whom urban planning was just one facet of a general reconstruction of society on socialistic lines. Indeed, Unwin may well be linked more closely than Howard to the mainstream of nineteenth-century idealism. Howard's main reference point was the minority interest of land reform which Henry George helped to revive from around 1880. Unwin, on the other hand, was linked through Edward Carpenter and the Barnetts to Morris, Ruskin, Christian Socialism and the new brands of Marxist-inspired socialism which flourished from the 1880s. Howard's guiding ideal was co-operation, but Unwin's view of the world had plenty of room for State socialism. Thus his growing involvement in municipal housing was not a betrayal; on the contrary, it allowed him to operate more effectively as a town planner after 1918 when the planning of private housing was generally of such a disappointing quality. Even after his transformation into a civil servant, Day maintains, Unwin retained his socialist vision and it provided the principal impetus to the whole of his career.

The enhancement of Raymond Unwin's reputation certainly does no harm to the view that planning was shaped by influential individuals. Indeed, Martin Hawtree argues that a number of influential planners, some of them unqualified in any of the professions or disciplines related to planning, did more to establish it than the architects, engineers and surveyors who, backed by formal professional organizations, had dominated land development and building before the planners appeared. Even Harrison identifies an important moulder of opinion and practice in yet another unqualified reformer, T. C. Horsfall. No doubt scope exists for a re-incorporation of these individuals into a more impersonal model of causation, and indeed Gaskell and Harrison suggest how this might be done. However, in the absence of perspectives broader than those adopted here, a successful conclusion seems a long way off. We shall return to this point below.

The question of the *character* of early town planning is addressed most directly by Hawtree. His main thesis is that planning, from the start, was an amalgam of ideas complicated by the conflicting ambitions of the interested professions. He sees the foundation of the Town Planning Institute as a brilliant compromise dreamed up by one of his most influential (and least qualified) founding fathers, Thomas Adams. Hawtree brings out very well the apparent convergence on statutory town planning of various approaches to the urban environment developed independently by a number of brilliant individuals. In this way he rightly leads us to ask whether there ever was a town planning *movement* as such. Of course, his argument can have two implications; on the one hand, it can suggest that a few leading individuals were the only true planners. On the other, it could convince those sceptical of the individual interpretation that planning emerged as a recognized approach to the urban problem only because the Liberal administration's decision to extend the participation of local authorities in urban land development produced an artificial closing of the ranks among interested parties. Anyone who drew this latter conclusion from Hawtree's work would have to turn to the political forces (and their economic and social context) which shaped the Government's legislative programme, and this would again force the individuals into the background.

Whichever conclusion one draws on this point, Hawtree's essay suggests more brutally than any of the others that town planning did not have a great deal of potential to change the urban environment, let alone contribute to a general reconstruction of society. In addition to its doubts, areas of ignorance and internal tensions, it remained, in the period studied here, largely restricted to residential development. There was little consideration before 1920 of the problems of betterment, industrial planning or full, city-wide planning. There was a general failure, as Martin Gaskell points out, to recognize the dangers of sprawl inherent in the low density ideal. The slow progress of urban planning in Britain between the wars may thus be attributed partially to a very poor start. This ground was made up after 1940 but much time had been lost.

While defects of planning technique could be corrected in time, fundamental conceptual weaknesses could detract from the significance of town planning indefinitely. In the formative years of planning at least three-quarters of Britain's population was composed of manual workers and their families. This majority's almost complete indifference to town planning cannot be ignored. Hawtree, unintentionally perhaps, portrays town planning as a middle-class, technical activity which looks back to nineteenth-century traditions of improvement. Harrison and Gaskell strive admirably to detect and measure working-class interest and participation in town planning, but even Harrison, in a thorough investigation of a leading industrial city, can find very little of it. Interestingly, Gaskell is prepared to accept that, at Fairfield at any rate, the majority of houses were planned for workers, but Harrison is able to show that, even there, working-class residents were in a small minority. On the contrary, Harrison demonstrates how far the planned garden suburbs, like Letchworth itself, were centres of faddism. Such tight, claustrophobic communities must surely have discouraged all but the most aspiring or deferential of working men. Even Michael Day, convincing in his assertion of Unwin's socialism, never faces the problem of why the main beneficiaries of socialism showed so little interest in planning.

A really convincing, all-embracing theory of environmental planning as a means of social reform ought to have enthused the working classes. Ebenezer Howard's garden city idea was sufficiently comprehensive, but it was not convincing enough to draw British society into a very costly and disruptive reconstruction of its entire urban system. Raymond Unwin, his eyes on more immediate concerns, never tried to elaborate such a theory. Thomas Adams was even more preoccupied with technical matters. This left the task entirely to Patrick Geddes, who took it up with gusto and made a complete hash of it. The resulting vacuum helped to allow the Garden Cities and Town Planning Association (later, Town and Country Planning Association), the heir to Howard's ideas, to play such an influential role between the wars, and in Patrick Abercrombie British planning at last produced a planner-theorist who had, and could convey, a general grasp of what town planning could do for society as a whole. Indeed, in the 1940s mass interest in town planning at last developed, in step with this new competence. In the 1960s and 1970s, however, the emergence of internal doubts coincided with a new loss of public respect. This chequered career might suggest a permanent uncertainty stemming from those early days in which the role, scope and objectives of town planning were never convincingly established. The formative years would thus contain the seeds of planning's current malaise. Indeed, taken together, this is precisely the conclusion that these four essays suggest.

A future for planning history

Planning historians will no doubt come to focus increasingly on the twentieth-century practice, and the associated theory, of statutory planning. However, these four essays demonstrate the continuing interest of the formative years. They also suggest, either positively or negatively, certain refinements of concept and methodology which will help those studying more recent periods.

First of all, the essays indicate how much enlightenment can be drawn from the increasingly intricate and detailed research which is now coming to mark planning historiography. All four draw on previously unused or even undiscovered sources. In their unearthing of key documentary materials these authors are representative of the whole school of planning historians. Individual efforts will no doubt continue to be the most productive, but the Planning History Group is already working on a number of fronts to safeguard or create planning history archives. Meanwhile, the growing involvement of fully-trained historians in planning history is raising the whole standard of research in the field. On the other hand, these essays demonstrate that the perceptions of trained architects and planners are essential to the development of a full historical understanding. On the evidence presented below, planning historiography merits the growing respect which it is acquiring within the historical sciences. Moreover, it is clear that growing technical sophistication can reinforce its relevance to planning issues in our own day. Competence and objectivity, in this as in other fields, secure their just reward.

At the same time, these essays suggest that more progress could usefully be made in the creation of a broader context for the study of planning history. Their anglocentricity is, of course, perfectly justified by the theme of the volume. However, just as our early planning pioneers drew much of their inspiration from outside Britain, we would now do well to pay attention to some of the ways in which planning history is studied abroad. Two major alternative approaches are available: the Marxist mode of analysis which dominates the continent of Europe, and the functional mode which characterizes much North American work. For the Marxist, planning is not a progressive force but just one of a number of activities designed to shore up the State in the interests of its creator, the bourgeoisie. This approach allows urban planning to be incorporated more fully into the history of general State activity, on the one hand, and into the processes of economic and social change, on the other. On this definition, planning can be detected much earlier in the nineteenth century than British orthodoxy normally allows, and a much stronger continuity is established between the nineteenth and twentieth centuries. Moreover, the Marxist interpretation makes the recurring disillusionment with planning much easier to explain.[24]

The North American alternative to the Marxist approach can best be described as functionalism. According to this view, planning is a residual activity undertaken by public authority in order to achieve what cannot be done in cheaper, more individualistic ways. It thus has no distinctive capacity to promote social progress or human happiness. This interpretation, too, allows extensive planning activity to be detected in the nineteenth century, well in advance of the formulation of a fully-fledged concept of 'city planning'. Moreover, like the Marxist approach, it evens out the oscillations between periods of euphoria and periods of disillusionment which loom so large in the orthodox British view of planning history. It roots the growth of planning in urban needs and realities, and plays down the role of individual leaders.[25]

Time alone will tell whether British planning historiography can respond to these and other new approaches. Marxist interpretations of episodes in British planning have already been set before the Planning History Group, and functionalism is beginning to make an appearance there.[26] Meanwhile, the essays in this volume provide an earnest of much vital new work in preparation. If British planning history, at the very least, can remain an area of keen debate, it can scarcely fail to evolve.

NOTES

1 See the occasional column, 'Planner-bashing', in the weekly publication *Planning*. It contains a rich selection of newspaper and magazine cuttings in which 'planners' are reviled.

2 T. Adams, *Recent Advances in Town Planning* (1932), 45; J.P. Reynolds, 'Thomas Coglan Horsfall and the town planning movement in England', *TPR*, xxiii (1952–3), 58; M.G. Hawtree, 'The origins of the modern town planner: a study in professional ideology' (Ph.D. thesis, University of Liverpool, 1974), 26.

3 See e.g. P. Lavedan and J. Hugueney, *Histoire de l'urbanisme: antiquité* (Paris, 1966); M. Morini, *Atlante di storia dell'urbanistica* (1963).

4 For a recent discussion of urban growth in the early industrialization period, see C. W. Chalklin, *The Provincial Towns of Georgian England: a study of the building process, 1740–1820* (1974), 4–54.

5 The most authoritative figures for the end of the nineteenth century, based on a reworking of the census, are provided by C.M. Law, 'The growth of urban population in England

and Wales, 1801–1911', *Inst. British Geographers Trans.*, XLI (1967), 125–44. The size of the urban population before 1700 is discussed in B.A. Holderness, *Pre-Industrial England: economy and society, 1500–1750* (1976), 15.

6 The fullest account is still Sidney and Beatrice Webb, *English Local Government: statutory authorities for special purposes* (1922).

7 The main authority is now R.H. Harper, 'The evolution of the English building regulations 1840–1914' (Ph.D. thesis, University of Sheffield, 1978).

8 See e.g. Adams, *op. cit.;* G. and E.G. McAllister, *Town and Country Planning* (1941).

9 See e.g. M.P. Fogarty, *Town and Country Planning* (1948); J.W.R. Adams, *Modern Town and Country Planning: a history of and introduction to the study of the law and practice of modern town and country planning in Great Britain* (1952).

10 See e.g. C. Stewart, *A Prospect of Cities, Being Studies Towards a History of Town Planning* (1952); P. Lavedan, *Histoire de l'urbanisme: époque contemporaine* (Paris, 1952).

11 See e.g. H.J. Dyos, 'Urban transformation: a note on the objects of street improvements in Regency and Early Victorian London', *International Rev. of Social Hist.*, II (1957), 259–65; C.M. Allan, 'The genesis of British urban redevelopment with special reference to Glasgow', *Economic Hist. Rev.*, 2nd ser., XVIII (1965), 598–613.

12 Ashworth himself gave a lead with his 'British industrial villages in the nineteenth century', *Economic Hist. Rev.*, 2nd ser. III (1951), 378–95. For the most famous of these villages, see R.K. Dewhirst, 'Saltaire', *TPR*, XXXI (1960–1), 135–44. J.N. Tarn, 'The model village at Bromborough Pool', *TPR*, XXXV (1965), 329–36, studies a more obscure example. For the influential experiments of the later nineteenth and early twentieth centuries, see J. Reynolds, 'The model village of Port Sunlight', *Architects' J.*, CVII (1948), 492–6; *One Man's Vision: The Story of the Joseph Rowntree Village Trust* (1954); Bournville Village Trust, *The Bournville Village Trust, 1900–1955* (1955); F.M.L. Thompson, *Hampstead: building a borough, 1650–1954* (1976); B. Grafton Green, *Hampstead Garden Suburb, 1907–1977* (1977).

13 The extreme view that 'utopian' planning was the only type of planning worth studying was advanced by Leonardo Benevolo, *The Origins of Modern Planning* (1967). The fundamental distinction between idealistic planning and the adjustment of existing towns has been developed to its fullest by F. Choay, *L'urbanisme: utopies et réalités* (Paris, 1965) and *The Modern City: planning in the nineteenth-century* (1970). Outstanding among the studies devoted to British urban idealism are: W.H.G. Armytage, *Heavens Below: utopian experiments in England, 1560–1960* (1961); A. Haworth, 'Planning and philosophy: the case of Owenism and the Owenite communities', *Urban Studies*, XIII (1976), 147–53; D. Hardy, *Alternative Communities in Nineteenth Century England* (1979).

14 For Howard, see especially D. MacFadyen, *Sir Ebenezer Howard and the Town Planning Movement* (1933); W.A. Eden, 'Ebenezer Howard and the garden city movement', *TPR*, XIX (1943–7), 123–43; R. Fishman, *Urban Utopias of the Twentieth Century: Ebenezer Howard, Frank Lloyd Wright and Le Corbusier* (1977). On the garden city, see E. Bonham-Carter, 'Planning and development of Letchworth Garden City', *TPR*, XXI (1950), 362–76; C.B. Purdom, *The Letchworth Achievement* (1963); F.J. Osborn, *Genesis of Welwyn Garden City: some Jubilee memories* (1970); M. Miller, 'Letchworth Garden City zwischen Romantik und Moderne', *Bauwelt*, LXX (1979), 96–109.

15 See especially C. and R. Bell, *City Fathers: The early history of town planning in Britain* (1969); G. Spyer, *Architect and Community: environmental design in an urban society* (1971); J.N. Tarn, *Five Per Cent Philanthropy: an account of housing in urban areas between 1840 and 1914* (1973); G. Darley, *Villages of Vision* (1975).

16 See e.g. P. Boardman, *Patrick Geddes: maker of the future* (1944); P. Mairet, *A Pioneer of Sociology: life and letters of Patrick Geddes* (1957); H.E. Meller, 'Patrick Geddes: an analysis of his theory of civics, 1880–1904', *Victorian Studies*, XVI (1973), 291–316; P. Kitchen, *A Most Unsettling Person: an introduction to the ideas and life of Patrick Geddes* (1975); P. Boardman, *The Worlds of Patrick Geddes: biologist, town planner, re-educator, peace-warrior* (1978).

17 J.D. Hulchanski, *Thomas Adams: a biographical and bibliographic guide* (Papers on Planning and Design, no. 15: Department of Urban and Regional Planning, University of Toronto, 1978).
18 J. P. Reynolds, 'Thomas Coglan Horsfall and the town planning movement', *TPR*, XXIII (1952), 52–60.
19 W.L. Creese, *The Legacy of Raymond Unwin: a human pattern for planning* (1967); M. Day and K. Garstang, 'Socialist theories and Sir Raymond Unwin', *Town and Country Planning,* XLIII (1975), 346–9; D. Hawkes, 'The architectural partnership of Barry Parker and Raymond Unwin, 1896–1914', *Architectural Rev.*, CLXIII (1976), 327–32.
20 Notably *Town Planning in its Social Context* (1970); *Urban Change and Planning: a history of urban development in Britain since 1750* (1972); and *The Evolution of British Town Planning* (1974). This latter study incorporates an official history of the Royal Town Planning Institute.
21 See e.g. R. Smith, *East Kilbride: the biography of a Scottish New Town, 1947–1953* (1979).
22 By J.B. Cullingworth, *Environmental Planning 1939–1969,* vol. I, *Reconstruction and Land Use Planning* (1975), and G.E. Cherry, *Environmental Planning 1939–1969,* vol. II, *National Parks and Recreation in the Countryside* (1975).
23 See e.g. S.M. Gaskell, 'Housing and the lower middle class, 1870–1914', in *The Lower Middle Class in Britain, 1870–1914,* ed. G. Crossick (1977), 159–83.
24 The most explicit application of Marxist ideology to planning history is provided in H. G. Helms and J. Janssen (eds), *Kapitalistischer Städtebau* (Neuwied/Berlin, 1970).
25 The functionalist approach is discussed at greater length in A. Sutcliffe (ed.), *The Rise of Modern Urban Planning* (1980), 3–4.
26 See reports of Group seminars in *Planning Hist. Bull.,* I (1979), no.1, 3–5; no.2, 3–4.

'The suburb salubrious': town planning in practice

S. MARTIN GASKELL

'The suburb salubrious': town planning in practice

S. MARTIN GASKELL

1 Introduction

The material on which this section is based is taken from a thesis presented in 1974 for the degree of Ph.D. at the University of Sheffield, entitled 'Housing estate development, 1840–1918, with particular reference to the Pennine towns'. The central concern of that thesis was the examination of changing attitudes to the development of housing estates in the Victorian period in order to analyse the factors which contributed to the establishment, by 1918, of the low-density suburban estate of semi-detached housing as the standard form of development for the working class. The study was therefore involved directly with the question of the relationship of housing reform and town planning. As the basis for the examination of that relationship it placed emphasis on the role of the individual estate of land, which it was argued was the determining factor in planning and urban improvement during this period. Housing development and reform were studied within its limitations and attention was thereby given to a range of responses.

The research for the thesis was concentrated within a particular geographical region, that of the Pennine towns. The reasons for this choice were twofold. On the one hand, it was considered important to examine in detail housing schemes within a definite area in order both to study local and regional responses to national developments and general problems, and also to demonstrate the ways in which local tradition served to modify national legislation and broader changes in aesthetic attitudes. On the other hand, it was felt that such a study of a provincial region would counter the heavy emphasis on London which had marked many earlier studies of the history of nineteenth-century housing reform and planning. This was not to deny the importance of developments in the capital or the extent to which ideas pioneered and implemented there influenced the process of reform throughout the country. The intention was rather to supplement material already available on housing reform and urban improvement in London; to extend the scope of housing history both in a geographical sense and by supplementing the attention previously given to model housing and philanthropic endeavour.

The consequence of this investigation was a study of the roots of the garden city and town planning movement in the early twentieth century which placed emphasis on the continuity of the nineteenth-century ideal of the suburban housing estate. It was an ideal that had filtered down from the aristocratic estate, through the exclusive middle-class villa estate, ultimately to the working-class suburban estate. It was an ideal that gained impetus, both locally and nationally, from the Victorians' reaction to urban living, and their increasing awareness of the virtues of fresh air and the need for open space. Its form was determined by a contemporaneous reaction to the housing conditions of the early nineteenth century, and more significantly by the reaction to the housing built under the first bye-laws with their concentration on sanitary reform. The application of the suburban ideal to working-class housing was made possible on the one hand by the improvements in urban transportation and in the slowly increasing affluence of the bulk of the working class, and on the other hand by the incorporation of new methods of estate layout and concepts of housing design. These were the culmination not of a process of national reform or legislation, nor indeed of any single strand of development; rather they owed their development and expression to the combination of a multitude of small and locally varying estate developments, and in particular to the combination of the concept of the industrial community with the planning, housing and financing exercises of the differing self-help bodies. This was the tradition on which the garden city movement and the early town planners were able to draw; it was this tradition which gave to British town planning in its formative years its particular quality and appeal.

> As is the case with all conventional phrases, 'town planning' has different meanings in different mouths. To the medical officer of health it means sanitation and healthy houses; to the engineer, trams and bridges and straight roads, with houses drilled to toe a line like soldiers. To some it means open spaces; to the policeman regulation of traffic; to others a garden plot to every house, and so on. To the architect it means *all* these things, collected, considered, and welded into a beautiful whole. It is his work, the work of the trained *planner*, to satisfy all the requirements of a town plan, and to create in doing so a work of art.[1]

Thus the Secretary General of the Town Planning Conference of 1910 introduced the transactions of the conference and reflected the importance which the RIBA attached, in the aftermath of the Housing and Town Planning Act of 1909, to the study of questions involved in the improvement and extension of cities. The proponents of town planning at this early stage argued not just for a 'new way' of undertaking town development but also for the need to approach that task in terms of a 'comprehensive' treatment of the physical environment. The expression of these values was demonstrated in the attention given at this inaugural conference not only to city extension and development, but also to the review of cities of the past, present and future, and in particular to the examination of the artistic and architectural qualities of the subject.

This stress on the total understanding and treatment of the physical environment was shared, with varying emphases, by the other constituent organizations of the town planning movement – the National Housing and Town Planning Council, the Civics Committee of the Sociological Society and the Garden Cities and Town Planning Association. In promoting this new order and new approach the protagonists were united in their condemnation of, and search for an alternative to, the urban environment of nineteenth-century England. Such activity built on the increasing public expression of concern, over the last two decades of the nineteenth century, for the deteriorating quality of life in big cities and the consequent effect both on the physical well-being of the population and the social stability of the country. As Ashworth summarized the situation at the beginning of the twentieth century:

> there were, then, an increasing sensitivity to the condition of the physical environment, increasing awareness of its relation to human experience, increasing doubt as to the possibility of achieving much more on the old lines of public health and housing policy. This was a state of affairs in which the minds of some naturally sought the more comprehensive approach, which they called town planning.[2]

Within the town planning movement, the four organizations already identified, while appealing to a comprehensive solution to urban problems in which physical reforms were both conceived of and carried out in an interrelated programme, at the same time approached the problem from the basis of different values and assumptions and through different means of achieving a solution. Within this debate, the practical demands of better organization were stressed by the National Housing and Town Planning Council. In achieving this, attention was drawn, particularly by T.C. Horsfall, to what was happening on the Continent and to the advantages which accrued from the adoption of building plans catering for the needs of the whole town. Emphasis was almost inevitably, however, placed on town extension and the means by which local authorities could control the laying out of new districts and so prevent their development in an haphazard, piecemeal fashion, which was arguably responsible for the evils of nineteenth-century urbanization. In this debate the economic attraction for municipalities was an important factor, stressed especially in the speeches and writing of those exponents of town planning who were involved in local government, such as J.S. Nettlefold, Chairman of the Housing Committee of the Birmingham City Council, who emphasized particularly the benefits for comprehensive organization of civic control and order.

Alongside this concern for the better ordering of the physical environment, developing essentially out of the sanitary and housing reform activity of the previous century, there was also an appeal to the attainment of fundamental changes in the ordering of society. This link between planning and sociology was pioneered through the Civics Committee of the Sociological Society by Patrick Geddes, who urged the need to view the question of urban extension and development within the context of the total town. The betterment of towns involved not just the environment but also the community. However, if Geddes was the most articulate advocate of civic development, the most influential pressure for the creation of comprehensively organized environments came from the Garden City Association. If the town had failed in the nineteenth century as an acceptable environment for living, Ebenezer Howard in advancing the idea of the garden city demonstrated the feasibility of combining the nature of town and country, and argued that out of this would be achieved the benefits of both.[3] The contribution of the garden city was its realization of the means of achieving a form of comprehensive order which was central to the whole town planning movement, along with its promotion of forms of development and architectural treatment with expressed accepted aesthetic standards in a tangible form.

It was the interrelationship and fusion of all these movements, and the ideas and ideals underpinning them, that forged the town planning movement in the first decade of the twentieth century. It was the support of many professional bodies and the needs of local authorities which ensured the favourable circumstances for the relatively rapid realization, in a legislative sense, of a measure of town planning. Behind this lay the interaction of different interests: the persistence of nineteenth-century arguments for urban improvement, the social and aesthetic reactions of the end of the century, and the continuation and modification of utopian idealism. With the mutual reinforcement of the ideas arising from these sources, the town planning movement of the first decade of the twentieth century laid stress on the need for a comprehensive and controlled response to the urban environment. The legislation generated, however, was at best a partial acceptance of the arguments advanced.

The statutory embodiment of town planning was first achieved in the Housing, Town Planning, Etc. Act of 1909.[4] Its very title establishes its roots in the reform tradition of the nineteenth century and gives an indication of the bill's emphasis. Under the terms of the Act local authorities were empowered to prepare, with the consent of the Local Government Board, town planning schemes in relation to land which was in course of development and appeared likely to be used for building purposes. 'With the general object of securing proper sanitary conditions, amenity and convenience in connexion with the laying out and use of land, and of any neighbouring lands', the Act in effect provided the means to regulate new suburban development.

In the passage of the bill through Parliament, the emphasis of the supporting speeches had been placed on the value of town extension plans and on what John Burns referred to as 'the suburb salubrious'. Speakers promoting the measure had reflected a belief in the process of suburbanization as a solution to the problems of the town. This belief owed its origin to Victorian middle-class practice. In identifying the benefits to be achieved through the legislation, supporters drew their examples pre-eminently from the garden suburbs of recent origin. Thus associated with the passage of the Act were certain assumptions about the kind of layout and the nature of development which went with town planning.

What was realized, therefore, with this legislation was a limited measure of general acceptability, which did not interfere with the interests of landowners through the extension of local authorities' compulsory purchase powers. The Act did extend and rationalize some of the existing legislation relating essentially to housing, particularly with regard to the introduction of stricter compensation clauses and the inclusion of betterment provisions in improvement schemes. It provided for a degree of supervision and control of rural housing and at the same time significantly extended the powers of local authorities with respect to house ownership. This was all, however, in a sense consolidation of previous housing legislation. The Act's contribution to town planning concerned a limited range of conditions, and it allowed no provision for the prevention of development where such development was not in the public interest. The Act facilitated only the establishment of general lines of local town planning schemes in areas of urban extension.

In these circumstances it was inevitable that the immediate impact of the Housing and Town Planning Act of 1909 should be limited both with regard to the number of schemes undertaken and with regard to the nature of the planning implemented. Far from the comprehensive ideals of the town planning movement, legislation provided within strict limitations for the planning only of a small proportion of the land, and in relation to the physical determinants, as distinct from the social considerations, of planning. The consequences of the Act were accordingly assessed by Ashworth:

> Though it had many and important antecedents, statutory town planning immediately after 1909 was a mild, uncertain affair. Town planning for all was a novelty which might be gingerly tried, but there was every deterrent to prevent any body from indulging in it to excess. There was now an act which permitted local authorities, if they were so disposed and if they obtained the consent of the Local Government Board, to prepare town planning schemes, but only for land about to be developed. What exactly constituted town planning was uncertain.[5]

In practice, the development that occurred under the Act over the following five years was essentially limited to residential estates developed along lines commonly associated with those garden suburbs whose advantages and amenities had been so frequently invoked in the promotion of the legislation. At least those lessons had been absorbed, even if their application involved some distortion. The achievement, however, meant that town planning in this initial stage became associated with a particular form of development. This emphasis of town planning in the years before the First World War was most clearly demonstrated in the examination of 'Modern town planning in England' in the first volume of the *Town Planning Review*:

> The contributions towards the modern town planning movement for which England is responsible up to the present have been largely due to private effort and not municipal enterprise; they have also sprung from the housing and sociological side of the subject. Housing reform rather than a desire for civic art or a study of traffic problems is at the root of the Garden City and Garden Suburb; and it is noteworthy that the two chief organisations which have been the mouthpiece of this movement have recently added the words 'Town Planning' to names which formerly stood for Garden Cities and Housing Reform. If it were not for the one great experiment of First Garden City at Letchworth, it might be said that the keynote of the revival of English Town Planning which has taken place during the past 20 years has been the creation of suburbs of small houses with a strict limitation as to the number per acre. This is sometimes called the 'Garden City idea', but erroneously.[6]

It is with the examination of this emphasis in town planning as it developed in this country that this section is concerned. Building on the basis of the research undertaken into housing estate development in the Pennine towns, the first part considers the character of the garden suburb and attempts to assess the significance of such suburbs in relation to the early town planning movement. Subsequently, with the passage of the first town planning legislation, certain schemes implemented under that Act are examined and the limited achievement of British town planning before the First World War is discussed. These case studies illustrate the significance of the suburban tradition, and in particular its development into the garden suburb, in terms of understanding the ideas and values underlying the early town planning movement and the way in which those ideas and values were transformed into prac-

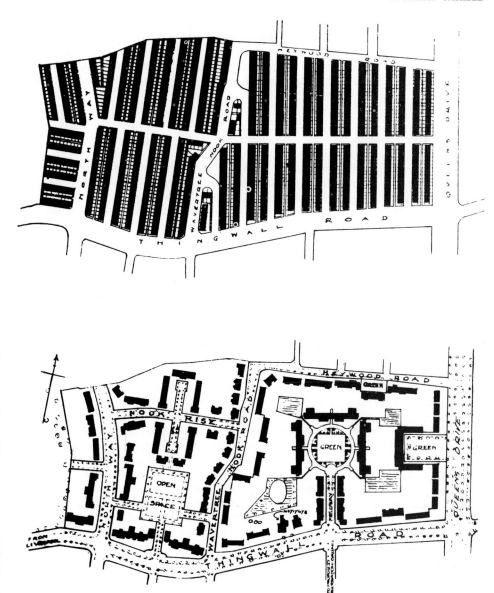

Figure 1. Alternative approaches to estate development. The diagrams illustrate the advantages of low-density layout under the Town Planning Act of 1909. The top plan carried the caption 'Twenty-five acres of Liverpool Garden Suburb as it might have been. The plan shows how the land could have been laid out to comply with the minimum requirements of the Liverpool Corporation's Acts, with 41 houses per acre.' The plan at the bottom was captioned 'Twenty-five acres of Liverpool Garden Suburb as it is. The first part of the Estate, showing 11 houses per acre.' (E.G. Culpin, *The Garden City Movement Up-to-Date*, 1914, 54).

tice. Against the complexity of the early town planning movement must be placed the simplicity of achievement under the first legislation, and in conclusion the section seeks to identify some of the characteristics of British town planning which derived from the juxtaposition of ideas and movements in the first two decades of the twentieth century.

2 The garden suburb

The growth of suburbs was the characteristic and inevitable form of urban development in the later half of the century, and produced what was perhaps the greatest single change in the living habits of the English people since the industrial revolution. In retrospect, it is possible to see that it was a natural consequence, first, of the separation between workplace and home, and second, of improving communications which continually extended the daily travellable distance between the two.[7]

By 1900 there was increasing awareness that the acquiescence in, and virtual encouragement of, such suburban development was causing irreparable damage. Green fields were being lost for ever, and the houses being built served neither the best interests of the individual tenants nor of the community at large. Intermingled with a certain degree of social alarm over the changing character of the suburban population and the debasement of property standards was an increasing realization that the accustomed pattern of suburban development left much to be desired in environmental terms. By the end of the nineteenth century there was then widespread disaffection both with inner-urban building standards, particularly with regard to housing, and with the pattern of suburban extension. Although the expansion of cheaper methods of public transport had brought the possibility of suburban life within the reach of a much greater range of the population, it required the stimulation of new ideas and new ideals before urban development and suburban estates could be conceived of and promoted along novel lines. It was also clear from the experience of earlier self-help housing schemes that it would be necessary that any such scheme should demonstrate economies in layout and design before it could be applied to estates planned for the majority of the population. Otherwise, builders would have continued to try to secure within the stereotyped pattern of the high-density terraced unit the greatest amount of accommodation and convenience possible for the minimum of capital outlay.

In these circumstances the need for rejuvenation in both the layout and design of suburban estates was widely voiced around the turn of the century, both by social critics and by architectural reformers. Against the background of national concern over the physical well-being of the population and over the quality of the environment in which people lived and worked, the 'question of the suburbs' became a matter of public debate in the years around 1900, as criticism spread beyond the columns of the architectural journals and both national and local newspapers began to carry various articles, commentaries and letters on the character of contemporary suburban expansion. In a major report in 1904 *The Times* fulminated against the 'appalling monotony, ugliness and dullness' of suburban extensions to London and urged the need 'to redeem the suburb from meanness and squalor'.[8] Aware of this critical mood, builders were increasingly receptive to new ideas on suburban devel-

22

opment which sought to transfer to housing estates designed for a broader section of the community the garden character of the arcadian suburbs of the Victorian middle-class élite.

The stimulus for a rejuvenation in the physical appearance of housing during the last decade of the century came essentially from the ideas of William Morris, which were transmitted in architectural terms by Philip Webb, W.R. Lethaby and their followers.[9] In practice, the first examples of the application of new ideas to working-class housing came from the two industrial settlements of Port Sunlight, begun in 1888, and Bournville, begun in 1895. Here were established the balance and scale that were to govern the layout of later garden suburbs. On both estates great attention was paid to the spatial qualities of layout – the straight street of the bye-law terrace was discarded in favour of a picturesque settlement of trees and gardens, with cottages built semi-detached or disposed of in units of five or six. The roads themselves lost the rigidity of the gridiron, for as W.A. Harvey, the architect of Bournville, commented, 'it is nearly always better to work to the contour of the land, taking a general sweep in preference to a straight line.'[10]

These preconditions anticipated two of the later principles of Parker and Unwin that were to guide the development of the garden suburb – low density on the land (five to eight houses per acre at Port Sunlight and seven to eight at Bournville), and a reduction in the number of streets necessary for residential development. The houses at the two villages also provided object lessons in grouping and design. A greater diversity of textures and colours was evidence of a desire for variety in the street picture. At Bournville the variety of bricks, hand-made tiles and careful roof ridging were all incorporated in order to obtain 'that rustic appearance suitable to a cottage', and were in definite reaction to the turgid repetition of the Birmingham bye-law streets.[11] At Port Sunlight the variety of materials and styles was even more impressive, and the danger of visual disintegration was avoided by the construction of up to ten house units within mansion blocks, which were designed so that there was the minimum of external demarcation between individual houses. These larger units provided new opportunities for grouping around open spaces and developing the concept of the superblock. With this different scale of approach, the architects at Port Sunlight had to angle the blocks at street corners and form courts out of the larger combinations, and in so doing they forecast certain planning devices which were to be adopted more widely over the next two decades.[12]

Yet though Bournville and Port Sunlight foreshadowed the type of layout that was to influence future suburban planning, neither was a stimulus to much direct imitation. Primarily this was a result of both developments' lack of economic viability. Lever never made any secret of the fact that the rents received at Port Sunlight did not cover the charges incurred.[13] At Bournville Cadbury always intended that the rents received should show a 4 per cent return on the capital expended. This meant that few of the houses were let at rents within the means of the poorer working man. An extravagant bye-law system insisted upon unnecessarily wide and expensive roads, and this involved a very heavy expenditure on estate development. As such costs had to be met by the tenants, it meant that large numbers of working men were excluded from the benefits which Cadbury had anticipated.[14]

It was essential that certain economies in development and layout be incorporated before the visual models of Port Sunlight and Bournville could be transferred to the working-class suburban estate. The catalyst that united the aesthetic and practical elements in a new approach to planning and which stimulated interest was, of course, Ebenezer Howard's *Garden Cities of Tomorrow*, first published under a different title in 1898. In that book Howard proposed the building in the heart of some agricultural district in England a town of 32,000 inhabitants where the most approved modern methods of engineering and sanitary science should be adopted, and the utmost attention devoted to securing healthy and beautiful houses and conditions of life and work for all classes of people. Howard showed that there was a general consensus of opinion that the continued growth of large cities, combined with a decline in the population of the country districts, was an unhealthy development. The resulting problem, according to Howard, was how to create, in the midst of the fresh air of the country, opportunities for profitable industrial investment and prospects of pleasant forms of social life more attractive than any to be found in the great towns and cities. This involved the organization of the voluntary exodus of people from the overcrowded towns to the new settlements, and in support of his argument he used a proposal of Alfred Marshall's that workmen should be induced through the efforts of a committee, aided by their employers, to migrate and form colonies in the country.[15] Howard incorporated into that proposal the idea that, as the migration of a large number of people to a given area in the country would be attended inevitably with a rise in the value of that area, provision should be made for securing the increased land value for the people whose advent caused it.

Another element in Howard's work was the combination of town and country life as expressed in John Stuart Mill's commentary on Wakefield's *A View of the Art of Colonisation*:

> Wakefield's theory of colonisation has excited much attention and is doubtless destined to excite much more . . . the system consists of arrangements for securing that each colony should have from the first a town population bearing due proportion to the agricultural and that the tillers of the soil should not be so widely scattered as to be deprived by distance of the benefits of that town population as a market for their produce.[16]

Howard carried this idea further by planning a system of towns separated from each other by agricultural belts, the smaller towns being satellites of the central city. It was his intention that when the garden city reached a certain size both in terms of population and of acreage, with 30,000 people living on 1,000 acres within the 6,000-acre 'estate' of the city, then the city should grow not by extending its built-up area into the countryside, but rather through the establishment of another garden city beyond its own zone of country. In this way clusters of garden cities would gradually come into existence.

Apart from this urban cluster concept, however, Howard's 'Garden City' offered little that was novel either in design or thought. It encapsulated aspects of the utopian communities envisaged throughout the nineteenth century and drew heavily on the ideas of earlier social reformers. It was probably this very eclecticism in Howard's thesis that was its strength. Land nationalizers, co-operators, liberals, conservatives, fabians, socialists, anarchists and housing reformers were all attracted by some part of the theory. The immediate and popular reaction to the garden city idea must be credited in part to its coincidence with the promotion of a variety of schemes for land reform and resettlement. In 1893 J.C. Kenworthy founded the English Land Colonisation Society, which attempted to organize a residential colony in the Home Counties for middle-class people anxious to flee from city life.[17]

Subsequent difficulties led to its transformation into a more general movement for helping the return of town-dwellers to the land. Several other socieities, including the Home Colonisation Society, the Allotments and Small Holdings Association, and the Association for Improving the Condition of the People, were concerned with the physical and moral deterioration of urban life; the earnestness of their endeavours goes far to explain the enthusiasms roused by the garden city movement. Yet, at the same time, there was increasing awareness of the impoverishment of contemporary rural life. With the depopulation of the agricultural areas and the decline of rural communities, the countryside was stagnating. It might provide a healthier and more attractive environment than the towns, but for most people this did not compensate for the restriction of opportunity and the limitation of interest. For the urban masses, life in the country was not a realistic alternative, whatever its apparent attractions. It was to this dichotomy that Howard directed attention, with his central concern for the integration of urban and rural patterns and his assessment of the need to revitalize both. As Mumford concluded:

> What was needed, Howard saw . . . as Kropotkin at the same time proclaimed. . .
> was a marriage of town and country, of rustic health and sanity and activity
> and urban knowledge, urban technical facility, urban political co-operation. The
> instrument of that marriage was the Garden City.[18]

However, few members of the Garden City Association looked for just one solution of these many social problems, and this resulted in a quiet watering down of the thesis until it became synonymous in the public mind, and in the minds of many early planners, with the garden suburb. Howard, himself, frequently commented on the misuse of the term 'garden city'. When the London County Council housing scheme at Tottenham was described as a garden city, he complained that the Act of 1911 covering the development had referred to the laying out of land on garden city lines because neither the framer of the bill nor the committee which passed it knew what the term implied.[19] Compared with the self-centred garden city, a garden suburb scheme sought to ensure only that the future growth of existing towns should be on healthy lines. Howard felt that such schemes, though useful, tended to drive the country yet further afield and did not deal with the root evil of rural depopulation. At the same time, while garden villages avoided some of the problems posed by the garden suburbs and were indeed garden cities in miniature, they nevertheless depended on some neighbouring city for water, light and drainage, they did not have provision for a protective belt and they were usually the centre of a single industry. But despite his reservations, Howard realized that all these types of development shared the impressive virtue of pre-planning:

> The essential thing is that before a sod is cut or a brick laid, the area must in its
> broad outlines be properly planned with an eye to the convenience of the
> community as a whole, the preservation of natural beauties, the utmost degree of
> healthfulness and a proper regard to communication with the surrounding
> district.[20]

The garden city movement, then, with all its ramifications and notwithstanding the dilution of the original intention, placed essential emphasis on planning, on overall design and the maintenance of certain minimum standards of layout.

These new concepts of planning and design were of particular importance in that they involved economies in construction which made estate development on what became so generally referred to as 'garden city lines' a possible alternative to traditional speculative activity. Firstly, it was demonstrated that great expense in estate development was incurred by the bye-law demands that all roads be finished in the most expensive and durable manner, irrespective of whether the traffic on them was likely to require or justify such expense.[21] The population of a group of cottages and the wheeled traffic visiting them might be very small, yet for such a service road most local authorities, under existing bye-laws, required paved footpaths, granite kerbs and channels and granite macadamized road surfaces, the whole from 40 to 50 feet wide and costing with the sewers from £5 to £8 per lineal yard. This excessive cost tended to limit the frontage of the houses, for where an attempt was made to build a cottage costing under £200, the charge of £3 per yard for the half share of the road became a serious matter and the houses suffered both in size and frontage to an unnecessary extent. It was admitted by Unwin that, where traffic was likely to be heavy and the estate roads served to link up main roads or were likely to develop into main roads in the future then suitable provision had to be made. But where, as frequently happened, the road was used only for the daily visits of the milkman and the rounds of the coal merchant's van, then a well-made track, more in the nature of a carriage drive with a grass margin on each side and, in some cases, a simple gravel or paved footpath of narrow width for use in wet weather, was all that was needed. With the small amount of traffic using such a road, it was argued that the maintenance against wear and tear would be no greater than in the case of the vastly more costly road usually required.[22]

To meet this difficulty to some extent, the Hampstead Garden Suburb Trust obtained in 1906 an Act of Parliament under which the width of the road to be constructed according to the bye-laws was limited to 40 feet and the Trust were allowed, if they made their roads of greater width than 40 feet, to devote the extra space to grass margins in which trees could be planted.[23] Another clause allowed the Trust to construct roads, not exceeding 500 feet in length, of a width of 20 feet, provided that the houses on each side of such roads should not be nearer to one another than 50 feet. These short roads were extensively used at Hampstead Garden Suburb and led to the formation of many groups of houses around greens, which could not practicably have been arranged without the powers given in the Act. Many of the roads on the estate exceeded the minimum of 40 feet, some being 60 feet wide, and in these cases grass margins with trees were provided.[24]

In other cases, as for example in the village of New Earswick and at the garden city of Letchworth, no bye-laws relating to the character of roads and streets were in force, and it was possible for Raymond Unwin to experiment with roads of various characters and widths (see figs. 22–5).[25] J.S. Nettlefold pointed out the results, in economic terms, of the absence of urban bye-laws at New Earswick,[26] for there the rents of the houses remained well within the means of the working man. At Bournville, on the other hand, the roads were much wider than necessary for the convenience of the frontages, and great expense was incurred in channelling and kerbing. The result was that the rents of most of the houses at Bournville were above the means of the ordinary working man.[27] The relaxation of urban bye-laws was thus a persistent theme of the Garden City and Town Planning Association.

The inevitable corollary of high-cost estate development was the fact that the ordinary landowner was compelled to put as many houses to the acre as the bye-laws allowed, in order to earn the maximum interest on the capital invested. Building bye-laws, as they operated in most English towns by the end of the nineteenth century, only indirectly limited the number of houses per acre by their regulations as to the minimum width of streets and the minimum space allowed to be left at the back of buildings. In the first place, they provided for an open space varying from 36 to 50 feet in front of the building, and this space was usually occupied by road and footpaths. Secondly, the bye-laws usually required that an area of at least 150 square feet be left free at the rear of the building, extending its full width and not less than 10 feet in depth where the building did not exceed 10 feet in length. The depth of this open space varied in proportion to the length of the building and so, for cottages which usually did not exceed 25 feet in length, the maximum depth of open space at the rear that was usually secured by the bye-laws was 25 feet. With the narrow frontages usually adopted for small cottages, it was possible to crowd as many as 50 houses on to the acre, or even more. This allowed no garden space, only a small yard attached to each cottage.

Raymond Unwin calculated that the desirable number of cottages per acre, from the point of view of health and comfort, would be between 10 and 20.[28] Near the

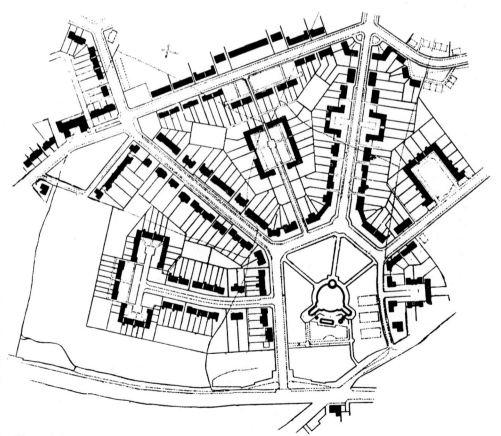

Figure 2. Part of the Co-Partnership Estate at Hampstead (E.G. Culpin, *The Garden City Movement Up-to-Date*, 1914, 34).

centre of a town densities would necessarily be higher than on the outskirts, but even here the number of houses per acre need not exceed 20. Wherever possible it should be restricted to between 10 and 12.

> Twelve houses to the net acre of building land, excluding all roads, has been proved to be about the right number to give gardens of sufficient size to be of commercial value to the tenants – large enough, that is, to be worth cultivating seriously for the sake of profit, and not too large to be worked by an ordinary labourer and his family.[29]

In his pamphlet *Nothing Gained by Overcrowding*, Unwin contrasted a plot of ten acres with 34 houses per acre with another of 15.2 houses per acre.[30] In the first scheme each house had 83½ square yards of ground, while in the second scheme the lower density allowed each house 261½ square yards. The roads in the first scheme would have cost £9,747 10s, compared with £4,480 in the second scheme. The result was that, though the number of houses had been reduced by half, the plot sizes had been tripled and the layout costs per house remained stable. As Creese has pointed out: 'It is not actually a principle of costing less then, that counts, so much as obtaining more for the money per family unit'.[31]

Unwin did demonstrate to landowners, however, the benefits, in financial terms, of low-density development, pointing out that it was better to sell two acres per year at £300 each than one for £500, and that land values are never lost, they merely migrate.[32] In general, however, Unwin was more concerned with the aesthetic possibilities low-density development provided through the use of culs-de-sac, courts, quadrangles and greens. It was S.D. Adshead who expounded most clearly that the greatest benefits of low-density building would be secured on the cheapest land.[33] On a suburban estate with low-cost roads, the land costing under £500 an acre and the houses not less than ten to the acre, the amount invested in land and roads was very low compared with that in bricks and mortar. Adshead showed that when land cost £300 per acre and was developed with ten cottages per acre in order to secure a 5 per cent return, then 7s. would have to be the weekly rent for each house, compared with 6s. 3d. if the estate was developed with 50 cottages per acre. But the extra 9d. in rent provided for a garden 144 feet by 21 feet and an allotment 50 feet by 21 feet. Once land cost £500 per acre, then it was necessary to build 15 houses to the acre if they were to be let at 7s. per week, and when land values rose to £1,000 per acre 25 cottages were required in order to allow a rent of 8s. a week to secure a 5 per cent return. Thus the cheaper suburban land allowed the developer to secure his expected capital return, with much lower development costs.

In addition to economies in layout, this freer development also made possible the rethinking of the plan of the house or working-class cottage. The houses described by Raymond Unwin in *Cottage Plans and Common Sense*,[34] and subsequently developed by him on the earliest part of the estate at New Earswick (begun 1902), adapted to working-class homes many of the innovations of Webb and Voysey.[35] In place of the narrow-fronted terraced house with a front and back room, the lower street costs enabled the introduction of houses with greater widths. This meant that, in the first place, it was possible to provide more variety in accommodation. Secondly, all the accommodation required was brought under the main roof, and long back projections or detached outbuildings were dispensed with, which effected a reduction of gloom and shade. Thirdly, the increased wall space admitted of more windows and allowed staircases, landings and larders to be placed on outer walls with direct light and ventilation. Lastly, the proportions of the buildings lent themselves to a treatment more pleasing to the eye. Breadth itself is a valuable aesthetic quality and when it was associated with the broad casement window of simple framing and the long lines of a well-pitched roof, then to some degree the homely appearance of the English country cottage was recovered.[36]

The emphasis in such cottages was on good design and on well-planned relationships. This was particularly true of the cheaper estate cottages. Unwin commented on the problem after the 1905 Cheap Cottage Exhibition at Letchworth, when many competitors, endeavouring to build a cottage for under £150, had produced models in wood and timber framing and a variety of patent materials, few of which were satisfactorily resistant to cold and damp, while others sought picturesqueness in such a confusion of shapes and levels that they were productive of designs wholly impracticable for living in.[37] He realized that if cottages were to be built cheaply, yet well designed in relation to their surroundings, then they had to be built in groups.

> Where groups of cottages must be kept absolutely simple, good results will depend largely on the arrangement of them. Here, as in so many other cases, our forefathers have shown us the right way. When they wanted to build a large number of small dwellings economically, we find they frequently adopted the quadrangle form, with the buildings either arranged all round, or on three sides; they knew full well that a degree of simplicity in design which would be wearisome if spread out in a long straight row may be extremely pleasant when the buildings are grouped round a square or green.[38]

In an environment which retained as much of its natural character as possible, it was essential that the building should harmonize with its site and surroundings, making it, as it were, part of the ground on which it stood. As Maurice Adams commented in *Modern Cottage Architecture*:

> Such qualities do not depend so much upon expenditure as upon an application of thought and good taste. They exist quite apart from elaborateness of detail and are mostly obtained by avoiding all ornamental excesses, while they must blend with the architecture of the hedgerow and coppice.[39]

The garden estate, therefore, required a degree of overall planning: roads and cottages not only related to natural conditions, but both conceived of together in economic terms. This was the approach to planning and layout that had become associated with the garden city movement. It was an approach which combined the views of architectural theorists with the practical endeavours of working men themselves to secure a better standard of housing, a better quality of design and a better form of layout. However, the rapid development of the garden city concept, of those patterns of housing inherent in it and of its extension into multifarious suburban schemes was, as has been pointed out, the result of the coincidence of Howard's original thesis with other social movements. In particular, on the organizational side, the garden city movement coalesced with new forms of public utility organization – the modification of financial arrangements pioneered in the earlier building societies, the freehold land societies and co-operative societies. This resulted during the last decade of the nineteenth century in the adaptation of the co-partnership idea to the process of housing estate development and planning.

This was a vital factor in the establishment and extension of garden suburbs, since other organs of self-help had largely lost the initiative in housing estate development. By 1890 the building society movement was dominated almost completely by the permanent society, with its emphasis solely on the financial security of individual properties.[40] Even when societies produced model designs for the guidance of members, as did the Halifax Permanent Building Society in 1891 and the Co-operative Permanent Building Society in 1896, they were concerned simply with the construction of single units, and the designs remained restricted by the conventions of the traditional terraced house.[41] As far as the building societies were concerned, the model cottage was just a more substantial version of the standard form with, perhaps, the embellishment of a bay window or an ornamental porch.

The co-operative societies continued to be unwilling to risk the investment of members' capital in estate developments other than those of a well-tried character.[42] In 1899 one of the great retail societies, the Royal Arsenal of Woolwich, embarked on the building of an estate that would hold 3,500 houses.[43] The houses were to be built by the Society and then sold subject to lease, with the Society providing a 90 per cent mortgage repayable over 30 years. The 1,052 houses built by 1912 had cost between £215 and £400 each and were described as being 'in accord with the prevailing style in Plumstead'.[44] Most of the houses had seven rooms and were built in terraces, generally two storeys in height, although there were a few with an attic bedroom in addition. Frontages were all quite narrow, varying from 13 to 16 feet. The layout was spacious, but the streets followed a simple parallel scheme; and though the houses were embellished with carved stone work, ornamental iron work and gabled bay windows, there was no attempt to handle the units as total architectural compositions. The design avoided little of the monotony of contemporary speculative housing.

The co-operative movement was consistently criticized for its failure to lay down higher standards or to attempt to educate working-class taste in housing.[45] The 1900 Conference of the Southern Section of the Co-operative Union was told:

> The great mass of people had no desire for better conditions . . . the habits of tens of thousands of our workmen would not allow them to live under better conditions if such were povided. They like to live in one room and it was the duty of co-operators to educate them to a better condition of things.[46]

The corollary of this criticism was that co-operative societies should not simply assist home purchase by the means of mortgage advances, but that they should make themselves responsible for the layout and design of the houses on an estate. Only through collective ownership could they assist in improving the standard of houses and further the attainment of co-operative ideals.

Despite criticism, however, no society set itself such objectives. Basically this was because such ideals did not appeal to members. There was, however, much that was attractive in the principle of a man having a sense of possession of the house in which he lived and an interest in the economical administration of the property.[47] It was in their attempt to accommodate this point of view that the Co-Partnership Tenants made their great contribution to the housing reform question, to the furtherance of the garden city movement and to the development of numerous garden suburbs. For the co-partnership ideal was to combine corporate control with a personal interest in the profits arising from a right and economical use of the property. The methods adopted by the Tenants Co-partnership Society were: to purchase an estate in the suburb of a growing town and to plan or lay out the same, so as to provide suitable playing sites for the tenants and their children; to insist on the reasonable limitation of the number of houses to the acre, so that each house might have a private garden, and on pleasing architectural effects in the grouping and designing of the houses; to erect substantial houses, provided with good sanitary and other arrangements for the convenience of stock-holders desiring to become tenants; to let these at ordinary rents, so as to pay a moderate rate of interest on capital (usually 5 per cent on shares, and 4 per cent on loan stock), dividing the surplus profits, after providing for expenses, repairs and sinking fund, among the tenant stock-holders, in proportion to the rents paid by them. Each tenants stock-holder's share of the profits was credited to him in capital instead of being paid in cash, until he held the value of the house tenanted by him, after which all dividends could be withdrawn in cash.[48]

In such societies an individual could obtain practically all the economic advantages which would have arisen from the ownership of his own house. Capital was obtained at a rate of interest below the level at which the individual could usually borrow to build or buy his own house, while the preliminary legal and other expenses were less than would be the case if incurred individually. Nor did the tenant share-holder run the risk of loss in the event of removal, for his security was in the stock of an association rather than in the deed of a particular site and house. His mobility was not restricted, therefore, by the possession of property.

The first housing society to adopt the system of sharing the profits with its tenants, after a fixed interest on capital had been paid, was the Tenant Co-operators Limited, which was registered in 1888.[49] The idea had been put forward originally by F.O. Greening in the *Co-operative News* in 1881, when he stressed the inability of the London worker ever to find the purchase money for a house, the high legal costs incurred by building societies, and the difficulties of selling for men forced to move for employment.[50] The idea was explained by Benjamin Jones to the Industrial Remuneration Conference in 1885 and developed by him in a pamphlet published in 1887.[51] The society was registered and its first prospectus published in 1888. Over the next eight years the Tenant Co-operators Limited established, either by purchase or erection, five estates: at Upton Park, with six houses; at Penge, with 37 houses; a block of 14 tenements at Camberwell; 32 maisonnettes at East Ham; 26 houses at Epsom. Originally, Jones planned a series of 50 estates around London, with the idea that tenants, as members of the society, would be able to move house around the metropolis as and when their work demanded, without too much difficulty or expense. The need for the working man to be mobile, particularly in the job market of late nineteenth-century London, was an important consideration. In addition, within this overall scheme, Jones anticipated a system of organized social and educational work. In practice, however, each estate was by itself too small to create any feeling of corporate life, and the lack of a clubhouse or central meeting place was a definite drawback.[52]

Nevertheless, although the Tenant Co-operators had not developed on the scale anticipated and although they continued to depend on voluntary organization, the initial activity had shown that the original ideal was capable of practical development. The fundamental principle of permitting tenants to become shareholders by the holding of one £1 share, such a holding entitling them to vote equally with any other shareholders, irrespective of the amount of capital held, continued throughout the lifetime of the society. In this respect other later tenants societies made a considerable departure from the original concept. The capital holding of tenants in other societies was to be generally at a higher level, and by 1912 the voting power of tenants in many societies had been restricted or removed entirely.[53]

The net profit realized by the Tenant Co-operators Limited over the first 25 years, after the payment of all charges, expenses, depreciation and interest upon loans and deposits, worked out at 6.7 per cent upon the amount of share capital. For 1912 it was 8.3 per cent. Interest upon share capital being limited by rule to 4 per cent, however, the surplus profits were distributed to tenants in the form of dividends rising to as much as 2s. 6d. in the pound.[54] Despite this modest success no further estates were developed by the Tenant Co-operators, and it was with the public interest and enthusiasm aroused by Howard's garden city scheme that the concept was taken up by others and combined with the idea of a garden city or suburb. This led to the establishment of numerous successful societies.

In 1901 there came into existence a society in west London, the Ealing Tenants Limited.[55] By concentrating its operations on one estate the Ealing Society was able to include many features, such as a model estate plan, an institute, recreation and playing sites, which would have been impossible if the property had been scattered in different districts. It thus established for itself the claim of being 'The Pioneer Co-Partnership Village', and under the title of 'Co-Partnership in Housing' the movement made a rapid advance in the following decade. By 1911 there were 14 societies, holding property to the value of about £1,005,000, and engaged in developing further property to the value of about £1,207,500.[56]

The Co-Partnership Tenants Limited was registered in 1907, and was instrumental in raising capital for federated co-partnership societies.[57] Over the first five years a total of £651,269 was raised in the form of shares, loan stock and mortgages. The society also developed the Co-Partnership Tenants Housing Council as a propagandist organization and as a source of information and assistance in technical, financial and architectural matters.[58] By 1910 a feature of the movement was the increasing number of cases in which advantage was being taken of the skill and experience of the society's staff by local societies who were able to raise their own capital. Thus two types of co-partnership societies developed – the one controlled from the centre, and the other where capital, initiative and therefore control were local. The Fifth Annual Report of the Co-Partnership Tenants Limited welcomed the development, for it felt that the more public-spirited men with business experience and public confidence were responsible for public utility housing societies then the greater would be the progress and also the variety and experiment.[59]

Raymond Unwin, the consulting architect to the society, considered that the Co-Partnership Tenants movement marked a new era in housing, for not only was the individual likely to procure for himself a better house and a larger garden by obtaining them through a co-partnership society than by any other means, but the introduction of co-operation opened up quite a new range of possibilities.

> Through the medium of co-operation all may enjoy a share of many advantages, the individual possession of which can only be attained by the few. The man who is sufficiently wealthy may have his own shrubberies, tennis-courts, bowling greens, or play places for his children, and may, by the size of his grounds, secure an open and pleasant outlook from all his windows; but the individual possession of such grounds is quite out of the reach of the majority. A Co-Partnership

Association can, however, provide for all its members a share of these advantages, and of far more than these. In fact, the scope of the principle is limited only by the power of those who associate to accept and enjoy the sharing of great things in place of the exclusive possession of small things.[60]

Clearly, in exceptional circumstances, an owner or a company had laid out an estate so as to provide for the common enjoyment of some of the advantages of the site, but usually everything was sacrificed which would not produce a revenue, and which could not be divided up into individual self-contained plots. The latter were described by Henry Vivian, the chairman of the Co-Partnership Tenants, as 'being marked by the maximum degree of detachment, which are so desired by those who know only of individual possession and have not learned the joys of sharing'.[61] Where a site was being developed on co-partnership lines, the whole position was changed. In place of a chance assortment of individuals, there was instead a whole to be thought of and planned for. It was aimed to make a home for a community with something like an organized common life. A centre was needed for this and was found in clubs, schools or places of worship. Consequently emphasis was placed on the siting of these in the planning of the estates. The site was thought of and planned for as a whole, and the certainty of some degree of co-operation allowed aspects of natural beauty and distant prospects to be preserved for the enjoyment of all. Play places and shelters for the children, greens for tennis, bowls or croquet could be arranged with the houses grouped around them, so that besides providing the tenants with recreational space they also afforded both more pleasant prospects from the windows and more attractive views along the streets. In this way, instead of the building on the estate consisting of endless rows or the repetition of isolated houses having no connection with one another, the property was grouped together to form units of interesting shape and form encircling the open spaces. The benefits for estate layout that accrued from the co-partnership development of an estate were summed up by Henry Vivian:

> The principle of sharing, therefore, not only causes each individual house to become more attractive, but gives to the whole area covered that coherence which, springing from the common life of the community, expresses itself in the harmony and beauty of the whole. This harmony of outward expression must in turn react on the life that flourishes under its influence, at once stimulating the growth of co-operation and giving wider opportunities for its practice.[62]

The extension of co-operation in estate development was noteworthy during the first decade of the twentieth century, and by 1913 it was estimated that some 60 estates, containing 11,479 houses already built, had been developed under co-partnership arrangements and in accordance with what were commonly designated as 'garden city principles'. These were the estates catalogued in 1914 in E.G. Culpin's *The Garden City Movement Up-to-Date*. They were scattered throughout the British Isles, depending for their promotion on the involvement of sympathetic landowners, dynamic local initiative or the demands of new industrial development. The distribution of these co-partnership estates, however, demonstrated considerable unevenness. As with the industrial villages of an earlier generation, regional patterns emerged, and local initiatives frequently served to stimulate similar ventures nearby. In examining this development in Lancashire and Yorkshire, the variation in practice is at once apparent. In Yorkshire there was no co-partnership development, and garden suburbs appear to have made little impression on the urban scene. To the west of the Pennines the impact was of a very different order. In 1910 the largest co-partnership estate was begun with the laying out of the 18 acres of the Liverpool Garden Suburb at Childwall.[63] At both Warrington and Oldham tenant societies developed out of the 'city beautiful' societies which, like those in other towns, had been established in the early years of the century to campaign on a comprehensive basis for the improvement of the urban environment along the lines pioneered by Octavia Hill and refined in the propaganda of the Civics Committee of the Sociological Society.[64] By 1912 the *Manchester Guardian* could note: There has recently been quite a remarkable and useful development of garden suburb schemes in the outskirts of Manchester.[65] Five estates were then in process of development on co-partnership lines.

The Manchester Tenants Limited was registered in 1907 under the chairmanship of the Manchester housing reformer, Councillor Marr. An 11-acre estate was purchased at Burnage on the southern extremity of the built-up area of the city and situated four miles from the city centre. The capital was raised by means of £10 shares, with no individual shareholder having more than £200 in shares. By September 1910, when the estate was officially opened, 136 houses had been completed at rents varying from 5s. to 14s. 6d. per week, excluding rates.[66] The site was simply laid out in the shape of a cross with extending culs-de-sac and with a large central common garden for the playing of tennis, bowls and croquet. The society made its roads of macadam, 18 feet wide and bounded with 7 feet of grass and trees and 5-foot flagged pavements on either side. The local authority bye-laws demanded a 42-foot road with 24 feet of the width metalled and with two flagged pavements of 9-ft width. But though the Corporation objected to the society's development, no attempt was made to enforce the objection.[67] The trees and the grass remained to characterize this estate, which was frankly a group of houses well planned and laid out on co-partnership lines within a suburb of Manchester, and which took part in the general life of that suburb.[68]

The success of this venture led Marr to undertake a further co-partnership housing scheme in Manchester – the Fairfield Garden Suburb. In 1908 a garden allotment scheme was started on 2½ acres of land lying half way between Manchester and Ashton-under-Lyne.[69] This was an area containing many large industries and there was a great demand for housing. The promoters of the original venture thus conceived of a more ambitious scheme, and in 1912 secured 21 acres of land adjoining the Moravian settlement at Fairfield. The company was registered with the Co-Partnership Tenants and through this organization secured capital to the extent of £20,000. Between 1913 and 1914, 46 houses were built facing one road with a small court with a green in the centre and a series of culs-de-sac.[70] The neighbouring houses of the Moravian settlement were of a plain, dignified Georgian character,[71] and the new houses, designed by the Manchester architects Sellars and Wood, mirrored that form but avoided monotony by their skilful layout.[72] The houses, in terraced and semi-detached units, were carefully sited on the sloping land with great care given to levels and aspects. The architects also paid much attention to details, giving the estate a unity through the treatment of garden walls and flagging. The houses, built in common brick, differed from the folksy cottages of other garden suburbs, and the development as a whole possessed a more urbane character. The architects carefully combined traditional forms with new layouts, and evolved a harmonious environment that clearly demonstrated the immense importance of layout, and the need for attention to details in planning and materials, if the design of housing was to be successful.

The Fairfield suburb was planned with the majority of houses for working men, with rents around 5s. per week, though there were other houses on the estate that let at up to 10s. per week rent. Few other garden suburbs, however, were able to cater principally for the working class. The directors of Chorltonville Limited, a garden suburb on the south-western edge of Manchester, grappled unsuccessfully with the problem.

Chorltonville Limited was a limited company established in 1909 in order to lay out an estate on 'improved lines'.[73] Unlike the co-partnership estates, it was not registered under the Industrial and Provident Societies Act, and thus could not obtain, under the Housing Act of 1909, advances at 3½ per cent interest from the Public Works Loan Commissioners to the extent of two-thirds of the value of the property. However, the company was organized in other respects along co-partnership lines, with every tenant holding at least two £5 shares. The moving force behind this venture was a local estate agent, J.H. Dawson, and the scheme originated from his involvement with the Hulme Healthy Homes Society.[74] He aimed to persuade the working men of Hulme to go to live in a better class district under healthier conditions, and in so doing to prove that it was possible to build a model estate on garden city principles as a succesful business proposition. Unfortunately for Dawson, when the first 20 houses were completed in Claude Street, none of his poor families could be persuaded to move from the area in which they were established. Consequently the estate had to be adapted for an altogether different class of tenants. So the remaining 272 houses that were built on the 35½-acre estate over the following three years were designed for middle-class needs, and let at rents of £23 *per annum* and upwards. The spacious semi-detached houses centred on a large grassy area known as the Meads, while bowling greens, tennis courts and a cricket pitch were also provided. The roads were of a similar make-up to those at Burnage, and again difficulties with the local authority meant that they remained under the private control of the Chorltonville Owners' Committee, to which each tenant contributed a voluntary levy.[75]

In the end this became but another successful business venture providing a suburban retreat for city business men and their families, for whom the nearby railway station and tramway provided ready access. In many ways developments such as this, which was typical of many undertaken by private builders or companies and described as 'garden suburbs',[76] were a continuation of the Victorian arcadian suburb in a new dress rather than a genuine interpretation of the co-partnership enterprise. Though the houses lived up to their reputation of being bright, well-ventilated and containing all modern conveniences, each was designed individually and with scant regard for the total effect or the creation of street pictures. Co-partnership, and its emphasis on the benefits for all in the individual care of communal property, became on such estates a further expression of Victorian suburban exclusiveness.

The comprehensiveness of both the garden city ideal and of the co-partnership organization meant that the term 'garden suburb' served to embrace a wide range of schemes, that were varied both in design and in motivation. If some were projected by landowners or business men, others stemmed from the grass-roots vision of a better world, which in turn stimulated local interest and activity. In many industrial towns and cities the early years of the twentieth century saw a growing awareness of the dreariness of the environment and the possibility of relieving the situation. In Oldham, the formation of the Beautiful Oldham Society was stimulated by the publication in 1902 of *Glimpses into the Abyss* by Mrs Higgs, a local social reformer and critic of urban squalor and deprivation.[77] Devoting its attention chiefly in the first instance to the preservation and cultivation of plants and flowers, the interest of members turned increasingly to the question of the beautification of the homes of the people. The movement gave an impulse to the desire for a better mode of living and a better style of house design, and out of it developed the efforts to create a garden suburb in the town. In 1906 a 52-acre estate was secured for only £150 per acre as a result of the generosity of the local benefactors – the Lees family.[78] The Society was registered and affiliated to the Co-Partnership Tenants Housing Council. Capital of £10,000 was raised by private subscription but, though the acquisition of shares was made easy for the working class by providing £1 shares payable at the rate of 2s. 6d. every three months, the response was disappointing, and by December 1908 only 349 shares had been taken up. However, the Society was able to secure a £10,000 loan on easy terms, and building began in the following year. By the outbreak of war, 156 out of a proposed total of 600 houses had been built.[79] The houses were of five designs, each having a parlour and a bathroom, though some only had two bedrooms. The rents varied from 5s. 6d. to 7s. 6d. per week. This was a real effort to provide a well-built and well-positioned house with a garden at a price that at least the better-off working man could afford. It must be recognized, however, that even this was made possible only through the subsidization of the original purchase price of the estate. In addition, the Society was attempting to fulfil a role that was central to the intentions of the Co-Partnership Tenants Housing Council – that of education.[80] The Oldham Society felt that its own estate, with its layout of open spaces and unified arrangement of cottages, would help to modify the ideas of local builders with regard to the design and planning of housing for the working class. In this way they saw themselves as benefiting the whole community.

The co-partnership movement sought to promote through its estates an example which it hoped would influence a wider audience. At the same time, the organizers believed that the pattern of community life encouraged on the co-partnership estates would provide new interests for the inhabitants and serve indirectly as an educational influence fostering different expectations and standards of behaviour amongst the tenants. The Co-Partnership Tenants Housing Council guided most of the educational and social work on the main estates and chronicled their activities in its monthly magazine *Co-Partnership*.[81] It also organized the Co-Partnership Festival which was held annually on one or other of the co-partnership estates and at which flower shows, children's competitions, pageants and other features were organized, with the express purpose of demonstrating the advantages of the co-partnership ideal as expressed in suburban life both for the individual and for the general welfare of the community.[82]

The possibilities of a co-operative life had been stressed since the early days of the pioneer scheme at Ealing: 'The purchase of several plots of land instead of so many isolated frontages had given the pioneers a glimpse of what could be done in co-operation.'[83] As co-partnership estates developed, arrangements were made to facilitate the achievement of such aspirations. With encouragement from the management, tenants organized themselves into committees and arranged flower shows, gardening contests, concerts and winter lectures. As the secretary of the

Liverpool Company explained to the first tenants on the estate: 'Living in a co-partnership suburb did not mean being isolated tenants, but that the whole of the social and recreative life of the estate would be managed by the tenants themselves.'[84]

On the larger estates there would be a central hall or institute, which provided not only games rooms, lecture room, reading room and library, but also facilities for the organization of other communal activities. Of the Lancashire estates, only the Burnage garden suburb was able to support such a facility.[85] On the other estates social activities were organized among the houses.[86] Everywhere the greatest prominence was given to sporting and horticultural activities, as was only to be expected in developments which placed such emphasis on the virtues of fresh air and the outdoor life. By such means, however unsophisticated, the co-partnership estates sought to foster a spirit of neighbourliness which it was felt had been suppressed by the long streets and high yard walls of the terraced dwellings. During the first decade of development, when the ideas were novel and the tenants fresh, the spirit of co-operation seems to have flourished throughout the co-partnership garden suburbs.

But though the Co-Partnership Tenants had been able to develop a community of spirit that had evaded the housing efforts of the Victorian co-operative societies, they were no more successful in solving the problem of housing for the poorest of

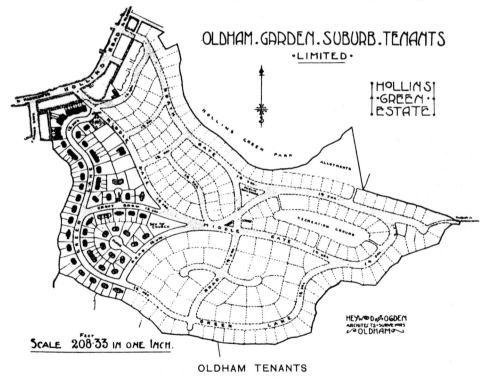

Figure 3. Design for Oldham Garden Suburb by Messrs Heywood and Ogden (*Town Planning Review*, I, 1910; PL: 47).

the working class. Out of 2,955 houses erected by societies connected with the Co-Partnership Tenants Limited by 1913, only 640 were rented for below 6s. a week; 1,913 were rented for between 6s. and 12s., while of the remainder, 247 were let for between 12s. and 20s. and 155 for over 20s. a week.[87] The societies appealed basically to middle-class tenants, and reflected middle-class values. Housing that could really meet the needs of the working class was built only by the Garden City Tenants at Letchworth, and on those estates where the development was subsidized by the landowner or promoter, as was the case at Oldham.[88] On none of the estates, moreover, was the dream of the promoters of the Hampstead garden suburb realized – that of creating a truly mixed and socially-integrated community.[89]

Of course the Tenant Co-operators had originally aimed to assist the working classes through the promotion of self-help, reflecting the view that even the poorest class did not value anything that was realized without effort or self-sacrifice of their own.[90] To enable the poorest members of the community to benefit from their scheme it was arranged that the participants in the Tenant Co-operators' scheme had to take up only one share to the value of £1.[91] In the co-partnership societies shares were usually of £10 and tenants ultimately had to take up at least five shares.[92] Thus later societies did not allow the tenants a really effective share in the management of the estates, and they excluded poorer participants by demanding a share qualification greater than they could afford.

The garden suburb had not been able to prove itself financially. Nor had it established itself as the undoubted and immediate panacea of the housing needs of the working class. The application of self-help to the garden-city principle had provided an example that others could develop; it could not provide a single solution to the housing problem. It did, however, demonstrate, albeit on a small scale, the possibility of an alternative approach to the design and layout of housing for the lower classes. It had provided a different standard of suburban expansion. It was the practical example of improvement which those who urged wider powers of urban control saw as a basis for change; it was a model that could be appreciated and adopted.

As such the garden suburb in practice overshadowed the garden city from which it derived its significant impetus and with whose name it was associated. The energetic activities of the co-partnership tenants and the skilful publicity of many promoters of garden suburb ventures ensured that some of the ideas associated with this form of development came to occupy a large place in the public mind. In the years before the First World War the garden city, other than through the one example of Letchworth, did not exert a direct impact on the development of urban areas in this country. What resulted indirectly was the creation of new suburban settlements by co-operative societies in conformity with certain standards of layout and design. That these were frequently confused with the garden city as such was largely the consequence of the involvement of many of the early advocates of the garden city, especially Raymond Unwin, in the establishment of garden suburbs. At the same time, support for the latter came from the garden City Association itself, and confusion in the terminology was inevitable. Frederick Osborn later reflected: 'And so the big woolly public, at first much taken with Howard's idea and wishful to pursue the subject, got thoroughly muddled between garden cities and garden suburbs.'[93]

Over the years leading up to the First World War writers on housing and planning increasingly adopted the descriptive term 'on garden city lines' to indicate the development of estates in suburban areas along lines exemplified by the garden suburbs. When in 1914 E.G. Culpin, the secretary of the Garden City Association, reviewed the development that had taken place in his book *The Garden City Movement Up-to-Date*, he listed a series of schemes none of which, with the exception of Letchworth, could justify the title 'garden city'. Though many of these housing and estate developments could quite properly have been regarded as owing something to garden city ideas, to call them garden cities was an abuse of what was originally meant by that term. This misuse of terminology reflected the extent to which people thought that to lay out a site with adequate garden space was to plan on 'garden city lines'. The effect of this confusion was summarized in retrospect by that lifelong campaigner for the ideal of the garden city and for the building of satellite towns, C.B. Purdom:

> the significance of the garden city as an alternative to the suburban growth of cities was overlooked, and the general public no less than technical men and writers in general, and even writers on town planning, took their idea of what a garden city was from the misapplication of the idea that was found in suburban land developments.[94]

3 The suburban estate legislated for

Notwithstanding the practical and organizational difficulties faced by the co-partnership societies, their co-operative garden suburb ventures had captured the public imagination during the first decade of the twentieth century and had come to dominate the counsels of housing reform. They demonstrated the possibility of a way forward that was not matched by any other organ of reform and they thus provided a frame of reference against which the town planning movement developed.

Admittedly, the co-partnership movement in the garden suburbs was primarily concerned with housing rather than town planning, and, as was argued at the outset, the town-planning movement owed its origins to a series of converging ideas and interests. What the garden suburbs had demonstrated through the kind of practical achievement surveyed in the preceding section was the way in which schematic and quantitative diagrams could be applied to site conditions, along with the advantages of the control of layout and design according to certain aesthetic and architectural standards. These the public could appreciate, for as Osborn later commented: 'the public, hailing the new standards with enthusiasm, and then as now able to visualize houses but not towns, identified the component with the total product.'[95]

It was then the model of the co-partnership garden suburb that was to the fore in the debate of 1909 and which was reflected in that first legislative formulation of town planning. In these circumstances, the practical possibility of town planning was, as Ashworth argued, to be virtually synonymous with 'suburban layout on garden city lines'.[96] The model employed was that of the garden suburb, not the garden city, and not even the model of the garden village or the suburban council estate.

This is not to suggest that the other formulations were not important either in their design or their financial aspects. The garden villages were particularly responsible for the articulation of many ideas crucial to the garden city concept and it was as a consequence of this contribution that in 1906 the Garden City Association enlarged its activities and interests, and adopted as its third objective: '*The building of Garden Villages*, as exemplified by Port Sunlight and Bournville, for properly housing the working classes near their work.'[97]

The tradition in which these communities must be placed is of course that of the model industrial village: a tradition that was clearly much older than the concept of the garden city. Industrialists such as Lever, Cadbury, and Rowntree had pioneered the ideas and forms that were now reflected in the Garden City Association's interpretation of planned development. These garden villages had provided clearly identifiable patterns of designs and standards of layout.

However, there were few opportunities for the creation of completely new settlements which could be laid out on 'model' lines. Some firms might be persuaded to move to the garden city at Letchworth,[98] or decide to migrate to the suburban areas of a city where there was room for expansion and land was cheaper, but isolated settlement was uncommon. The experience of the early twentieth century suggested that the industrial financing of planned residential schemes had limited applicability on anything but a very small scale.

On the other hand, the municipal suburban estate established itself as a significant factor for the future in the town planning and housing reform movement, even though the number of council estates developed before 1914 was very limited. The 1890 Housing of the Working Classes Act had enabled municipal bodies to extend their interest in housing beyond that of simple demolition and reconstruction and to become land purchasing and house building agencies.[99] The possibilities for action that the Act had authorized had led to much discussion and argument over the following decade between those who felt that local authorities, as the representatives of society, should take all possible action to remedy the evils created by that society and those who were alarmed by the potential effect of the growth of municipal power.[100] The basis of such concern was that the growth of local authority housing might impede the flow of capital into the private sector and that the more council housing that was undertaken, the less incentive there would be for private enterprise to build, and that this might lead to a time when the private builder ceased to build altogether. In addition, there were widely voiced fears over municipal ability to control standards, secure good workmanship and maintain financial efficiency.[101]

During the two decades following the passage of the Housing of the Working Classes Act municipalities advanced hesitantly in housing matters, with only a few authorities making some cautious experiments. Though some civic leaders showed a new awareness of housing problems and possible municipal solutions, in quantitative terms council houses remained a relatively unimportant feature in the urban scene. Prior to 1909 about 98 per cent of the housing stock catering for the working classes had been provided by other means than through the agency of local authorities.[102] Even after the Housing and Town Planning Act of 1909, they built few houses. Between 1909 and 1915 approximately 11,000 houses were built by local authorities at an average cost of £235 per house, whilst a total of over 200,000 houses were erected by private enterprise.[103] And it must be remembered that during this period private enterprise in the provision of workmen's houses was much discouraged, notably by increased costs of labour and materials, the greater attraction for the investing public of industrial and commercial undertakings and the baneful influence of the 1910 Budget on the building trade.[104]

It was, therefore, the experience, the standards and the features of the co-partnership garden suburbs which predominated in the early twentieth century. In the intensifying debate over the need for wider powers of control and direction in the field of housing development and town planning, this approach was promoted

most strongly by the two most influential bodies involved, the Garden City Association and the National Housing Reform Council. As a consequence of the influence
and relative success of the garden suburb it was argued by 1909 that previous
housing legislation should be extended to include the planning of new suburbs. The
1909 Town Planning Act built on this basis and brought forward legislation to
encompass suburban expansion.[105] The experience of the enforcement of the Act
demonstrated the limitations of that conceptual basis, particularly in terms of the relationship of the individual estate to the total pattern of urban growth, and in terms
of its financial feasibility. The 1909 Act built largely on nineteenth-century experience of estate development, self-help and extending local control. In growing from
these roots, it determined the character of much ensuing twentieth-century housing
and planning legislation.

The 1909 Town Planning Act endorsed at a national level the combination of local
government oversight and some of the ideas and practices enshrined in the garden
city ideal. Local authorities were to have the power to control the standards of
layout and impose conditions of development on new estates if they so chose. Under
that umbrella, development was conceived essentially in terms of the physical and
aesthetic qualities established in the co-partnership garden suburbs. It was then a
compromise of attitudes, a pragmatic proposal reflecting a commitment only to
what had been demonstrated to be achievable. As Campbell Bannerman had
remarked at the time of the debate on the bill: 'The proposal might properly be
regarded as perhaps the greatest common measure of agreement in the opinions of
well-intentioned men on this subject throughout the country.'[106] On the suburban
estate, it was widely believed, there would be realized the joint benefits of town and
country which Howard had preached. C.F.G. Masterman characterized the current
mood when he wrote that suburban life was 'the healthiest and the most hopeful
power for the future of modern England'.[107]

The result was that, under the first town planning legislation, the garden suburb
became synonymous with town planning. Although the Act did contain provision
for the implementation in a more efficient manner of improvement schemes in built-
up areas, Part II, which was the most important and novel portion of the whole
measure, applied only to the development of new areas so that it was concerned
with town expansion rather than town redevelopment. The failure to face the difficulties of land reform and to introduce a system for the compulsory acquisition of
land meant that in practice planning was limited to suburban extension.[108] Though
John Burns, in introducing the bill, indicated that he envisaged a more comprehensive interpretation, extension plans, such as those in force in German towns, were
impracticable without more thoroughgoing reform.[109] The Local Government
Board, however, gave no lead in this respect, and the encouragement of planned
redevelopment on a larger scale was delayed.[110] Public opinion and parliamentary
support was limited to an indiscriminate approbation of the concept of the garden
suburb. Geddes rightly commented:

> Though some find fault with Mr Burns for not giving complete and immediate
> powers in his Act to scheme out vast future areas in German fashion, his caution is
> also to be praised. We are not ripe for such magnificent schemes; we are not to be
> trusted with such sweeping changes.[111]

Under the Town Planning Act the community was empowered, through its local authority, to make a plan laying down the lines upon which part or all of the land surrounding a town, not yet built upon but likely to be built upon in the future, should be developed. In practice, a town planning scheme, as approved by the Local Government Board, usually provided for the layout of a particular area or estate. But within the boundaries of that designated area an authority was able to exercise unique and novel powers. The plan would define the direction, position and width of the roads, and could make provision for the local authority to develop any of the roads which were urgently required for the public need or were necessary for the subsequent implementation of the plan as a whole. Any bye-laws or other statutory enactments might be varied by the town-planning scheme, so far as was necessary for its proper execution, with a view to securing better sanitary conditions, amenities and convenience. This meant that the local authority could depart from the standards established by its own bye-law system in order to create the new and wide highways which were becoming increasingly necessary with the growing amount of vehicular traffic, while reducing the width of minor streets serving residential areas. The scheme might also make restrictions on the number of buildings which could be erected on each acre of ground, determine their height and character, and prescribe the space around buildings. Land could be compulsorily purchased for open spaces and other purposes in connection with the town planning scheme. The local authority was thus enabled to control both the disposition of individual buildings and the zoning of different functions. Finally, it could establish a maximum density over the whole area covered by the scheme. This was basic to determining the character of the area since the Local Government Board insisted on conformity to the density standards acceptable in garden city practice.[112]

Raymond Unwin considered that, if these powers were used carefully, it would be found that there was little of what was required for the ideal development of the growing town that could not be secured under one or other of these headings.[113] One of the special features of the Act was to empower the local authority to make agreements with the owners of land on any subject bearing upon its development. The local authority was put in a favourable position for making such agreements because it had not only the power to restrict within certain limits the use to which the owner might put his land, but it also had the power very greatly to facilitate development by the suitable laying out of roads, or by prohibiting objectionable buildings on adjacent property, or by modifying many existing restrictive bye-laws which had been formulated to suit other conditions of development.[114]

Here then, for the first time in this country, local authorities had the powers and the means to secure the organized growth of a new area and to plan for the 'suburb salubrious' as Burns described it.[115] Under this legislation, the garden suburb, as a form of housing and rehousing for all classes of the community, received official commendation.

It is not surprising, therefore, that in examining schemes submitted under the Act in Lancashire and Yorkshire it should be found that the schemes which were the earliest to be approved by the Local Government Board were those which centred upon a precise piece of suburban estate planning along garden city lines. At Middleton the Lees Trustees had been desirous of developing the Alkrington Hall Estate on garden-city lines, and though the Garden City Association had been unable to form a company to acquire the estate, they had proceeded to secure a plan for laying out the 600 acres along those lines.[116] When the local authority was applied to for exemption from the bye-law restrictions, it decided to make the estate the focal point of a larger scheme which would be submitted to the Local Government Board for approval.[117] This larger scheme covered a suburban residential area that was being opened up by improved communications, and ultimately a joint scheme was proposed by Middleton and Manchester, whose Blackley estate was contiguous to that of Alkrington Hall.[118] The scheme, as approved by the Local Government Board in 1912, made possible the planning of 1,300 acres and included the laying out of a much-needed wide arterial road through north Manchester and the development of residential property along garden-city lines on the land adjacent.[119] The plan provided for houses laid out at a density of 12 per acre and for roads varying in width from 65 feet to 25 feet in accordance with the volume of traffic in the district. Another bye-law requiring modification was that which demanded a minimum height of 9 feet for all rooms. In the case of an estate so sparingly planned, there was no need for such lofty rooms and the scheme allowed a minimum of 8 feet 6 inches, which was, in fact, the maximum height of the rooms in the houses on most of the garden-suburb schemes. The plans, drawn up by Pepler and Allen, included 2 acres of public open space and 3.8 acres of private land which was to be kept open. This open land included the protection of the Alkrington Hall Woods on the southern side of the estate.[120] These conditions and the relaxation of the bye-laws were particularly effective in the Manchester part of the scheme, where the already-completed part of the Blackley council estate had been severely criticized on the grounds that it adopted unnecessarily expensive methods of development and made quite inadequate provision for open spaces.[121] The scheme showed, on a limited scale, the possibilities under the Act for the control of development on the land of several owners by means of some unified planning (see fig. 10).

The initial stimulus, however, had come from one owner, and in many cases town planning schemes were actually restricted to single estates. The first such scheme submitted to the Local Government Board by a landowner was that for Jesmond Park in Rochdale.[122] The estate was the property of a Mr Smethurst who had been a strong advocate of housing reform in this district and who desired, in the development of his estate, to show what might be done by private enterprise on a practical business basis to solve the question.[123] The 30 acres set aside for the scheme were to be developed with houses averaging 16 to the acres, and all the roads were to be at least 40 feet wide and consist of a 16-foot carriageway with 5-foot pathways and 7-foot grass verges planted with trees and shrubs. Bowling greens, tennis courts and recreation grounds were to be provided, including a small sunken garden which was formed in an existing hollow. A small shopping and communal centre with an institute as its central feature was made the axial point of several of the principal roads, while the five other roads converged on a circular place enclosing a site for a church or other public building. The main lines of the layout were influenced to a large extent by the considerations of aspect and the contour of the land – several of the roads being formed in existing hollows which were to be only partially filled in, with the land rising upon either side – while existing roads and cottage property which cut into the estate at several points dictated the lines of some of the new roads. The houses, which were mainly in pairs with an occasional group of three or four, varied in cost from about £200, and it was proposed that tenants should buy their own houses on a system by which they would pay about 5s. 6d. per week for the cheapest type.

This scheme for the development of an estate was first submitted to the Rochdale Town Council under the existing building bye-laws. While the Council expressed itself in favour of the plans in principle, it refused to sanction the scheme as certain of its proposals contravened the bye-laws. In order to circumvent this restriction, and with the encouragement of the Rochdale Housing Reform Council, the local authority decided to adopt Mr Smethurst's plan as a town planning scheme and to submit it as such to the Local Government Board for approval under the new Act.[124] The extension of the scheme by the local authority made it possible to develop the Marland area on lines approved by contemporary housing reformers. However, this was an unusual case, and like the Ruislip-Northwood scheme in London, as Ashworth pointed out, came about because of the coincidence of the opening up of a new suburban residential area, vigorous local pressure and the involvement of the landowner in model estate development. 'The Act was not likely to be working very often in such a favourable combination of circumstances.'[125]

Yet the editor of *The Garden City* considered that the facilitation of such schemes

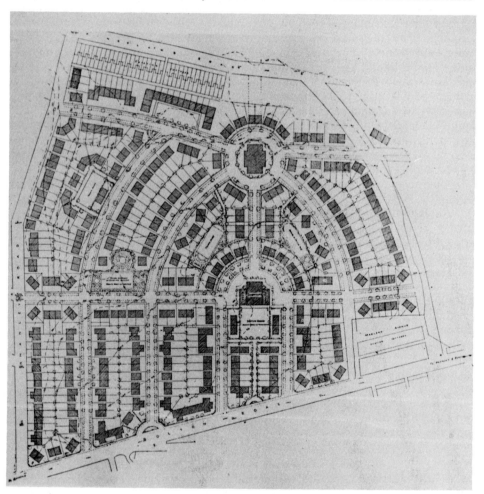

Figure 4. Design for Jesmond Park Garden Suburb by Gilbert Waterhouse (*Town Planning Review*, II, 1910; PL: 74).

was a most important function of the Act and that the submission procedure for them required simplification, so that owners would not be deterred from any efforts at improved development.[126] An owner ought rather to be encouraged if he went voluntarily to the great expense and trouble of laying out his estate on model lines, when he could with greater profit to himself have developed it upon the old haphazard methods.

The positive results of early town planning appear restricted, but it was argued that it was more important to secure a limited practical achievement than to be engaged solely in the preparation of more comprehensive schemes that had no immediate impact.[127] There was always need for layout and design on improved lines actually to be carried out and serve as an example. This was important not simply because much housing was continuing to be laid out under irrelevant bye-laws, but more significantly because developers and authorities misunderstood and misused the terminology associated with the town planning movement. Thus frequently the label 'garden city' or the descriptions 'model' and 'planned' were applied to estates without justification, but as means of advertisement. For instance, in 1909 a plan was drawn up for the Fearnville Park Garden City at Roundhay in Leeds and this shows streets arranged in a parallel manner, with houses in terraces and the only concession a somewhat larger than average amount of garden space.[128] Here was a not uncommon example of an estate which called itself a 'garden city' but which was laid out with virtual disregard of all garden city principles and where the straight line had been pressed at the expense of any natural beauties. There were numerous other examples of estates, consisting perhaps of no more than two parallel streets of terraced or closely-packed detached dwellings, which gloried in the name of 'garden city'.[129]

And if landowners and builders were reluctant to alter radically their style of development, local authorities were often equally loath to be flexible and reinterpret the standards of control. In 1913 the Health Committee of Bradford City Council organized a competition for laying out a 50-acre estate on garden-city lines.[130] Competitors interpreted this to mean the type of layout which had hitherto been associated with this terminology, until the Committee made their intentions clear in a circular.[131] It stipulated that the width of streets and the proportionate width of carriage and footpaths were to be strictly in accordance with the bye-laws, which did not permit of grass margins and which required roads to be of a minimum width of 42 feet. Culs-de-sac were not allowed, and all houses had to be served by a back road, for the building regulations did not allow covered passage-ways between houses. Open space was not to be provided for specific purposes such as bowling greens and recreation grounds, and land was not to be set aside for allotments. Sites were not to be reserved for a recreation room, library, club or other such building and no provision was to be made for churches, chapels or schools. This was to be purely a residential area laid out under traditional restrictions: 'The Building Regulations must be strictly adhered to and competitors are not allowed to depart from the literal interpretation of the bye-laws.'[132]

Thus, although the Town Planning Act appears in retrospect as a very timorous and hesitant measure, it had to battle against widespread uncomprehending opposition, even under its most limited interpretation as a guide to estate layout. As a result, those who envisaged the Act as primarily a means of relieving, if not completely solving, the housing problem had necessarily to stress the economies involved in layout under a town planning scheme, as compared with that under the bye-laws. J.S. Nettlefold wrote:

> Local authorities must recognize the fact that working men will not get, at the old rents, houses surrounded by gardens, allotments, playground and playing fields without charge to the ratepayers, unless the old official bye-law methods are superseded by business-like give-and-take agreements between progressive landowners and enlightened public bodies.[133]

He concluded that the extra cost of bye-law estate development over town planning estate development represented about 9d. per week on the rent of a 6s. 6d. house. The public health and aesthetic aspects of town planning must not be forgotten, he conceded, but in the end it was the economic aspect that was most important, for it was this that would govern the ultimate success of town planning.

However, there were those who looked beyond the immediate necessities of estate development and realized the dangers and inconsistencies inherent in anything less than total urban planning. George Cadbury was severely critical:

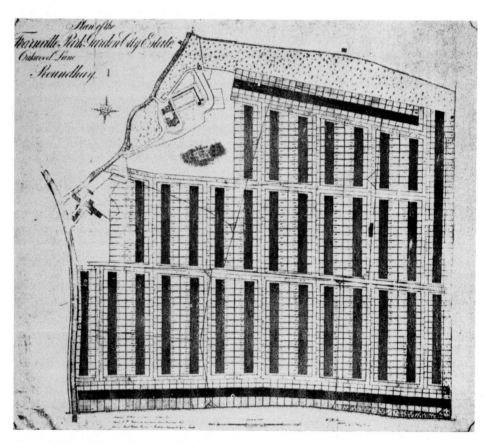

Figure 5. Plan of Fearnville Park Garden City Estate, Leeds. An illustration of the abuse of the term 'garden city' (W.H. Beeres' plan of 1908, Leeds City Library).

46

I believe that town planning is infinitely more important than anything else in the Bill, and on that nothing definite will be done. Miserable, monotonous suburbs will still be built all around our towns, spoiling the beautiful face of the country. When I think of the numbers of little children who will be brought up in these dismal suburbs, it is enough to make my heart bleed. Suburb planning is of the greatest importance to towns of 50,000 inhabitants or over. Every town and the District Councils within a radius of ten to fifteen miles should form a Housing Board. No new street should be allowed to be made in their neighbourhood without a plan being submitted or prepared by this board as to how the unused land in the neighbourhood is to be laid out, and when passed by the Housing Board it should be sent up to the Local Government Board. No new street would be allowed to be made until the plans had been submitted and playgrounds provided, as is the case in Germany, by a fair contribution from every landowner, whose land would be improved, in proportion to the area he held.[134]

Estate planning needed to be placed in context, and such criticism focused attention on the problems that the Act occasioned when it was applied to single estates or limited areas of a town. If, for instance, it was applied to just one or two suburbs within a town, it would probably check building operations in these areas whilst leading to increased building in adjacent areas which were free from restriction and yet which might be separated simply by the width of a road from the planned suburbs. In short, it would not stamp out the disease but only remove its locality. Furthermore, as E.M. Gibbs pointed out in Sheffield, restrictions under the Act might be placed on landowners in, say, two suburbs from which their counterparts in other suburbs were free, and yet as ratepayers they would have to pay their share of the cost of the preparation and operation of the schemes which imposed these restrictions.[135] So he concluded that if, for the public good, undesirable building was to be stopped and justice done to all, then a town planning scheme should be made to apply to all suburbs with no intervening areas exempt.

Nowhere in the country, however, was planning conceived of on such a scale prior to the First World War. Birmingham, the most advanced city in the preparation of plans, submitted schemes only for two limited areas to the east and west of the city, affecting some 2,300 acres.[136] By the outbreak of war, Manchester had prepared schemes for the 300 acres at Blackley adjoining the Middleton scheme in the north and for a second residential area of 10,000 acres in the south.[137] Sheffield was the most ambitious city in its planning and by 1913 three schemes had been sanctioned and a further two prepared.[138] These aimed to control all the suburban growth to the west and north of the city but left exempt the development to the south and east.

Thus in practice the Town Planning Act catered for restricted suburban estate development, and the consequence of its implementation was the control of urban expansion by the surrounding of the built-up area with such estates, laid out to low-density garden city principles with segregated areas of industry. Patrick Abercrombie reflected the current attitude in 1915:

All the energies of our town planners, seeking to make use of the Act, have been devoted to devising schemes which will prevent the Bye-Law Suburb from continuing its cancerous growth over the face of the land; under the clauses limiting the number of houses to the acre, the garden city principle of house density has been generally acquiesced in; and whether or not one agrees with the more drastic proposals of the garden city itself, it can hardly be denied that it is desirable that the next century's cincture of growth round our existing towns should be one of gardens rather than one of red brick and macadam.[139]

The implication of this orthodoxy was clearly a form of residential development that was greedy for land and which served to increase greatly the rate of expansion of large cities. So surely did low density seem to represent all that was healthy and beneficial environmentally, that the dangers of such suburban growth were unheeded. The early town planners, in their enthusiasm for the novelty of layout, or at least in their concern to secure some fragments from the despoliation of the countryside, seemed oblivious of the threat of endless suburbia which their policies involved. Even so sensitive and perceptive a planner as Raymond Unwin does not seem to have realized the ultimate consequences of low-density residential development. In 1912 he argued that the difficulties inherent in the increasing size of towns and the wider distribution of population would be much less than had at first sight appeared.[140] Town planning would provide for the better distribution of population and thus the more economical use of land. The further a town spread, the smaller was the increase in its diameter required by the development of a given area of new land. Unwin clarified his contention by demonstrating that if Manchester, with a radius of 2¼ miles, required over a ten-year period 100 acres for dwellings each year, with the houses built at a density of 34 per acre, then the radius of the town would increase to 2½ miles; but if the houses were built at a density of 15 houses per acre then some 227 acres would be required each year, which would serve to increase the radius only to 2¾ miles. Thus the extra distance to be travelled in that case would be only a ¼ mile further after ten years of 'wholesome development' and every addition would have a proportionally smaller effect.

Such growth, however, was not simply to be condoned but to be actively encouraged, for Unwin considered that the lower-density development would secure a greater total return to the owners of land in terms of the incremental value of land due to building operations.[141] Developing his calculations based on Manchester, he estimated that land increased in value from £50 to £500 per acre when transferred from agricultural to building purposes. Thus if 34,000 houses were to be built at the rate of 34 houses per acre this would produce an increment of the value of £45,000. But if the same number of houses were built at the density of 15 houses per acre then 227 acres would be required, and this would lead to an increment of £102,150. Unwin, seemingly concerned only to promote the extension of planned housing schemes, was attempting to encourage landowners to accept town planning ideas. He concluded his naive argument thus: 'Yet the owners of land are afraid of Town Planning. Why, the Town Planning Act may prove to be the handsomest gift this country has made to its landowners for a very long time.'[142]

Unwin was later to realize the pitfalls of his earlier commitment to the concept of continuous urban expansion with rings of garden suburbs. The healthfulness and density of the population of the whole city was not dependent on a simple overall layout of ten houses per acre. By 1938 he was to acknowledge that the city pattern required and permitted an almost unlimited variation:

This movement proposes that every dwelling, whether central or not, should have enough ground for healthy family life, and should be within reasonable distance of some open land. With this secured, the need for excessively low density to obtain further protection is greatly diminished. There is nothing in garden city principles that calls for scattering, or even semi-detachedness; nor is there anything with which the crescents of Bath or the squares of Bloomsbury would be inconsistent.[143]

Aware of the evils of the 'dreary suburb', Unwin was arguing that each part of the town ought to have its own significant form. However, in the years before the First World War, the emphasis on practicalities, and Unwin's particular involvement with form, meant that the wider implications of suburban estate development were disregarded. The only concern was expressed by a handful of critics who were worried by the interpretation of planning as being simply the addition of planned suburbs to the existing town. In particular, C.B. Purdom attacked the substitution of the garden suburb for the ideal of the garden city, which he considered was 'too good an idea to be confused with inferior practices'.[144] As Howard had always maintained, one of the essential strengths of the garden city was its completeness – designed as a self-contained whole, providing its own social resources.[145] With the 'dilution of town planning', the spreading garden suburbs were in danger of providing, instead of Howard's ideal of the combination of the best in both town and country, a suburbia of semi-detached houses in a landscape that presented all the worst features of town and country without any of their respective benefits. This line of attack against the unrestrained adoption of low-density housing patterns was developed by the architectural critic, Trystan Edwards. He considered that the idea of a 'suburb' implied something that was second rate and that of all suburbs the garden suburb was probably the most shoddy and depressing:

It has neither the crowded interest of the town nor the quiet charm of the country. It gives us the advantages neither of solitude nor of society. And the great inconvenience of this manner of living must also be noticed. The working man does not want to traverse long distances to see his friends after his day's work is done. Some of these suburbs are so big that trams are needed for the inhabitants but cannot be employed without sacrificing the rustic concept which is so much desired. As people of very limited means have not got private carriages or motor cars, they should not have their dwellings scattered far from each other.[146]

Edwards then turned the attention of critics to the dangers of abandoning the urban tradition. He argued for the planning of compact towns with 'nature undefiled' immediately beyond. This concept seemed more attractive than the 'monotonous diffuseness' of garden suburbs:

There will presently be a reaction against such a manner of building, and it will be realized that they love nature best who love the town. The time will come when the area set aside for houses will be severely restricted, so that the beauties of nature may be reserved for communal enjoyment. Such an enactment is highly necessary, for at present we find little houses springing up in the most charming spots. It is very nice for people who come first . . . but when everybody else does the same the advantage disappears. A spirit of extreme individuality is shown in this movement – individuality that often defeats its own ends.[147]

The drawbacks of dispersion inherent in the overgrowth of suburbs were paralleled by the dangers of diversity. In the period following the introduction of town planning legislation, however, Edwards was virtually a lone voice crying against the results of the low-density policy in urban growth. On the other hand, his appeal for the coherent and controlled layout of estates was shared by most contemporary planners. Whatever their approach to the situation in terms of design and style, planners were generally in agreement in the period prior to 1914 that a satisfactory layout could not be achieved simply by the indiscriminate scattering of detached houses of the most various design and then trusting to a little greenery to give the effect of composition. T.A. Lloyd, the architect to the Welsh Town Planning and Housing Trust, highlighted such attributes in reflecting on developments in 1917:

> town planning alone and the laying out of an estate on the right lines are not sufficient to carry us very far along the road of progress. Nor will the mere codifying of sets of model regulations or bye-laws suffice if we do not give the fullest consideration to the planning of individual houses and their arrangement in relation to adjacent buildings, roads and open spaces.[148]

The estates that were developed under the Town Planning Act and the schemes applauded by the early planning bodies demonstrated essentially this approach with its re-presentation of the ideas of Camillo Sitte and the stress on the visual qualities of town planning. The treatment of 'planned' estates up to 1914 inevitably incorporated in varying degrees a commitment to a sense of balance between buildings and their site. The first English planners, following essentially the lead of Raymond Unwin, adopted the ideas of enclosure and community, and the concern for securing visual interest through the exploitation of topography and the use of curves and breaks in street alignments. The closing of vistas, the enclosing of spaces, the avoidance of straight lines, the variation in the building line: these were the features typified in the early planning ventures. They were in turn a reflection of Sitte's concern to recapture the apparently accidental beauty of the medieval urban scene. The emphasis which early town planning placed upon this notion was an indication of the extent to which town planning, as it had emerged in this country, valued the artistic and architectural qualities of such endeavour on a small scale.

4   Conclusion

British town planning as it emerged in its first legislative formulation and as it was practised under that legislation demonstrated a particular interpretation of the art of urban planning. It is this interpretation and the reasons behind it which this essay has been concerned to investigate. The emphasis established has been on the central contribution of the garden suburb as being of essential significance for the understanding both of the nature of the first town planning legislation and of its impact.

The early town planning movement owed its origins to a variety of interacting ideas and interests, and leading advocates of planning in the years prior to the First World War were critically aware of the comprehensive function of town planning. Beauty of design and layout, though arguably of prime importance, was to be attained in consort with the practical aspirations of convenience and efficiency. Improvement in the aesthetic quality of the layout of new urban areas was only a part of the total fabric of town planning. The constituent components of the early town planning movement placed different emphases and values on different elements within the process of planning, ranging from the restructuring of social forms to the realignment of transport systems, and from the physical determination of new developments to the economic distribution of resources and services. The early town planning movement embraced all these expectations and encompassed a range of views as to how they would be achieved. Nevertheless, the aspirations of its supporters were of a comprehensive order; the underlying commitment to this ideal was identified by Raymond Unwin in 1910:

> Mr John Burns' Town Planning Act has wisely concentrated the attention of town planners in England mainly on the development of the still unbuilt-on areas round

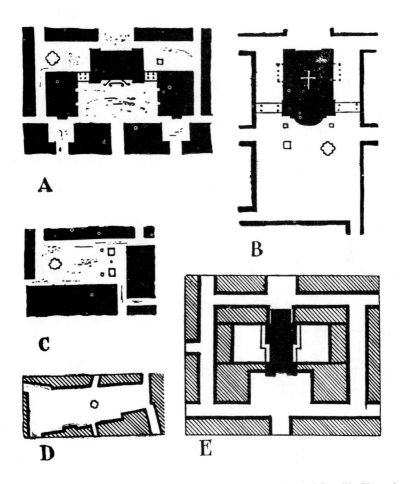

Figure 6. Raymond Unwin's demonstration of the recommendations of Camillo Sitte with regard to enclosure and the relationship of buildings in urban planning. The visual appreciation of such ideas greatly influenced notions of layout and site planning among the early practitioners of town planning in this country (R. Unwin, *Town Planning in Practice*, 2nd edn, 1911, 222).

the existing towns where the greatest damage is now taking place. We must, however, not suppose that we can consider the suburban areas by themselves. City planning really involves the whole problem of the proper organisation of city life. The high degree of specialisation upon which modern industry and life depend points to the probability that a very large proportion of the population of civilised countries will continue to live in, or immediately about, great city centres . . .

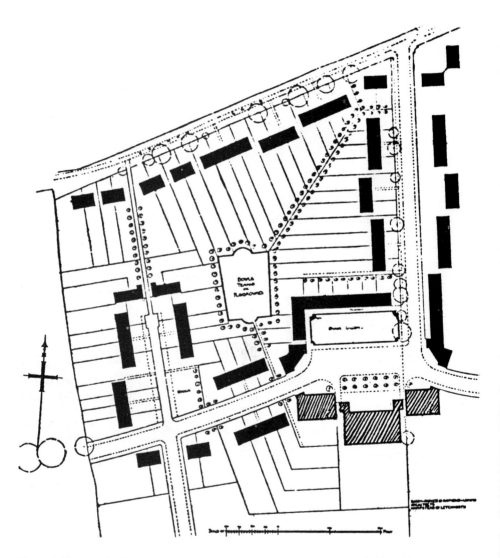

Figure 7. The application of the ideas represented in figure 6, as demonstrated in Parker and Unwin's design for the Leicester Anchor Tenants' Estate, with its concern for the creation of street pictures, balance and proportion, and a sense of enclosed space (R. Unwin, *Town Planning in Practice*, 1909, 232).

We need to bring into our city life that guiding oversight and direction in making the best of the facilities which its position affords, and that proper correlation of all the different parts, which are found so essential in a great modern industrial concern.[149]

In practice, however, the emphasis was on what could realistically be attained. The appeal of the Victorian suburban tradition and the garden city ideal combined in the practical achievement of the garden suburb. The product of voluntary corporate action, this form of development provided a realizable alternative to the limitations of nineteenth-century housing practice. But it also had a wider appeal. The movement to the suburbs, the greater extension of building faciliated by new methods of transport, and the chaotic conditions produced by business developments in inner-city areas stirred up many different reactions in different groups of people. In consequence such people, becoming increasingly conscious of the particularly distasteful symptoms of the course of urban development, began to look to town planning for help, without grasping the problem as a whole.

The effect of this partial approach was not only a dilution of the expectations of the early town planning movement, but also a confusion between the garden city and the garden suburb in which the significance of the garden city as a planning alternative to urban extension was overlooked. Indeed, though the Town Planning Act of 1909 seemed to pay lip-service to the garden city movement, in effect it did little more than encourage suburban growth at low density. This approach to planning carried with it the general acceptance, and to some degree complacent acceptance, of suburban growth as the principal mode of urban development. This was the legacy which early town planning bequeathed to post-war Britain. It was a legacy overtaken by events, since, with the increasing expansion of towns owing to better transport facilities, the garden suburbs ceased to be able to maintain any separate identity, and planned expansion became increasingly merged into the urban framework. Thus the end product of planning reform was unwittingly the suburbia of the 1930s. By then, however, the concepts that had been developed to meet certain particular circumstances were applied and extended within a very changed urban situation. With the expansion and dilution of the garden city idea, the final product became less well designed and ultimately increasingly monotonous. The idea of the coherent estate maintaining a balanced development was seemingly forgotten, and the result was urban expansion pressing out aimlessly into the countryside along the main roads. As the interstices were gradually filled in, towns became surrounded by the suburbia of semi-detached houses with their own gardens, which destroyed assiduously the balance between town and country that had been at the heart of the garden city concept.

The town planning that was handed down from these formative years was then one in which the major emphasis was laid on housing rather than the overall shaping of the town. The legislation of the inter-war years made advances in terms of the subsidisation of housing and the provision for council house building; at the same time, it enshrined the ideas of early town planners in their commitment to low-density development. The planning legislation of the inter-war years did not, moreover, involve any change in the concept of planning from that pioneered in 1909. The preparation of schemes was, admittedly, made obligatory and some of the procedural difficulties were removed; but the essential concentration on raising the standards of new residential development remained. British town planning continued to exercise rather vague and certainly restricted control; it was not until the Act of 1932 that planning powers were extended to land of any type and legislation directly concerned itself with the remodelling of existing towns or the replacement of badly planned areas.[150] Even this and later measures, however, remained inadequate, and it was not until the Second World War that the pressure of events provided the necessary stimulus for a comprehensive extension of town and country planning powers. The consequence was that throughout the inter-war period development proceeded indiscriminately and British town planning, building on its initial experience, remained essentially concerned with the unit of development rather than the totality; the central concept of the early town planning movement, of the town as a comprehensively conceived community, receded.

That convergence of ideas in the early town planning movement had not, however, been realized in legislation or in planning activity in the period prior to the First World War, and it was this early achievement and practice which informed the subsequent development of British town planning. The basis for a comprehensive approach to planning, particularly in terms of its values, was, however, already present in the early movement. In the subsequent realization of town planning it had a relatively minor place, until re-identified in more recent years, with the need to move practice away from the discredited suburban image. In the intervening period, the product of the pattern accepted in the formative years had been at the macro-level both limiting and to a large extent ineffectual. At the micro-level, however, the position established in those initial years meant that British town planning maintained a quality in terms of the detail of treatment that was one of its greatest strengths.

The impact of the garden suburb on the early planning movement, and in particular the scale of activity of the co-partnership societies, meant that while civic design was slow in reaching its full development, considerable advance was made in that aspect of it which was concerned with the planning of residential areas. Attention to the details of site planning was a major achievement of town planning as it emerged, and standards were established in those early years which owed much to the conjunction of town planning and suburban improvement.[151] As Gordon Cherry has pointed out, the principal notions of the emergent town planning activity were in fact being formulated in the course of the actual development of estates.[152] Inherent in the notion of the garden city was the emphasis on the preparation of advance schemes and the need for careful surveying of any site to be developed. The artistic and architectural aspirations of the garden suburbs reinforced the commitment to the detail of small-scale planning. It was encapsulated pre-eminently in Unwin's study of town planning which looked so clearly to historical precedent and to an analysis of the relationship of buildings and spaces based on romantic and physical concepts. Unwin's ideas were essentially concerned with physical enclosure, and through his interpretation of the garden suburb came a comprehension of planning which devoted particular attention to the grouping of buildings and architectural organization.

It was this approach, enshrined in the early garden suburbs, which constituted the finest achievement of British town planning in its formative years. From those examples came the fundamentals of site planning that were to characterize the future development of town planning at the micro-level. Of these perhaps no single feature had so great an influence upon the character of site planning as the limitation of density. But along with this went a much greater freedom in road location

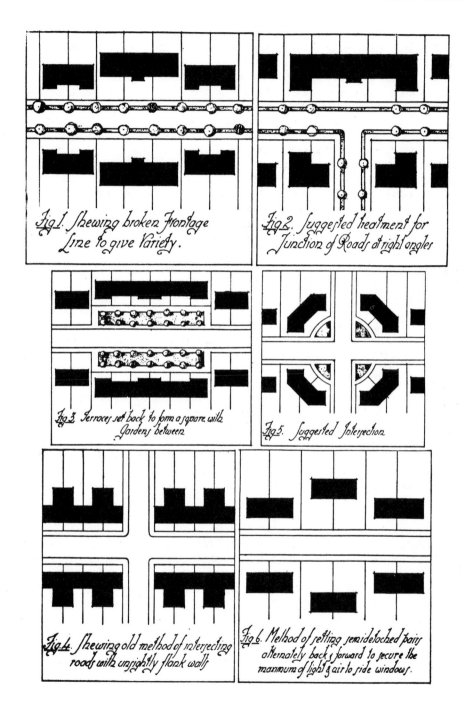

Fig 1. Shewing broken Frontage
Line to give Variety.

Fig 2. Suggested treatment for
Junction of Roads at right angles

Fig 3. Terraces set back to form a square with
Gardens between

Fig 5. Suggested Intersection.

Fig 4. Shewing old method of intersecting
roads with unsightly flank walls

Fig 6. Method of setting semidetached pairs
alternately back & forward to secure the
maximum of light & air to side windows.

Figure 8. Diagram prepared by H.C.Lander, demonstrating 'Some of the Principles of Town Planning in Garden Cities and Suburbs' (E.G. Culpin, *The Garden City Movement up-to-Date*, 1914, 68).

and design, which was facilitated by the increase in the size of the house plots. This resulted in the abandonment of the stereotyped system of parallel streets and in the adoption of the much more rational procedure of adapting the layout plan to the contours of the site. The planning practice that emerged in this country at its best paid the closest attention to detail, whether in the contouring of roads to enhance the topographical features of the site, the disposition of buildings to give character and distinction to each street, the use of natural features to secure more effective groupings of buildings, or the subordination of individual houses to the harmony of the whole. British town planning had arguably been most successful when concerned with such details as the arrangement of buildings to give the feel of a built-up corner or the disposition of houses in a cul-de-sac to give the sense of enclosure. Inherent in this approach is the appreciation that every site has its own peculiar problems which cannot be solved by the application of a ready-made plan, and that in every scheme the differentiation between the functions of the various parts should be reflected in the type of layout adopted.

This then was the positive contribution of early town-planning practice. It was a reflection of the importance of the architect in the moulding of that practice and of the absence of standardized municipal control; it was a development of the tradition of the garden city and a consequence of the interaction of that movement with notions of planning; it was a consolidation of what was actually achieved in the first planning ventures; it was the corollary of the failure to realize in practice the comprehensive vision of the early town planning movement. It meant in fact that, as a consequence of this formative experience, British town planning assumed a particular quality and developed in a very definite direction:

> The British concept of new town design, as it was beginning to emerge in the first few years of this century, was neither the City Beautiful nor the Futurist vision of a mechanistic Valhalla. It was not what Muthesius imagined either: it was a curious distillation of English characteristics, particularly the love of the house and the garden . . . The nature of planning might best be described in this country as an attempt to grasp the idea of community structure and to seek out a new language for expressing the idea of the home.[153]

NOTES

1 RIBA, *Town Planning Conference, 1910, Trans.* (1911), iv.
2 W. Ashworth, *The Genesis of Modern British Town Planning* (1954), 174.
3 E. Howard, *Tomorrow: a Peaceful Path to Real Reform* (1898); republished as *Garden Cities of Tomorrow* (1902).
4 9 Edw. VII, c.44.
5 Ashworth, *op.cit.*, 188.
6 *TPR*, I (1910), 18.
7 J. Burnett, *A Social History of Housing 1815–1970* (1978), 187.
8 *The Times*, 25 June 1904.
9 R.T. Blomfield, *Richard Norman Shaw, R.A., Architect, 1831–1912* (1940), 33–6; N. Pevsner, 'Architecture and William Morris', *JRIBA*, LXIV (1957), 172–5; N. Pevsner, *Pioneers of Modern Design* (1960), 48–60; A.R.N. Roberts, 'The life and work of W.R. Lethaby', *J. Royal Soc. Arts*, CV (1957), 355–71; R.N. Shaw, 'The home and its dwelling

rooms', in *The British Home of Today*, ed. W. Shaw Sparrow (1904), cv–cvi; L. Weaver, *The Country Life Book of Cottages* (1919), *passim*; *Studio*, IX (1896), 189–90.

10 W.A. Harvey, *The Model Village and its Cottages: Bournville* (1906), 63.

11 *Ibid.*, 57; J.H. Whitehouse, 'Bournville: study in housing reform' *Studio*, XXIV (1902), 170–1.

12 W.L. George, *Labour and Housing at Port Sunlight* (1909), 66–7; M.E. Macartney, 'Mr Lever and Port Sunlight', *AR,* XXVIII (1910), 43; J. Reynolds, 'The model village at Port Sunlight', *JRIBA*, LV (1948), 495.

13 W.H. Lever, 'The buildings erected at Port Sunlight and Thornton Hough', (paper read to the Architectural Association, 1902); George, *op.cit.*, 93–6.

14 Bournville Village Trust, *Sixty Years of Planning* (1943), 7, Cadbury Brothers Ltd, *Bournville Housing* (1922), 5; J.S. Nettlefold, *Practical Housing* (1908), 53.

15 A. Marshall, 'The housing of the London poor', *Contemporary Rev.*, XLV (1884), 230.

16 J.S. Mill, *Principles of Political Economy* (2nd edn, 1849), I, 147.

17 W.H.G. Armytage, *Heavens Below* (1961), 336.

18 L. Mumford, 'The garden city idea and modern planning', in E. Howard, *Garden Cities of Tomorrow*, ed. F.J. Osborn (new edn, 1965), 34.

19 *Daily Telegraph*, 21 June 1919.

20 Quoted in D. MacFadyen, *Sir Ebenezer Howard and the Town Planning Movement* (1933), 129.

21 Nettlefold, *Practical Housing*, 112–13.

22 R. Unwin, *Town Planning in Practice* (1909), 299–307.

23 6 Edw. VII, c. cxcii.

24 S.E. Rasmussen 'A great planning achievement', *Town and Country Planning*, XXV (1957), 286; M.H. Baillie Scott *et al.*, *Garden Suburbs, Town Planning and Modern Architecture* (1910), 15; Unwin, *Town Planning in Practice* (1909), 393; *idem, Town Planning in Practice* (2nd edn, 1911), 353.

25 Unwin, *Town Planning in Practice* (1909), 308–10.

26 Nettlefold, *op.cit.*, 53.

27 E.G. Culpin, *The Garden City Movement Up-to-Date* (1914), 20, 32–3; Harvey, *op.cit.*, 11–12; J.E.B. Meakin, *Model Factories and Villages* (1905), 436–8; W. Thompson, *The Housing Handbook* (1903), 198–9.

28 This is a net measurement referring to building land excluding roads.

29 Unwin, *Town Planning in Practice* (1909), 320.

30 R. Unwin, *Nothing Gained by Overcrowding! How the Garden City Type of Development may Benefit both Owner and Occupier* (1912), *passim*.

31 W.L. Creese, *The Search for Environment* (New Haven, 1966), 174.

32 Unwin, *Town Planning in Practice* (1909), 328–31; *idem* 'Housing and planning' (paper read at the Health Congress of the Royal Sanitary Institute, 1936), 2–4.

33 S.D. Adshead, 'The economies of estate development', *TPR*, III (1912), 273–5.

34 R. Unwin, *Cottage Plans and Common Sense* (Fabian Tract no. 109, 1902), *passim*.

35 B. Parker, 'Site planning at New Earswick', *TPR,* XVII (1937), 2–9; L. Weaver, 'Cottages at Earswick', *Country Life*, LVIII (1925), 681.

36 B. Parker and R. Unwin, 'Cottages near a town', in *The Catalogue of the Northern Art Workers' Guild* (1898); P. Houfton, 'The raw material of town planning', *Garden Cities and Town Planning*, IV (1910), 292; *BN*, LXXXV (1903), 196; XCVII (1904), 5–6.

37 *ACR*, LXXIV (1905), 23, 57–9; LXXV (1906), 37; 'The Letchworth experiment', *BA*, LXIV (1905), 107–8; 'The garden city exhibition from the architect's viewpoint', *BN*, LXXXIX (1905), 716–18; 'Is the cheap cottage a myth? Practical results of the exhibition at Letchworth', *GC,* n.s.I (1905), 91–3.

38 R. Unwin, 'Cheap cottages', *GC*, n.s.I (1906), 109.

39 M.B. Adams, *Modern Cottage Architecture* (1912), 13.

40 S.J. Price, *Building Societies: their origin and history* (1958), 266, 313; E.J. Cleary, *The*

Building Society Movement (1965), 152.

41 Halifax Building Society, Directors' Report, 1891 (quoted in letter, 24 June 1971, from Mr N.S. Watson, Secretary of the Halifax Building Society); C.R. Hobson, *A Hundred Years of the Halifax* (1953), 48; *CN*, xxvii (1896), 1063; xxviii (1897), 182; A. Mansbridge, *Brick Upon Brick: The Co-operative Permanent Building Society, 1884–1934* (1934), 59.

42 *CN*, xxvii (1896), 253; xxix (1898), 1288; xxxi (1900), 331, 451, 1475; Mansbridge, *op.cit.*, 39.

43 *CN*, xxxi (1900), 102.

44 W.T. Davies, *The History of the Royal Arsenal Co-operative Society Limited* (1918), 83. Compare also the co-operative cottages built on the Thorn Estate at Bacup in 1908. See *CN*, xxxix (1908), 293.

45 *CN*, xxv (1894), 1314; xxvii (1896), 1063; xxix (1898), 1288, 1366; xxxvii (1906), 1212; xl (1909), 92; *LCP*, ix (1903), 78.

46 *CN*, xxxi (1900), 102.

47 *Ibid.,* xxxi (1900), 1475; xxxiv (1903), 360.

48 H. Vivian, 'Garden cities, housing and town planning', *QR*, ccxvi (1912), 512; H. Vivian, *Co-Partnership in Housing in its Health Relationship* (1908), 5–6; E.B., *Co-Partnership in Housing* (1910), *passim*.

49 J.E. Yerbury, *A Short History of the Pioneer Society in Co-operative Housing* (1913), 22.

50 *CN*, xii (1881), 99.

51 *St James Gazette*, 21 October 1887; *The Times*, 29 March 1888; B. Jones, 'Address on co-operation', *Co-operative Congress 1889*, 16; B. Jones, 'Outlines of a proposed co-operative dwellings association', reprinted in Yerbury, *op.cit.*, 14–16.

52 Culpin, *op.cit.*, 49; Yerbury, *op.cit.*, 54–6.

53 Yerbury, *op.cit.*, 58.

54 *Ibid.*, 60; Culpin, *op.cit.*, 49.

55 *LCP*, vii (1901), 186.

56 Culpin, *op.cit.*, 50; Vivian, 'Garden cities', 512; *TPR*, ii (1911), 340.

57 *LCP*, xiii (1907), 113.

58 *LCP*, xiv (1908), 129; xv (1909), 21.

59 *TPR*, ii (1911), 340.

60 *LCP*, ix (1905), 189.

61 Vivian, 'Garden cities', 512–13.

62 *Ibid.*, 513.

63 *TPR*, ii (1911), 79, 242.

64 *TPR*, ii (1911), 112–13; *CN*, xl (1909), 50.

65 *MG*, 26 June 1912.

66 Culpin, *op.cit.*, 53; *MCN*, 26 March and 1 September 1910; *MG*, 26 June 1912; *LCP*, xiii (1907), 12, 129; *LCP*, xiv (1908), 175; *LCP*, xvi (1910), 102.

67 *TPR*, i (1910), 120; *CN*, xl (1909), 1187.

68 *Burnage Journal*, 1930; *Manchester Evening Chronicle*, 25 May 1939 and 14 June 1964; E.W. Sidebotham, *Burnage* (1925), 19–24.

69 *MG*, 26 June 1912.

70 *Co-Partnership*, xvi (1910), 102; xix (1913), 96; Culpin, *op.cit.*, 28.

71 Creese, *op.cit.*, 6–9; Manchester Society of Architects, *Manchester Buildings* (1966), 42–3.

72 J.H.G. Archer, 'Edgar Wood: a notable Manchester architect', *Trans. Lancs. and Ches. Antiq. Soc.*, lxxiii (1964), 182.

73 *MCN*, 20 March 1909; *MG*, 26 June 1912; *Chorltonville: programme of official opening, 7 October 1911* (1911).

74 *MCN*, 20 November 1937.

75 *MCN*, 26 May 1927 and 29 April 1939; *Manchester County Express*, 10 August 1941.

76 *MCN*, 9 July 1904, 31 August 1907, 4 November 1911, 19 April 1913.

77 M. Higgs, *Glimpses into the Abyss* (1902), *passim*; *Oldham Chronicle*, 11, 12, 18 and 21 December 1901, 28 July 1922; *Oldham Standard*, 27 March 1936; H. Bateson, *A Centenary History of Oldham* (1949), 186.

78 *Oldham Chronicle*. 29 August 1941; *LCP*, xiii (1907), 12.

79 *Oldham Chronicle*, 3 and 9 August 1908, Bateson, *op.cit.*, 186–7.

80 *CN*, xl (1909), 506–7; *Oldham Chronicle*, 7 April 1906 and 3 March 1908.

81 *LCP*, i (August 1894) – xiv (December 1908); *Co-Partnership*, xv (January 1907) – xxv (January 1918).

82 Culpin, *op.cit.*, 50–1; *Co-Partnership*, xviii (1912), 154.

83 *TPR*, i (1910), 24–5.

84 *TPR*, ii (1911), 128.

85 *MCN*, 17 September 1910; *Co-Partnership*, xvii (1911), 37.

86 *TPR*, ii (1911), 242; Yerbury, *op.cit.*, 56.

87 Culpin, *op.cit.*, 50; *TPR*, iv (1913), 65.

88 'Great need of labourers' cottages', *GC*, i (1906), 55; Culpin, *op.cit.*, 53; *TPR*, i (1910), 27–9.

89 H.O.W. Barnett, 'A garden suburb at Hampstead', *Contemporary Rev.*, lxxxvii (1905), 231, 234–5; S.A. Barnett, 'Of town planning', in *Practical Socialism* (1915), 266.

90 E.R. Dewsnup, *The Housing Problem in England – its statistics, legislation and policy* (1907), 253–4.

91 Culpin, *op.cit.*, 49.

92 Yerbury, *op.cit.*, 58; *MCN*, 17 September 1910; *MG*, 26 June 1912; *Chorltonville: programme of official opening, 7 October 1911*, 12.

93 F.J. Osborn, *Green Belt Cities: the British contribution* (1946), 39.

94 C.B. Purdom, *The Building of Satellite Towns* (new edn, 1949), 42.

95 Osborn, *op.cit.*, 39.

96 Ashworth, *op.cit.*, 164.

97 Culpin, *op.cit.*, 16; *TPR*, i (1910), 21.

98 Howard wanted a well-balanced and self-contained community in the garden city, so provision of industry as employment for residents was as important as the agricultural belt and the gardens. To attract industry the company entered into a considerable amount of correspondence with firms in and around London for both propaganda purposes and to obtain information as to industrialists' needs. The industrial area was planned in relation to workers' homes, transport, power and the whole town. See Purdom, *op.cit.*, 103–17.

99 53 and 54 Vict., c. 70.

100 E. Bowmaker, *The Housing of the Working Classes* (1895), 33–8; Dewsnup, *op.cit.*, 253–62; T.R. Marr, *Housing Conditions in Manchester and Salford* (1904), 80–91; Nettlefold, *Practical Housing*, 14–34; W. Thompson, *The Housing Handbook* (1903), 153–78.

101 *Trans. NAPSS*, (1884), 477; *Architect*, lxiii (1900), 221; lxiv (1900), 374; lxvii (1902), supplement 23; *BA*, xxxviii, (1892), 163; *Builder*, lxxvi (1890), 79–80; J. Parsons, *Housing by Voluntary Enterprise* (1903), 57–67.

102 B.S. Townroe, *A Handbook of Housing* (1924), 6; *ACR*, lxxxi (1909), 256.

103 F. Howkins, *An Introduction to the Development of Private Building Estates and Town Planning* (1926), 8–9; Townroe, *op.cit.*, 7; *BN*, cvi (1914), 259.

105 9 Edw. VII, c.44.

106 Bournville Village Trust, *op.cit.*, 14.

107 C.F.G. Masterman, *The Condition of England* (1909), 95.

108 *ACR*, lxxxiv (1910), 28–30; *BN*, xcvi (1909), 422, 664, 703; G. Cadbury Jnr, *Town Planning* (1915), 139–52; Nettlefold, *Practical Town Planning* (1914), 136–78.

109 Parliamentary Debates, 4th ser., CLXXXVIII, col. 958; *ACR*, lxxxiv (1910), 29; *TPR*, i

(1910), 41–3.
110 P. Geddes, *Cities in Evolution* (1915), 298; Nettlefold, *Practical Town Planning*, 179, 202; P. Boardman, *Patrick Geddes: maker of the future* (1944), 244.
111 Geddes, *op.cit.*, 207–8.
112 6 Edw. VII, c.192; Hampstead Garden Suburb Trust, *The Hampstead Garden Suburb; its achievements and significance* (1937), 5; Local Government Board, Memorandum with respect to the provision and arrangement of houses for the working classes, 1911; Revised memorandum, 1913; *BN*, CIV (1913), 466.
113 P. Waterhouse and R. Unwin, *Old Towns and New Needs: also the Town Extension Plan: being the Warburton Lecture for 1912* (1912), 50.
114 *ACR*, LXXXIV (1910), 29; *BN*, XCVI (1909), 422; *Garden Cities and Town Planning*, n.s. (1911), 36.
115 Parl. Debates, 4th ser., vol. 188, col. 949.
116 *GC,* n.s., I (1906), 214; *BA*, LXVI (1906), 303.
117 *BN*, C (1911), 630.
118 *BN*, CI (1911), 149; CII (1912), 652; *Garden Cities and Town Planning*, n.s. I (1911), 98; *MCN*, 5 August 1911.
119 *MG*, 26 June 1912; *TPR*, I (1910), 115.
120 Alkrington Garden Village, *Prospectus* (no date), Mattley Collection, Rochdale Public Library.
121 *BN*, XCIV (1908), 301; CIII (1912), 647; *TPR*, II (1911), 159.
122 *Garden Cities and Town Planning*, n.s., I (1911), 36–7; *TPR*, II (1911), 160.
123 *BN*, XCIX (1910), 895.
124 Rochdale Borough Council Minutes, Paving, Sewering and Building Committee, 28 December 1910, 10 January 1912, 24 April 1913; Health Committee, 17 May 1911; Borough of Rochdale, *Rochdale (Marland) Town Planning Scheme* (1915), *passim*; Rochdale Housing Reform Council, *Tenth Annual Report* (1911), 3–4; *Rochdale Times*, 21 September 1912; *TPR*, VII (1918), 256.
125 Ashworth, *op.cit.*, 192.
126 *Garden Cities and Town Planning*, n.s., I (1911), 36.
127 *CN*, XL (1909), 506–7; *TPR*, I (1910), 18–22; Unwin, *Town Planning in Practice*, 13.
128 The average size of the plots was 550 square yards: W.H. Beeres, Plan of Fearnville Park Garden City Estate, Oakwood Lane, Roundhay, 1908, Leeds City Library Local History Collection; Culpin, *op.cit.*, 34.
129 Sheffield City and County Borough Alteration of Boundary Representation and Local Government Board Inquiry, 1911, evid. G.P. Talbot, A.A. 5118–34; evid. R.W. Fowler, A. 5269; evid. Sir Alexander Rose Stenning, A.A. 5334–5; *BN*, XCVIII (1910), 776; *CN*, XXXIX (1908), 234; *GC*, II (1907), 359, 477; *Sheffield Independent*, 31 July 1912.
130 City of Bradford, *Particulars and Conditions of the Competition for laying out a site of about 50 acres at Southfield, Odsal, for and including the erection of workmen's dwellings on Garden City lines for the Health Committee of the City Council, 1913*; Bradford City Council Minutes, Health Committee, 5 February, 9 April, and 4 June 1913.
131 City of Bradford, *Proposed Workmen's Dwellings, Southfield, Odsall, Competition, Replies to Enquiries* (no date); *Garden Cities and Town Planning*, IV (1914), 63–6.
132 *Garden Cities and Town Planning*, IV (1914), 4.
133 *TPR*, II (1911), 108.
134 Bournville Village Trust, *op.cit.*, 15.
135 E.M. Gibbs, *The Future Extension of the Suburbs of Sheffield: A Lecture delivered to the Sheffield Society of Architects and Surveyors, 9 March 1911* (1911), *passim*.
136 *TPR*, II (1911), 99–111. G. Cadbury Jnr, *op.cit.*, 89; Nettlefold, *Practical Town Planning*, 105–24; C. Gill and A. Briggs, *History of Birmingham*, II (1952), 162.
137 *BN*, CII (1912), 758; CIV (1913), 74; H.M. McKechnie, *Manchester in 1915: British Ass. Handbook* (1915), 25; Waterhouse and Unwin, *op.cit.*, 51.

138 C.F. Wike, *Description of Town Planning and Housing in Sheffield: Paper read at a Conference . . . of the Institute of Municipal and County Engineers, July 1913* (1913), *passim*; *TPR*, III (1912), 125–32.
139 *Architects' and Builders' J.*, suppl., 29 December 1905.
140 Waterhouse and Unwin, *op. cit.*, 59–60.
141 *Ibid.*, 52–6.
142 *Ibid.*, 56.
143 R. Unwin, *Address to Royal Sanitary Institute* (1938), 16–17.
144 *Garden Cities and Town Planning*, n.s., IV (1914), 125.
145 D. MacFadyen, *Sir Ebenezer Howard and the Town Planning Movement* (1933), 127–8.
146 *TPR*, IV (1913), 155.
147 *Ibid.*, 155–6.
148 *ACR*, XCVII (1917), 204–5.
149 R. Unwin, 'The city development plan', in RIBA, *Town Planning Conference, 1910, Trans.* (1911), 247.
150 22 and 23 Geo. V, c.48.
151 See, for example, F.L. Thompson, *Site Planning in Practice* (1923).
152 G.E. Cherry, *Urban Change and Planning: a history of urban development in Britain since 1750* (1972), 124.
153 J.N. Tarn, 'Housing reform and the emergence of town planning in Britain before 1914' (unpublished paper given to the First International Conference on the History of Urban and Regional Planning, London, 1977).

The emergence of the
town planning profession

MARTIN HAWTREE

The emergence of the town planning profession

MARTIN HAWTREE

1 Introduction

The following essay is a condensed version of a thesis entitled 'The origins of the modern town planner: a study in professional ideology', which was submitted for the degree of Ph.D. at the University of Liverpool in 1975. The research was carried out between 1970 and 1972 and arose from a previous study of the history of the *Journal of the Town Planning Institute* and its reflection of the developing subject and profession of town planning. Gordon Cherry was then engaged upon a history of planning and the Town Planning Institute in particular. In the light of his work the research was then concentrated on the origins of the town planning profession.

The thesis sought to contribute to the current debate on the state of the planning profession by examining its origins, with particular reference to its professional status and independence. Through much of its history the planning profession has been faced with the problem of reconciling its undisputed character as a federation of established skills with its need to demonstrate possession of a distinct, new skill in order to secure recognition of its individuality and status. This ambivalence was epitomized in the founding of the Town Planning Institute: the Institute was designed to foster co-operation amongst the established professions concerned with planning, yet at the same time was modelled on the institutes of well-recognized, fully independent professions.

The thesis explored the origins of the town-planning profession through the writings of early town planners, including reformers, propagandists, members of the professions, and a small group of practitioners who took a leading part in founding the new Institute. The thesis made no particular use of any sociological model of professionalization for its analysis, although the concept of professional ideology was introduced to clarify and intensify the theme of self-asserted professional status. It attempted simply to register the dawning self-awareness of town planners as professional people. The thesis concluded that the formation of the Town Planning Institute did not simply mark the founding and regulation of one more profession; it also expressed a rich amalgam of social, planning, and administrative idealism.

The present essay does not have space fully to investigate the outlook of these pioneers, and much of their biographical and ideological roundness has had to be sacrificed. The three main frames of reference for the thesis are, however, preserved: the developing ideal of town planning and its professional implications; the outlook of the established professions; and, finally, the careers of those early practitioners who succeeded, first of all, in translating the ideals of their patrons and employers into physical plans, and then went on to commute their own physical planning into ideals of professional organization. Overall, the content of the work is a fairly free development of the main ideas and conclusions of the thesis, narrowed slightly to concentrate on the period 1900 to 1914 and the founding of the Town Planning Institute.

My thanks to all those who offered help and encouragement in the preparation of the original thesis must be restated: to David Massey, my supervisor, for his unfailing advice throughout; and to the staff and students of the Department of Civic Design, in particular Ian Masser, and John Jones, for their many helpful discussions. I had most rewarding discussions outside the Department with the late Sir Frederick Osborn, the late Francis Longstreth-Thompson, with Michael Simpson of the University College of Swansea, engaged at the time upon a biography of Thomas Adams, and with Stephen Ward, who was kind enough to allow me to read the drafts of his research papers now incorporated into Gordon Cherry's book *The Evolution of British Town Planning*.

The business of research was rendered a good deal easier and more congenial by the assistance of librarians at the Department of the Environment, the Royal Town Planning Institute, the Royal Institution of Chartered Surveyors, and the Institution of Municipal and County Engineers. I am particularly grateful to the very helpful archivists at the Town and Country Planning Association, the National Housing and Town Planning Council, and the University of Liverpool.

Finally I must thank more recent counsellors, especially the editor of this volume whose encouragement and good sense has done so much to improve the casting of this essay.

'Who is to select the town planner?', asked Patrick Geddes in 1908. 'How can even the best-intentioned of Streets and Building Committees really make sure of its choice?'[1] At the time when Geddes asked this question – and it was perhaps the first time anyone had ever proposed the title 'town planner' – Parliament was considering legislation to secure the proper development of towns and, more particularly, their suburbs. Town planning looked back to nineteenth-century modes of social and public health reform and forward to new standards of development; in the words of the President of the Local Government Board, 'the home healthy, the house beautiful, the town pleasant, the city dignified, and the suburb salubrious'.[2] All agreed that the achievement of this ideal involved a daunting administration; very few recognized any need for a distinctive, professional skill.

Early advocates of reform in town development had made little reference to any major technical impediments to their ideals. Three well-recognized professions – architecture, engineering, and surveying – were actively engaged in the development of land and in building. To the extent that garden suburbs and town planning schemes were to involve the design of roads, the valuation of land, and the design, construction, and cost-control of housing schemes, these professions would indeed continue to be indispensable. But it was precisely because of their long establishment that these professions could appear feeble or even incompetent in view of the lack of dignified cities and salubrious suburbs in late nineteenth-century Britain. 'There are few in this country who know much about town planning' said Alfred Lyttleton. 'If you had twenty schemes to organise, I doubt whether you would be able to get the expert advice necessary before they could be put forward in even the most elementary stage.'[3] The real concern of Geddes and Lyttleton was that town planning, even granted the administrative equipment, might produce results not substantially different from those of the past. How were the great ideals which had underlain the town-planning campaign to be given visible form?

The Housing and Town Planning Act of 1909 allowed local authorities to plan suburban areas and created an opportunity for local authorities and private landowners to co-operate. The response of local authorities was disappointing, partly because they were slow to make headway through the many administrative procedures. In nearly every case the work was handled by the town clerk and borough engineer. By 1916, only seven outside consultants had been engaged in the whole of the country.[4] Yet within five years of the Act, something approaching a new professional organization had emerged in the form of a Town Planning Institute. In view of the anxiety expressed by Geddes, Lyttleton and a few others in 1909, and the subsequent low level of planning consultancy, the causes of the Institute's rapid emergence, and the provenance of its members, are matters of much interest.

This essay is particularly concerned with the technical development of the early town planning idea, and with the origin of the modern 'town planner'. What were the professional implications of the new (or rediscovered) power to plan towns? The broad answer was the need for co-operation: co-operation of intellects and skills. Three phases in the development of the idea of professional co-operation will be investigated here, interpreted first by the originators of the town planning idea, the reformers; second, by the existing professions, to whom reformers were looking for assistance;[5] and third, by those few people before 1910 who practised town planning and who instituted the discussion of a new breed of experts. The three analyses contribute to a single interpretation, that the Town Planning Institute and the professional identity which it represented were simultaneously the result of failure by the existing professions to find a basis for mutual assistance, and success on the part of a few early 'town planners' in founding a new practice and subject, inspired by distinctive ideals.

Although the Institute bore a family resemblance to other professional institutes of the time, it differed from them in having developed very quickly. Town planners were professionalizing themselves long before they had anything much to be professional about, either in terms of integrity, technical expertise, or even continuous employment. There was no official demand for 'town planners'; only professionals who would 'town plan' or help 'town plan' were sought. The proposal for a Town Planning Institute was largely idealistic, a by-product of the overall town planning campaign. Town planning juxtaposed professions which had been schooled in isolation, brought them together in a vision of controlled, scaled, co-ordinated urban development. It was largely the inspiration of one man, Thomas Adams, to recognize that neither the theory nor the practice of town planning were likely to coordinate the professions; they would co-operate, or so he hoped, only through being re-elected as 'town planners'.

2　Reform and the need for co-operation

Town planning, however multi-faceted it sometimes appeared in the literature of the early 1900s, sought something quite simple – the achievement of new standards of domestic and related environments. Between Edwin Chadwick in the 1840s and John Nettlefold in 1906 – when the phrase first appeared[6] – there had grown up an idea which combined the concept of a healthy, convenient, attractive, and economic layout of towns with the principle of government intervention in the interest of public urban good.

Chadwick, a spearhead of the public health movement, had been a prime agent in linking the principle of intervention with a number of important, mainly sanitary, defects of town development. The Public Health Act of 1848 provided rudimentary means of establishing order in the larger towns. During the second half of the nineteenth century reformers and philanthropists broadened the application of the principle to include not only main drainage schemes and other services but the planned redevelopment of slum areas. Here was some recognition that poor environment stemmed from lack of system and co-ordination in town development; so the restrictive convenants of private contract were increasingly emulated in local bye-laws, regulating new housing development.

About the turn of the century, housing reform gained much impetus from the experimental developments of George Cadbury, W.H. Lever, Mrs Henrietta Barnett, and Ebenezer Howard. Improved standards, particularly in architectural design, were realized on far larger scales than before. Thomas Horsfall and John Nettlefold, reformers preoccupied with the effectiveness of local government, urged that these standards be applied to towns as a whole by municipal action. They went beyond the simple diagrammatic concept of the planned town, which had satisfied so many of their forerunners, to envisage preventive planning and creative foresight as continuous local authority activities. Horsfall and Nettlefold attempted to municipalize the example of Cadbury and Mrs Barnett.

Once, however, planning acquired a statutory basis, the simplicity of this interpretation lost its appeal (though it survived in the didactic literature of planning until well into the 1940s).[7] Town planning was handed to, or was taken up by, a number of professions already involved in urban development, and each tended to view planning in the light of its own history and aspirations.

The earliest discussions of professional competence in the exercise of new powers of environmental control date back to the beginnings of the urban reform debate in the 1830s and 1840s. The advocates of new powers – civil servants, industrialists, landlords, social workers, local politicians, and others – were in a sense planning's earliest amateurs. They needed professional support to put their ideas into effect, while the professionals contributed to the development of their ideas. Co-operation with the professions, and between the professions, was the keynote of these discussions.

Edwin Chadwick had strong views about the kind of professional he required. His writings are remote in time and spirit from the early 1900s but his 'town surveyor' was a clear forerunner of the town planner. The stress which Chadwick laid on the physical defects of towns as the chief cause of public health problems drew him naturally to an engineering solution. Chadwick knew that there were few trained engineers to serve the new local boards of health. He had nothing but contempt for the old town surveyor, commonly appointed on political rather than technical grounds.

He was even scornful of the Institution of Civil Engineers but the conclusion to his *Sanitary Report* was unequivocal: 'that for the protection of the labouring classes and of ratepayers against inefficiency and waste in all new structural arrangements for the protection of the public health, and to secure public confidence that the expenditure will be beneficial, securities should be taken that all new local public works are devised and conducted by responsible officers qualified by the possession of the science and skill of engineers.'[8]

The scarcity of trained people inevitably led to abuse of the new posts. As late as 1914 a Local Government Board report had serious criticisms to make of John Voisey who held the combined office of surveyor, inspector of nuisances, and water engineer to the Borough of Dartmouth. He had been a councillor, resigning office in order to take up the new post. He had been a builder in the past, held no certificate of the Sanitary Institute (whereas a good many of the 108 applicants for the post were thus partly qualified) and had no knowledge of water engineering.[9] However, some progress had been made; in 1873 there had been founded the Association of Municipal Engineers, the first attempt by engineers to professionalize Chadwick's 'town surveyor'. Devoted to a specialist interest of the senior Institution of Civil Engineers and designed to qualify a surveyor or engineer for the post of Borough Surveyor or Engineer, the Association slowly promoted the status of the resident technical officer. The Borough Surveyor became the main agent of environmental and housing legislation and would have unhesitatingly continued with borough planning had not architects and other professionals begun to take an interest.

By the end of the century the idea of what constituted an adequate urban environment had been vastly broadened and enriched. The city not only required healthiness, but light, beauty and convenience, together with a new range of outlets for civic pride and responsibility. The idea was the product of a new generation of reformers, very different in outlook from Chadwick and his contemporaries. Consequently, their concept of the necessary professional support was also very different from Chadwick's.

The most spectacular and persuasive image of the new environment was provided by George Cadbury and W.H. Lever at Bournville and Port Sunlight.[10] Both men involved themselves with the detailed planning of their industrial villages. Cadbury employed the most competent professional advice and consulted anyone whose experience was valuable, but it was he who planned the roads, the grouping of the trees, the elevations of the houses, the widths of the pavements, the amount of garden space, and the proportion of land allocated to parks and playgrounds.[11] Lever similarly laboured over the plan of Port Sunlight, as well as the plans of the new works and public buildings in the village, and in many cases the houses too.[12] As co-ordinators of architects and surveyors, Cadbury and Lever were filling a directive role similar to that assigned nowadays to the professional planner. However, in their lack of professional training they remained amateurs, however lively and intelligent.

Walter Creese, writing about Hampstead Garden Suburb, found similar difficulties in allotting responsibility for some of the details of the scheme between Mrs Henrietta Barnett and her architect, Raymond Unwin.[13] Mrs Barnett established her authorship of the suburb quite as much as Cadbury and Lever did at Bournville and Port Sunlight. Few residents had any doubt about whom they had to thank or perhaps fear for those 'right' conditions of their environment. The decision to place the church and school at the highest point of the site was apparently hers. But she confessed that 'the ideals so clamorously occupying my mind had to be set out in architectural drawings and business phraseology.'[14]

In the case of Ebenezer Howard there was rather less connection between his own garden city idea and Raymond Unwin's and Barry Parker's physical creation of Letchworth. Howard regarded planning as a feat of engineering, scientifically and artistically related to the proposed site of the town. The future of town planning was therefore bound up with technology: 'though the reader is asked not to suppose that the design is put forward as one likely to be strictly carried out in the form presented: for any well-planned town and, still more, any well-planned cluster of towns, must be carefully designed in relation to the site it is to occupy; though as the science and art of engineering advances, less and less account is taken of natural obstacles and more and more completely does mind become master of matter, and bend it and its forces to the service of man.'[15] If the implication was that his concentric, symmetrical design for Garden City would increasingly come within the power of technology to create, we can perhaps forgive this flight of a utopian's egotism. But whatever the form of town, Howard was in no doubt about the extent to which he would need to draw on professional skills to carry out his experiment. It would, he stated, be the work of many minds – of engineers, architects, surveyors, landscape gardeners and electricians.[16] Howard was announcing the basic planning team which in one form or another has lasted to the present day.

The importance of this experimental work from Port Sunlight through to Letchworth and Hampstead was threefold. First a tradition of *de novo* settlement was being revitalized. Something approaching a new unit of urban development was established in which the efforts of housing reformers, until now battling mainly against existing civic disorder, could find freer, bolder, more exemplary expression. Second, the reformers defined, as far as the working classes were concerned, an entirely new environmental character, revolutionary in its openness, in its standards of architecture and amenity. Third, the experiments were strongly self-conscious and by 1905 enough of them were running simultaneously for them to gain strength from one another. Increasingly they became expressions of a wider confidence in the possibility of controlling and improving Britain's suburban development.

The schemes have been taken out of chronological sequence to delineate more forcefully the potential hiatus between an ideal and its technical realization. All were clearly the product of redoubtable enthusiasm. The exact role of technical competence depended on the temperament of the creator, the size of the project, and the relation between ideal and realization. Cadbury and Lever discovered the ideals of village planning only in the process of building, and in recognizing an identity of spirit and purpose between their two villages. They were also the financiers. Both Mrs Barnett and Howard formulated their ideals in advance, but they had to advertise their ideas and gain the respect and support of many people before the first bricks could be laid. Naturally, they all needed assistance and they were concerned to get the right assistance – there can hardly have been a better match for Mrs Barnett than Raymond Unwin who had himself worked at Toynbee Hall in East London with the Barnetts when a young man. However, only when their views formed part of a wider programme of reform, such as Howard's, were they obliged to consider the role of the technical professions in more general terms.

The phrase 'town planning', implying a responsible, continuous administration as well as a physical style of suburban development, emerged only as the initiative passed to the local authorities. It was Thomas Horsfall who first presented the idea of town extension planning as a distinctive mode not only of housing reform, but of wise local government.

> The chief reason for the very great difference between the new districts of German towns and those of our towns is, that German municipal authorities, in common, so far as the Author can learn, with those of every other civilized country except our own and perhaps the United States, have the power to control the growth of their towns by making town extension plans, the arrangements indicated on which must be complied with by all owners of the land which is within the boundaries of the town, and by all who build on it.[17]

Wide travel, direct engagement with the problems of Manchester, and the absence of bias derived from professional or political interest, contributed to the simplicity and coherence of Horsfall's statement. Indeed these were the most important and novel qualities of his thinking.

From Germany, too, came clear directives about the technical competence which planning required. Horsfall noted that the development plan was generally prepared by an official who had received a surveyor's training and whose experience gave him some knowledge of engineering, and of the tasks of the architect – an adaptive technician like his English counterpart, the borough surveyor, but one drawing on a richer professional experience. A recent statement from Germany had suggested that 'no town of any importance fails to submit its building plan for revision to one of some six or eight well-known men who have acquired a high reputation for their skill in preparing plans which make new districts wholesome, convenient and beautiful.'[18]

John Nettlefold, a Birmingham city councillor, followed up Horsfall's memoranda by developing a comprehensive idea of town planning with an identity and scope of its own.

> Town-planning may be considered as an endeavour to do for a town what an architect does for a house, when he sits down to draw out the plans before digging his foundations. He considers what he wants, and then does his best to fit in his various requirements to a harmonious whole. It is only by this means that he obtains what is required at a reasonable cost. If it is necessary (and everyone recognises that it is) to plan a house as a whole before starting to build, then a thousand times more is it necessary in the interests of public health, public convenience, and public economy, to plan out towns as a whole before new developments are allowed.[19]

Like Chadwick, Nettlefold was very concerned to justify a new public venture on grounds of public economy, but he did not go on to specify a particular professional expertise to ensure economy, as Chadwick might have done. He required simply the assistance of first-rate experts co-opted onto town planning committees; although, characteristically, he wanted them to have had 'business experience'.[20] It was Raymond Unwin who was to take up in his book, *Town Planning in Practice*, published the year after Nettlefold wrote, the full implications and challenge of Nettlefold's requirements.

By 1909 most of these reforming voices had been harmonized, albeit deceptively, in a general campaign for town planning which was organized by a number of pressure groups including the Co-Partnership Tenants Housing Council, the Mansion House Council for the Dwellings of the Poor, the Workmen's National Housing Council, the Rural Housing and Sanitation Association, and a number of local associations at York, Oldham, Rochdale, Plymouth and elsewhere. The interest in town planning was led and co-ordinated chiefly by the Garden City Association – although its role was theoretical rather than political – and the National Housing Reform Council; the latter put much effort into publicizing the views of Horsfall and Nettlefold and, with the aid of a strong parliamentary committee, set to work on converting ideas into legislation.

Town planning, then, was not conceived and brought forward as a new or even long-forgotten skill which now required the status and protection of a profession. It was rather an assembly of values, powers, principles and methods, demanding an equal range of intellectual, political, administrative, legal and technical skills for its successful operation. The increasing scope of the idea, its co-operative nature, and the scale of the enterprise suggested that all interested professions should be involved. With the exception of Chadwick, none of the reformers considered so far came anywhere near formulating the need for a new profession. As the values of health, convenience, beauty, and economy came to frame the developing idea of town planning, so the demand for professional assistance assembled the municipal engineer, the land surveyor, architect, landscape gardener, quantity surveyor, valuer, and businessman. Nevertheless, around the core of reformers and patrons there had already begun to gather a group of professionals whose allegiance went beyond mere interest. Was not Raymond Unwin, for instance, one of the first British counterparts of those planning experts whom Horsfall had come across in Germany?

Seen as a reform process, town planning did not require a separate profession to support it. Town planning might have grown up simply as a value system served by a variety of professionals in their time-honoured roles. This did not, however, happen. Instead, certain individual professionals became increasingly attracted to the idea of town planning; they sympathized with the cause of reform, took an active and leading part in the creation of new villages and suburbs, and began to perceive the peculiarities and complexities of a new and distinct activity. But the emergence of Unwin and perhaps four or five other comparable practitioners could not easily expand into the group of one hundred or so dedicated town planners who would be needed to found a new professional organization and who would cope with the demands of the Town Planning Act. The established professions, once they had recognized the implications of the new enterprise, were bound to demand consideration.

The interested professional institutes were naturally concerned to safeguard the rights of their members but the dangers seemed to them even greater – town planning appeared to attack the very basis of their time-honoured roles. There soon emerged a debate between three major professions, each of which claimed to be considered as *the* veritable town planners, rather than as mere contributors to a respository of town-planning skills. But their reasoning was unashamedly self-interested; they were respectively concerned with establishing what was distinctively architectural about town planning, or why town planning was really a question of engineering or of surveying. So professional histories and outlooks, sharpened by a certain fundamental, and normally healthy rivalry, began to complicate the reformers' plea for co-operation. Planning required a degree of exorcism of these shibboleths before there could arise a more profound and useful understanding of what was new and distinctive. It is to these frequently intransigent terms of professional reference, which are still with us today, that we now turn.

3 The response of the professions

The architects

Before the mid-nineteenth century, the dominant protagonist in what might be termed the pre-history of town planning had been the architect. Who indeed would have denied the dream of Sydney Smirke?

> Fairer still is the field for architectural achievements, when the establishment of a new town on some tract hitherto subject only to the labours of the husbandman, or to the casual visits of the woodsman or the hunter, offers to the enviable founder a *carte blanche* upon which he may lay out his squares and parallelograms, his circles, polygons, crescents, piazzas, and boulevards, with no other check to the expatiations of his genius than the limits of his paper, or the superficial area which it represents.[21]

Such 'architectural achievements' had not in fact always been the work of architects (even allowing for the imprecision of that title before the nineteenth century). Moreover, the very process of professionalization in the 1830s and 40s, and in particular the need to segregate architects from engineers and 'town surveyors', tended to narrow the range of the architectural profession. But once the expression 'town planning' had been adopted during the early 1900s as a generic description for the business of laying out towns, there could begin to emerge a coherent heritage of civic design stretching back through Nash, Craig, the Woods, Wren, Jones, Alberti, Vituvius, and so to Hippodamus of Miletus. Within this historic, international tradition, architects recognized the dream of Smirke, and were eager to uplift and ennoble the aims of English town planning as it had been practised or malpractised by engineers and surveyors for the previous 50 years.

In 1904 John Belcher, president of the RIBA, introduced the germ of the modern town-planning idea to the profession in his presidential address. Both his phraseology and his ideas suggest that Belcher had read Horsfall or was at least familiar with German municipal practice.

> The lungs of London, as they are rightly regarded, must not consist solely of the few open parks . . . but of wide channels and routes for currents of air to flow freely through. This is a matter I commend to the attention of our Town Councils . . . In the extensions of suburbs of cities and towns the public health demands that the buildings should be farther apart and the open spaces larger the further they are removed from the centre.[22]

Public health, town extension, low densities, the relation of architects to local authorities, were here flickering through the mind of the architect, moderated by the unassailable uniqueness of his art: 'its meaning is hidden behind the veil of outward symbol.'[23]

In April 1905, 15 months before the first clear use of the term 'town planning', John Simpson and Beresford Pite, senior members of the profession, threw out the phrase 'city planning' in the first general discussion at the RIBA of the ideas of the German civic designers, Camillo Sitte and Joseph Stübben (the RIBA had recently acquired the French translation of Sitte's book *Der Städtebau nach seinen künstlerischen Grundsätzen*). Simpson and Pite clearly defined the relationship between the architectural profession and town-extension planning:

> while such matters as public health, control and acceleration of traffic,
> improvement of ground values, restrictive Building Acts, and the like, have been
> exhaustively treated (and that to the public advantage), the artistic side of city
> planning has been almost entirely neglected in England, and I do not suppose that
> our authorities even realise its existence. The laying out of new streets and roads
> is nowadays looked upon as purely technical engineering.[24]

The problem, however, was more than simple adjustment of attitudes; it implied a substantial redeployment of professional skills.

The RIBA's reception of the town planning idea was complicated by a major issue of the same period, namely 'municipal' architecture and the want of proper architectural employment in this sphere. Town planning was first discussed in precisely the same way, as a question of architects forcing an entry into the realm of public, municipal works. The first phase of the campaign was to propose a new dimension for town planning; it was the dimension of framed spaces, proportion, and enclosure. So the eyes of the world, and most especially those of the engineer, were to be opened to the apt, the unexpected, the tasteful, the engaging. The plain field of town planning was to be charged with the devices of civic design.

After 1907, there emerged a more vigorous strain of professional architectural thought. No longer content with merely civilizing the town planning idea, there were some who pretended to the government of the whole enterprise. Simpson himself, commenting on the resolution by the House of Commons in May 1907 calling for town planning powers, had written: 'The Royal Institute of British Architects should at once recognise its great responsibility in this, which is essentially an architect's question.'[25] By 1909 the Chronicle of the RIBA Journal was reporting with plain untruth: 'That the matter of town planning is essentially an architect's question has been repeatedly insisted upon in Presidential Addresses at the Institute, in Sessional Papers, and in contributions from various hands to this Journal.'[26] What had been insisted upon was the importance of the architect's contribution and nothing more. However, in 1909 the more extravagant claims of the architects were being widely stated. The *Standard* editorialist, for instance, wrote: 'The business of town planning belongs to the architect and not to the amateur. Unless the Local Government Board is prepared to call in architects of the highest distinction, and to follow their advice, it were better to leave ill alone.'[27] The *Builder* saw the foundation of the Liverpool University Department of Civic Design as a snub to the opponents of the RIBA's new pretensions. England had been in danger of falling between two stools – the practical, sanitary considerations on the one hand, and the ultra-sentimental ideas of the Garden City Association on the other; the necessity for architectural treatment of the subject had been neglected.[28] The fullest expression of this architectural ideology quite simply equated town planning with town or civic design.

In all of this the pen of one or two architects may be suspected but in 1910 they were to lead the whole profession into a monumental attempt to establish town planning, once and for all, as an essentially architectural activity. Architects were virtually excluded from local authority planning activity and therefore had to rely on indirect means of influencing the course of town planning. The RIBA's Conference and Exhibition on Town Planning in 1910 could leave no one in any doubt that, if this exhibition was what town planning was truly about, then architects were the only professionals capable of realizing its full potential.[29] But there were soon indications that a number of architects were changing their tactics, recognizing the dangers of begging the question of architectural supremacy. The movement culminated in the RIBA's Town Planning Committee Memorandum of 1911.

This Town Planning Committee had been set up some years before and had recently begun collecting papers on town planning. Many of the authors had been keen spokesmen for architectural planning in the past, but they were now starting to write of location, geographical considerations, the effects of growth, city typologies, the relation of transport to housing and industry, and the siting and arrangement of schools. Here was the perception of a new subject, resulting from direct, even if theoretical, engagement with the reality of town planning practice.

The memorandum, *Suggestions to Promoters of Town Planning Schemes*, set out to rectify the architectural emphasis of the 1910 conference. The image of dreamers created there had begun to rebound against the profession; and the Municipal Engineers' Conference the previous month, which had capitalized on this point, demanded an answer. The memorandum identified three stages of town planning. First, survey of existing conditions; second, analysis of requirements and the settling of general lines of development; third, the design of a town plan. The work of the surveyor and architect interconnected in the second stage:

> The preparation of all the data upon which the design must be based hardly falls within the province of the architect; and it would seem that this formulation of the city's requirements, and of the limits within which the design must work, is the proper sphere of the surveyor (aided of course by the engineer, the valuer, the economist, the sociologist and the antiquarian). He should survey the conditions, suggest the requirements, and should be consulted as to the methods of satisfying them; but for the design of the town plan, the architecturally trained mind is as essential as for the design of a single building; for the work consists in applying upon a wider field and with greater scope the same principles which govern the designing of individual buildings.[30]

More emphasis was placed on the pre-design stage than in any previous writings produced under the aegis of the Institute. There was no longer so striking a confusion of the part of architecture for the whole of town planning. The authors could not refrain from ending with a flourish, stressing relations of masses to voids, points of emphasis, parts of a harmonious whole, rhythm of plans, ordered elevations, and the grandeur of cities. But none of this grandiloquence obscured the basic motive, to define the role of the architect in town planning. The committee was rewarded by the endorsement of John Burns for their code of practice; architects had made clear what they were best able to do and where they would fit into the work. Burns went on to ask surveyors and engineers to supplement the code from their points of view.[31]

Certain spokesmen, then, had come to understand that much more than aesthetics was involved in the architectural approach to planning. However, aesthetics still provided the firmest ground for the actual employment of architects in planning. The profession was still in much the same position as in 1904, but attitudes had matured. The early approach had been characterized by a headlong rush into the city, armed with some old, and some new, principles of civic design. Since then, the RIBA had established itself as a profession with enthusiasm and initiative for the whole activity of town planning. Moreover, the achievement of a fuller understanding and clearer definition of their role helped architects to adopt a more tactful approach to other professions. Architects began to recognize with less resentment the contributions which those professions could rightfully make to town planning. However, the more architects acknowledged the need for co-operation, the more they saw themselves as the rightful leaders of the team.

The whole development of the ideology was marked by two related characteristics (which contrast with the outlook of the municipal engineers). First was the architects' paramount fear of being left out of town planning; second, the tendency to discuss town planning and their own employment from the point of view of timeless ideals and principles. The municipal engineers, for their part, had no fears of being left out and they derived their ideas directly from the Town Planning Act.

The municipal engineers

Engineers had few claims to a venerable tradition of historic planning, or to any particular skill, such as civic design, which bore an immediate family resemblance to town planning. They had serviced towns through site works, roads, bridges, fortifications, ports, water supply, and drainage. Some had even discussed theoretical aspects of town layout and others had been involved with specific planning ventures in the past, but none of this was strikingly relevant to the engineers' adoption of modern town planning. There is no signal connection between the towns of Stourport, Barrow and Ullapool other than the fact that all three were influenced by engineers. Consequently it is not surprising that the generation of town-planning awareness should take place within a new branch profession set up to deal with public health and municipal problems, the municipal engineers.

Recognition of the need for some kind of residential development plan emerged from the earliest engagements with public health in the 1840s. Captain Vetch, of the Royal Engineers, Butler Williams, a professor of geodesy, and James Newlands, borough engineer to Liverpool Corporation, all contributed to the formulation of the elementary planning concepts of access, density, uniformity of land use, open space, direction and width of streets, ventilation, and sunlight. But the positive planning context which had seemed to be emerging during this formative period of enthusiasm very soon crumbled; what remodelling there was, took the form of more piecemeal changes achieved by the politically weathered bye-law. Standards were set and attained, but not through a single physical plan.

As the century progressed the Borough Engineer and Surveyor accumulated ever-widening responsibilities. No amount of controversy in 1909 could upset those 60 or so years of local government experience: 'constant additions to the statutes we have to administer, the gradual abolition of the contractor, and the continuously growing demands by the public for greater convenience, healthiness, and beauty in connection with all public works, have enormously increased our duties.'[32] The full range of reform values had been absorbed, through the engineer, into the everyday practice of municipal work.

The Association of Municipal Engineers began to discuss town planning in 1906 when Horsfall himself addressed the Association. The discussion which followed his paper was mixed and unbalanced; sometimes suggesting that members had not fully grasped Horsfall's idea; at other times that they had been thinking along similar lines for many years and only lacked the power to carry these ideas into practice. They agreed, however, that towns should be extended according to plans and that the main thoroughfares should be predetermined at all costs.[33] These were narrow terms of reference, partly induced by the suspicion that the very existence of the town planning idea implied some want of foresight and general competence on the part of engineers. Not until 1909 did the wider implications of the subject come home to them.

By this time the town planning campaign, as conducted by the National Housing Reform Council and the Garden City Association, was reaching its climax and shifting from propaganda to the means of execution. For engineers, the dual necessity to understand quickly the implications of the new Act and to understand it sufficiently well to counter the pretensions of other adventurous professions whose threat was only then being noted, meant that the work and ideas of the two major town planning associations (which were specifically turning their attention towards the borough engineer and the surveyor) provided needful sustenance. Apart from their staple concern with roads, engineers advanced no specifically engineering philosophy or theory of planning; they simply reiterated the latest housing reform and garden city ideals, regarding them as no more than a new or additional frame of reference for their customary work.

A number of engineers attended the Garden City Association's Conference on Town Planning at the Guildhall in 1907 but the profession (whether civil or municipal) was not officially represented. By 1909, however, Ewart Culpin, Secretary of the Garden City Association, was welcoming the increased participation of the engineering professions at the Association's November Conference, significantly entitled 'The Practical Application of Town Planning Powers'.[34] The National Housing Reform Council arranged a similar conference and had earlier in the year organized two trips to the Continent, involving 90 members and officials of local authorities. Borough engineers and surveyors, having listened to explanations of the Act and also to definitions of the architect's role in town planning by Beresford Pite and Raymond Unwin, simply staked their claim to the preliminary matters of roads, survey work, drainage, and levels. W.R. Davidge, district surveyor of Lewisham, felt that many professions would co-operate in planning but that it would rest with the engineer to sift the good grain from the large mass of cereals in his possession.[35] The claim was a modest one in itself but there was some additional emphasis on the co-ordinating role of the engineer. The borough engineer would get out the draft plan which could be boiled down gradually and come out as a plan to be adopted by all those interested.[36] Engineers, however, did not secure theoretical acceptance for this view.

The problem was evidently more than one of simple co-operation; two very different outlooks had to be united. *Engineering* carried a forceful editorial on the controversy over the proposed St Paul's Bridge, in London.

Architects and engineers, perhaps, inevitably regard the subject of town planning and of city improvements from opposite standpoints. The engineer considers a new roadway as essentially a fresh artery for traffic, whilst to all appearance, the average architect is more concerned in providing the citizen with a picturesque perspective than lessening the labour by which he earns his daily bread.[37]

The architect was more concerned with the sightseer than with transport between north and south London. Architects required persuasion that 'the bread and butter of utility must have precedence over the meringues of art'.[38]

Appeals based on the engineer's practical, down-to-earth good sense were certainly effective, but the engineer's strongest qualification lay in his privileged, municipal experience. The new Act could not be effectively applied, wrote Stilgoe, city engineer of Birmingham, without the engineers' intimate, local knowledge. 'We must drive forward the engineering works, the others will follow.'[39] Albert Greatorix, president of the Municipal Engineers in 1911, continued the argument:

Who, after all, is better able and qualified than the local surveyor, by reason of his knowledge of not only the internal working of the Act, but by his general knowledge as to what is necessary as regards the development of the district, and the lines which it should take; but we must show ourselves able to fulfill these duties.[40]

Outshone by the RIBA's Conference and Exhibition, the municipal engineers began to sense that they could no longer expect their knowledge and experience to go unchallenged. Nevertheless, when they did turn, rather late, to consider the basic material of town planning (issues concerning the area to be included within a plan, theories and designs for roads and communication systems, allocation of areas for definite purposes, the provision of open spaces, the limitation of numbers of houses to the acre and its economic implications for landlords and tenants, water supply, tramway systems, location of public buildings, and the modification of bye-laws), they had the advantage over architects of discussing the subject in the context of their everyday lives.

By 1912, the municipal engineering profession had a firm grasp of the new subject. They regarded town planning more as a question of organization and arrangement than as a new skill. Like architects, engineers recommended travel as the best method of acquiring any additional experience needed; although, by 1914, they understood that more was involved, for in that year they set up the first town planning examinations. This inclination to go ahead with examinations, without consultation with other bodies, at once showed the degree of isolation of the Institution of Municipal Engineers from other professional institutes, as well as a simple determination to get on with the business of qualifying its members for certain new activities which, irrespective of any arguments of architects, were undoubtedly falling into engineers' hands.

Support professions

Part of the success of municipal engineers resulted from their being very much more than just engineers and surveyors, and from their everyday involvement with the issues which formed the theory of town planning. Those professional institutes whose skill and area of concern were not fundamentally related to the town as a whole had correspondingly less to say about town planning, and less need to stake a major claim to town planning work. Private surveyors, however, affiliated to the Surveyors' Institution (set up in 1868), had a strong, historical justification for claiming a part in the new work. Not only did they share some of the skills practised by municipal engineers, but, in name at least, surveyors had been responsible for some of the finest town-planning achievements in the past, notably the large private estate developments of London and other cities. Leslie Vigers, president of the Surveyors' Institution in 1910, proposed his members as candidates for the new work.

> In the past the responsible work of laying out our towns has been almost entirely in the hands of the surveyors representing the large and small landed estates adjoining the more populous centres, and on the whole I do not think it can be contended that the work has been otherwise than well done . . . I agree, then, in the opinion . . . that there is already a large body of men having wide experience in this work, and that it is to them rather than to their confrères, the surveyors to the local authorities, that we must look for the successful carrying out of this part of the Act. While I should be the first to acknowledge the excellent work done by the latter for the health of the community, I do not think I should be dealing unfairly with them if I said that as a rule they have neither the time nor the special experience necessary for drawing up the details of a town planning scheme.[41]

Surveyors, however, as a profession, made no attempt to master the subject of town planning. They welcomed the Town Planning Act, sympathized with the garden city/garden suburb movement, and had useful things to say about the financial and fiscal implications of land reform and town planning, in particular compensation and betterment values. With the coming of official recognition that individual estates needed to be developed in harmony, they foresaw merely a new context for private estate planning, one which, as F.M.L.Thompson has noted, would cast them in the role of defenders of private interests.[42] Surveyors had no universalizing art with which to transcend the private interests of their clients, and they did not share with the borough engineer and surveyor a public administration which was equipped to harmonize a variety of interests. Furthermore, the surveyor's skills in valuation, measurement, land economics, management and plan-making, however necessary, were only part of a new planning ideal which laid stress on health, physical design, and layout. Town planning needed to focus more strongly than it did in 1909 on the problems of land and its uses before surveyors – and later geographers and economists – could play a more initiating role.

One might have expected two further professions to be involved in the struggle for town planning work, those of the medical officers of health and lawyers. The medical officer, however, reflected the preliminary, diagnostic role that the public health movement as a whole had played in the genesis of town planning. That role was related to housing administration rather than town planning, and in terms of the 1909 Act, the latter was concerned only with land not yet developed. Among the municipal officials, the town clerk was much more involved, as he was responsible for piloting the new 'town planning schemes'. However, neither the town clerks, nor the legal profession from which they were drawn, stated a desire for recognition as 'town planners'. When the Town Planning Institute came to devise the category of

Legal Membership of the Institute it simply recognized the statutory and administrative basis of town planning; it did not convey the right of the legal profession to 'practise' town planning. Thus none but architects, municipal engineers, and private surveyors entered the lists for the title 'town planner', and the main contest lay between the first two of these.

In all three cases what had started out in 1905 or 1906 as a simple, unrhetorical plea for the right to participation was by 1909 more or less elaborately transformed into an institutional suit at the bar of municipal enterprise. The structure of town planning employment prevented very much co-operation. So there was no perception, based on experience, of a simple, mutual contribution of skilled services; only the confusion of partial, theoretically divisive viewpoints. Each profession at times claimed leadership of a team which did not exist and one which none of them possessed the resources or real inclination to create. After 1912, however, there would be signs that institutional attitudes were losing their relevance. The new Town Planning Institute would permit the continued exchange of professional views, now in the context of joint commitment to a new activity rather than self-interested defence of an historically-based ideology. The creation of that context would be made possible by the recognition of certain distinctive characteristics of the new activity, characteristics not ultimately derived from the categories of architecture, engineering, and surveying. These new terms of professional reference were generated principally by those who had actually practised town planning before 1910. The names of Adams, Unwin, Geddes, and Mawson were to stand out in sharp relief from the professions of architecture, engineering, and surveying; not because they were outstanding members of those professions, but because they were doing something new. What they were doing may have been less inspiring than the creation of dreams of magnificent city designs, transport networks, or high-class estate developments, but it had the distinction of being directly related to the aims of the town planning movement.

4 Early town planning practices

In 1912 *The Builder* commented: 'Modern requirements are thus resulting in a new type, the town-planning specialist, who, whatever his previous training has been, as architect, engineer, or surveyor, must, above all, in this practical age still be a visionary.'[43] Between 1900 and 1910 there had emerged a small group of individuals devoting much if not all their time to garden city and town planning work. They shared certain beliefs in civic and social improvement which identified them in various ways with housing and town planning reform. When the Act of 1909 began focussing the attention of architects and engineers on the possibility of their professional involvement, this small group of early practitioners had already started to come to terms with the new work and could start directing that larger involvement, not through the institutional, technical, and ideological mentalities of architect, engineer, or surveyor, but through the experience and ideals of the town planner.

Who, then, were these pre-statutory 'town planners'? They were enthusiasts, men who had the ability and vigour to make a creative response to the challenge of the housing reformers and who pioneered the techniques and art of laying out the new city and suburb. They developed the experimental work at Bournville and Port Sunlight into a general practice of garden suburb planning, and, through their energy and breadth of vision, established a reputation as town planning consultants. They had a keener sense than most that town planning was something quite new, and this judgment, unlike that of the professions, was based firmly on planning experience.

In 1900 Patrick Geddes was 46; Thomas Mawson, 39; Raymond Unwin, 37; and Thomas Adams, 31. They were not personally known to each other and indeed as biologist, landscape gardener, architect, and farmer, there was little reason why they should be. Geddes and Adams were both Scots, living and working in and around Edinburgh. Mawson had a small family business in the Lake District, and Unwin worked in partnership with his brother-in-law, Barry Parker, in Buxton. Not surprisingly, they came to town planning along very different routes. For each, however, town planning was to be the practical expression and culmination of previous interests and ideals.

Nowhere is the range of influences wider and more complex than in the case of Patrick Geddes. Indeed the range was wider than many scientists, professionals, and academics of the time could bring themselves to respect. Geddes linked the romantic revolts of Carlyle, Ruskin and Morris, through his scientific training under Huxley, with the positivism of Auguste Comte. He shared Comte's belief in social progress as the gradual unfolding of truth through scientific description, which was to remain fundamental to his later ideas of civics and the civic survey. Darwin's image of struggle and competition had been the correct one for the brute industrialism of the early nineteenth century – the 'paleotechnic' era of hunters – but Geddes saw dawning the more ordered, refined, socially benign culture of a 'neotechnic' age:

> What we need is constructive peace and constructive peace simply means
> rebuilding this world, village by village, city by city, and region by region in terms
> of Geotechnics and evolutionary ideals. We must get beyond the Stone Age of
> predatory economics and its accompaniment of mutual slaughter to the new age
> of co-operation, of tending our own gardens and our nation's, with mutual aid as
> our ideal. It is high time to be leaving forever the Paleotechnic era of slums,
> poverty, and war and be fighting for Neotechnic and Geotechnic culture: the
> tending of life both by the objective work of reconstructing the environment and
> by the subjective expression of individual and social ideals. In other words this
> simply means that agriculturalist, architect and politician will be working out the
> visions of a Ruskin, a Tolstoi, a Walt Whitman.[44]

– or indeed of Howard, one might add. The quotation returns from the language of science to the simple relationship between vision and realization, reformer and technician. However strange Geddes's music may sound, his theme of geotechnic culture would find a precise purpose and image in the garden city.

Raymond Unwin, too, began his career with a high degree of social and political awareness of nineteenth-century surroundings. He was 'privileged' as he put it, to hear the voice of Ruskin declaiming against the disorder and degradation resulting from *laissez-faire* theories of life; to know William Morris; and to imbibe the thought and writings of James Hinton and Edward Carpenter.[45] Unwin had actively participated in reform movements to secure order and justice in society, to contrast the simple, community life of the country to the miseries of the city, to establish the dignity of labour, and, in particular to secure the return of 'beauty' as a condition of life and work. His outstanding contribution to town planning was to develop these ideals in conjunction with the means of their architectural expression. To design a town or suburb was to be the ultimate expression of his ambition to recreate a sense of community.

Thomas Mawson had a different pedigree. He did not approach town planning through social reform. His work was not inspired by the bleakness of the city, the material and social poverty of city life, but by the simple desire to create beauty through nature and art. His career began in Windermere where he and his brothers had set up a nursery and contracting business. In 1889 Mawson was able to separate the nursery from ihe landscaping side of the business and establish his own landscape gardening practice.[46] The major influences on his early life were the landscape treatises of Horatio Brown, Uvedale Price, and Humphry Repton. Town planning as an art was to be for Mawson as much a flowering of those influences as it was for Geddes and Unwin. Town planning was a natural and artistic expression on the very highest plane.

Thomas Adams, the youngest of the four, developed closest to the garden city ideal. He began his career as a dairy farmer in Midlothian. From his teens onwards he wrote and published articles on the need for reform of land tenures and rural development as a means of social improvement. That Adams was ready to be inspired by Howard may be judged from the following, written in 1897:

> The fact seems to be that agriculture is no longer capable of supporting so large a population, and that, by land being sown down with permanent pasture, or fenced in for the preservation of game, the people are driven to the city from sheer want of means to earn a living. The causes of this are, not only that much land, that was once arable, is now sown down to grass, and that improved transit and better education make the labourer yearn for the social attractions of the town, but also that the landlords do not provide nor maintain dwellings of a habitable kind on their farms and estates.[47]

The Scottish land reformer confronted absentee landlords, lawyer-factors, and a range of encumbrances peculiar to Scottish land law. While yet unaware of Howard's comprehensive solution to the problems of city and country, Adams followed the Liberal philosophy of free trade in land, and called for changes in law to ensure the proper management of land and ease of transfer. So garden cities and town planning would be an apt extension of Adams' interests in social improvement and land management.

There were, then, links between those worlds of biology, social reform, architecture, landscape gardening, and land reform. All shared a common heritage of nineteenth-century criticism and literature. What transformed these connections into a common impetus to practical work was the emergence of town planning as a sharp focus, or even final synthesis, of previous interests and ideals.

In 1900 Adams came to London to take up journalism. Alderman William Thompson, one of the foremost housing reformers of the time, was to say, many years later: 'I was one of the original members of the committee of the Garden City Association which appointed Mr Thomas Adams, then a young Scotsman entirely unconnected with the Housing Movement, as the first paid secretary of the Association.'[48] Only youth, solidity, very considerable ambition, and, by this time, profound inspiration from Howard's book of 1898, had recommended him.

Howard was also central to Raymond Unwin's introduction to the town planning movement. 'What sociable people wanted were country villages', argued Unwin in 1901, small centres of life large enough and varied enough to give them interesting society. The suburb offended in coming 'between town and country'.[49] The State or the landlord might relieve the overcrowding in towns by developing hamlets and villages in the outlying districts wherever suitable land was available. Unwin and Parker had become involved with the design of the Rowntrees' industrial village at New Earswick, near York, in 1900. Literature, ideals, and practice now began to fuse, promoting their identity not merely as cottage architects but as community designers. The late Sir Frederick Osborn maintained in discussion with the author that Unwin's Fabian Tract, 'Cottage plans and common sense', was the main reason why Parker and Unwin were invited to take part in the restricted competition for a plan for Letchworth, a competition sponsored by the Rowntrees. This same tract also caught the attention of Mrs Henrietta Barnett.

Patrick Geddes and Thomas Mawson were recruited to town planning not via the garden city, but through their relatively obscure work at Dunfermline. The future development of Pittencrieff Park, as the main subject of a competition organized by the Carnegie Trust in 1904, was appropriate to the involvement of a botanist and landscape gardener. However, Geddes was already launched on the scientific study of societies and cities, and Mawson had already begun to consider issues of urban design in the building circumferences of town parks which he laid out in Hanley and Wolverhampton, and estates which he developed at Windermere and at Wellington in Shropshire. Both used the Dunfermline opportunity to the full, publishing two very different reports but establishing similar reputations as consultants on city development.

These four pioneers were to stand out from a good many others involved in a professional capacity with early town planning ventures, simply because they were to develop a more fundamental connection between the ideals of town planning and their own active lives. Apart from Geddes, they were to do more town planning than most, and all were to write about the subject more than most. In turning now to the way in which they transformed chance opportunities into completely new developments of their careers, we shall continue to treat them individually, partly because they did not have the force of a group, and partly because what common force they exerted was to broaden the conception of town planning by their very differences of approach. They were not consciously tying together a new subject, but coming to terms with the broad outlines of a new field, in relation to their own special skills and gifts.

Thomas Adams

Between 1900 and 1906 Adams was, in effect, articled to the Garden City Movement. He became secretary to the Pioneer Company when it was formed in 1902, and took a leading part in visiting sites all over the country and ultimately in the selection of Letchworth for the first garden city experiment.[50] He became secretary of the First Garden City Ltd in July 1903, and for the next two years acted as manager of the Letchworth estate. He carried through negotiations with manufacturers, finding out their requirements and then inducing them to settle in Letchworth.

At the same time, however, Adams recognized that the Garden City Association would not achieve its potential influence on the environmental reform movement if it restricted itself to the pure milk of Howard's philosophy and the Letchworth experiment. Buder has perhaps gone too far in suggesting that, even in this early period, Adams wanted the Association to become a professional planning group, actively involved in the preparation of specific schemes and in the advocacy of legislation.[51] There is no doubt, however, that Adams' planning philosophy was essentially a practical and even mundane one. This sense of the practical was reflected in the expansion of the Association's activities and propaganda which he brought about. Early on, he saw advantage in identifying the Garden City Movement with the work of Cadbury and Lever, and arranged conferences at Bournville and Port Sunlight in 1901 and 1902. Later, he established links with Hampstead Garden Suburb.[52] Through him, the Association developed a catholic interest in order and good design in urban development.

Adams' broadening planning interests, combined with his growing experience at Letchworth, led him to recognize the need for supporting professional expertise. In April 1905 he announced the appointment of an Advisory Committee of Experts to offer counsel to individuals, firms, or public bodies proposing to build houses or factories, or to develop land on garden city lines.

> This new committee is designed to meet a new need. It is an indication of the wider notice the movement is receiving. We are becoming better known as an Association which stands for design and development, as opposed to chance and chaos in urban growth. And the result is that for some time now we have been receiving requests for our advice and opinion. A contemplated Orchard Village, a firm moving its iron works, a possible Garden City in Turkey, and the Hampstead Garden Suburb scheme, are the kind of questions our Advisory Committee considers.[53]

The new committee, then, was presented as the natural offshoot of a propagandist association rather than, as Buder suggests, a basic change of direction under the influence of a professional. However, Adams' recognition of the need for professional expertise had by now brought him to a position where he felt the urge to involve himself more directly in the design and development of garden cities and garden suburbs.

Adams resigned from the Garden City Company in 1906. Purdom has suggested that Letchworth was failing to grow as fast as expected. Adams had control of the estate 'taken out of his hands' and put into those of W.H. Gaunt, who had previously been involved with the Trafford Park Industrial Estate in Manchester.[54] From a letter of Sir Richard Paget it appears that Adams had been considering a move for some time. Paget had been asked by his father to look into the improvement of 400 acres of property to the north-east of Wolverhampton. 'Being interested in the Garden City Movement, I visited Mr Adams . . . and asked him to recommend some young man with Garden City Ideals who would become resident agent for the Old Fallings Hall Estate.'[55] Adams proposed himself. He saw in Paget's request a clear opportunity to gain further practical experience in land management and to promote the example of orderly suburban development he had so ardently campaigned for. But he did not stay long at Wolverhampton. The next few years were to establish Adams' name as one of the few town planners before 1909.

Adams set up an office at No. 3, Pall Mall East, and described himself as a consulting surveyor. After developing a plan for the Fallings Hall estate in association with the architect Detmar Blow, Adams was called to Glyn-Cory, a model village near Cardiff, first planned by Mawson and entrusted to Adams when Mawson left for a tour of America. Adams' essentially practical mind is well illustrated in his report on this scheme some years later. In contrast to Mawson, Adams dwelt little on the bold aesthetic conception of the development in concentric tiers up the slope of the hill. He chose rather to mention the cost of constructing the approach bridge, the widths of the two main crescents, and the letting out to contract of a gravitational water supply and sewage disposal scheme.[56]

The first plans which Adams prepared entirely by himself were for suburbs near Manchester, towards the end of 1908. At Alkrington 700 acres had been offered to the Garden City Association some years previously but no arrangements had been made for forming a company. The trustees asked Adams to prepare a garden suburb scheme to contain 30,000 people. Adams' design incorporated a number of features the value of which he had come to appreciate in his associations with Detmar Blow at Fallings Park, Mawson at Glyn-Cory, and Lutyens at Knebworth, including free-flowing arcs and crescents, long, tree-lined avenues, and a formal square situated at the highest point in the centre of the estate. Adams seldom dwelt on the aesthetic side of his town planning, however, perhaps in deference to the architectural profession for which he had an undoubted admiration. He spoke mainly about coherent development and low density; at Alkrington, at Newton Moor, Stockport, and again at Shirehampton, Bristol, his professional task was simply to prevent poor, untidy, mindless development on the outskirts of cities. For him there was a sharp, easily-grasped distinction between developments on the wrong lines and those on 'right lines'.

These schemes allowed Adams to progress towards the status of 'town planner' in two important ways. First, he established himself as more than an estate manager, as someone fully capable of preparing complete suburban layout plans for local authorities and private landowners. Second, he successfully established himself as a consultant rather than as a resident surveyor or architect. Adams, in fact, was neither architect, engineer, nor fully qualified surveyor. His reference points were derived, not from professional training, but from the ideals of the garden city and housing reform movements. It was, then, as a garden city/garden suburb practitioner that he made his name, in the face of very little competition.

Raymond Unwin

Raymond Unwin worked closely with Thomas Adams at Letchworth and on the Advisory Committee of the Garden City Association. Like Adams, Unwin was inspired by his earlier reform ideals and he became associated with nearly every front of the town planning campaign: the National Housing Reform Council, Letchworth Garden City, Hampstead Garden Suburb, co-partnership housing schemes, and the RIBA. It was the link between housing reform and its architectural means of expression which justly established Unwin's reputation as the father of modern town planning. Unwin's career is described in detail elsewhere in this volume (pp. 156–93) and discussion here can be confined to a single example of his philosophy and professional activity.

Figure 9. Plan of Knebworth Garden Village, Herts.

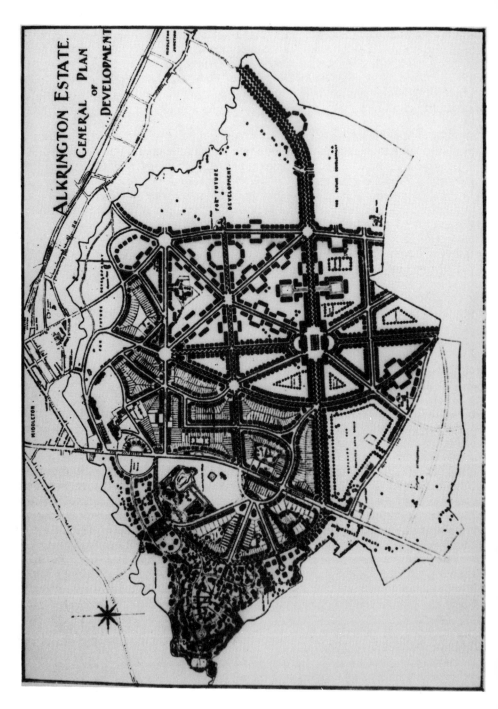

Figure 10. Plan of Alkrington Garden Suburb, near Manchester.

In 1905, the Co-Partnership Tenants Housing Council was formed under the guidance of Henry Vivian (chairman), Frederick Litchfield (secretary), Sybella Gurney, and John Nettlefold. It was a central committee and sponsor of local tenant societies. Unwin was selected as the Council's consultant architect and the objects of the Council were peculiarly fitting to the kind of architectural expression Unwin was beginning to develop.

> Instead of thinking and planning for only a chance assortment of individuals there is now a whole to be thought of. A home is now to be planned for a community having an organised life . . . The site can be thought of and planned as a whole; . . . In this way instead of the buildings being mere endless rows, or the repetition of isolated houses having no connection one with the other, they will naturally gather themselves into groups, and the groups again clustered around the greens will form larger units, and the interest and beauty of grouping will at once arise. The principle of sharing, therefore, not only causes each individual house to become more attractive, but gives to the whole area covered, that coherence which, springing from the common life of the community, expresses itself in the harmony and beauty of the whole . . . How much the architectural beauty of old cities and villages spring from their being the outgrowth of an organised civic life is perhaps little realised, but the ugliness and dreariness of the towns and suburbs which have resulted where such common life is lacking are but too evident to all.[57]

For Unwin, then, architecture was the expression of community values. The co-partnership housing movement gained much strength from this injection of garden city theory, and particularly garden city design. Unwin's general advice and his practical work for tenants associations at Ealing, Leicester, and Sevenoaks encouraged the development of small, village communities characteristically arranged around village greens, allotments, or recreation areas such as tennis courts and bowling greens.

Hampstead Garden Suburb was a much larger exercise. An early book about the Suburb carried, as a frontispiece, a plan drawn in the fashion of sixteenth- and seventeenth-century ichnographical maps of European cities. The drawing has much of Camillo Sitte about it, with the sequence of streets and squares leading up to the central square surrounded by the main buildings. Yet the plan lacks the concentrated urbanity of Sitte. Unwin had injected his own Englishness: greens rather than piazzas formed the backbone of the plan.[58] It was an early draft, perhaps formalized by Lutyens when he became associated with the suburb. Nevertheless Unwin succeeded in imparting an historical as well as aesthetic sense of community to the suburb; the walling and turretting of the south side of the suburb symbolized not so much an archaic concept of community, as the freedom of the artist to draw upon a richness of architectural and historical allusion. Community design was after all an individual art.

Unwin and Adams were very much at the centre of the small, developing world of town planning. They approached that world from the standpoint of garden city and garden suburb ideals but both went beyond them. The culture and inspiration of the architect led the one into design of new communities; the practicality and sense of order of the surveyor led the other into model estate management and planning. The sense of urgency in both cases produced propagandists as well as practitioners.

Geddes and Mawson, on the other hand, had no fundamental commitment to the garden city or garden suburb ideas. They gave, respectively, scientific and artistic enrichment to the town planning idea. If the science of the one and the artistry of the other were a little too heady for many, both nonetheless added to the sense of a new subject, a new field which had a definite complexity and deserved recognition as a discipline of its own.

Patrick Geddes

Geddes began his practical work as a housing reformer in Edinburgh's Royal Mile during the 1880s; he campaigned for the cleaning up of Edinburgh's streets; he played a leading part in founding a university settlement in Edinburgh, the model for which had come from the Barnett's Toynbee Hall in East London.[59] As a consultant he drew up a 'timely and thorough design' for Dunfermline in 1904. Here a close-knit methodology and visual perceptiveness had been combined with a quaint romanticism:

> consider whether the crooked little Old Town would not thus become no less beautiful in its way than the more formal New Town upon the lower levels towards the sea. That would have its stately avenues, its long perspectives, its charming garden city also, with its blossom-covered cottage houses, but this would have the still greater antique charm of variety, picturesqueness, unexpectedness, which can never fully be designed. With its high views, its sunward slope, it should even be the more healthful and attractive of the two.[60]

Geddes's subsequent contribution was, however, to lie in the field of civic science rather than civic design. From the day he had abandoned plant taxonomy after only a week at Edinburgh University, he had been searching for a social direction to scientific investigation. He had at first found this in sociology. In time, however, the city itself became the focus for both his investigation and active work. Geddes's Edinburgh Outlook Tower, a social-geographical observatory which he had started in the 1890s, symbolized this search for coherence. It was the growth, progress and decay of human societies – as presented in cities – which constituted the central problem to which all the sciences led up, on which all the arts converged, and to which all the problems of the individual were related.[61]

Geddes's essential contribution to town planning lay in the synthesis of knowledge about the workings of cities and their regions, their historical development, and the logic of their future. Orderly description had to precede rational action. The growing town planning campaign in the early 1900s concentrated Geddes's mind on urban issues. By 1909 he had done no further practical design, but he had worked out more fully his idea of 'civics' and the 'civic exhibition'; and its appearance in the report of the Cities Committee of the Sociological Society in 1909 came in time to shed light on (or perhaps obscure) the implications of the Town Planning Act.

The civic exhibition was a means of achieving awareness of a city's past, present, and future, the harmonizing of which Geddes described as the new and mighty riddle of the sphinx of destiny. The kind of survey and exhibition he had in mind included the following categories: *situation*: the regional context, geology, topography, climate, soil, vegetation; *communication*: the natural and historic pattern, present state and expected developments; *industry*: the native industries and commerce: *population*: its health, density, distribution, movement; *town conditions*: a detailed history of town's development, material survivals, survey of the present state of the streets and open spaces, services, housing, and sanitation; and finally, *town planning*: suggestions and designs including examples of other town plans and general ideas about how the town might be extended, improved, and, with alternative treatments, set out in detail.[62]

Geddes occupies a linking position in the professionalization of urban reform. He produced few town plans before the First World War, and none of the professions or disciplines to which he was attached were keen to take up town planning. Geddes did more than anyone else to explode the myth that town planning had some necessary connection with established professional curricula. As a wide-ranging intellectual and social scientist, Geddes most emphatically registered town planning as a new area of professional expertise.

Thomas Mawson

Mawson first came into contact with town planning through his competition entries for town parks in the late 1890s. Hanley Park, Staffordshire, and East Park, Wolverhampton, included small building estates on their fringes, later termed miniature town planning schemes by Mawson.[63] However, the application of the highest aesthetic principles to the resolution of civic problems was to be the outstanding feature of Mawson's career. Landscape and park designs first flowed outwards into the surrounding buildings and estates, developed into monumental groups of buildings, and eventually formed parts of the larger coherent whole – the town itself. Ultimately, Mawson was undertaking projects of immense scale such as the re-planning of Salonika in 1917. Simple faith in, and understanding of, design was always the foundation of his participation in those increasingly ambitious undertakings. At the roots of the design process lay the everyday starting point of the landscape gardener – the site. Design flowed from an appreciation of the possibilities, the problems and the excitements of the site, not from any arbitrary formulation of social and economic needs. Even when Mawson began to confront these wider, social issues in his city planning work in Canada after 1912, his artistic inspiration never deserted him.

1904 was the year of Mawson's first serious engagement with planning. His report on Dunfermline belonged to a considered tradition of planning which included Wren's plan for London, Edinburgh New Town, the Birmingham improvement scheme, the remodelling of Paris after 1848, the Vienna Ringstrasse, and the improvements to Budapest. 'True architectural dignity is only secured when each individual building acts as a complement the one to the other. To accomplish this, the entire site should be first properly planned with the ultimate end in view.'[64] His scheme included a mile-long boulevard, playgrounds, street planting, removal and opening up of slum and congested property, cottages for the old, an orphanage, several schools and other institutes, allotment grounds, a new park road and scheme for Pittencrieff Park, and detailed treatments of approaches to the city. Mawson also considered the possibility of purchasing land at a low agricultural price, developing it by municipal initiative, and then giving to each purchaser the benefit of the increased value. The ideas of Cadbury, Lever, and Hartley (of Aintree) were also in the back of his mind. He suggested acquiring a piece of land which would be easy to

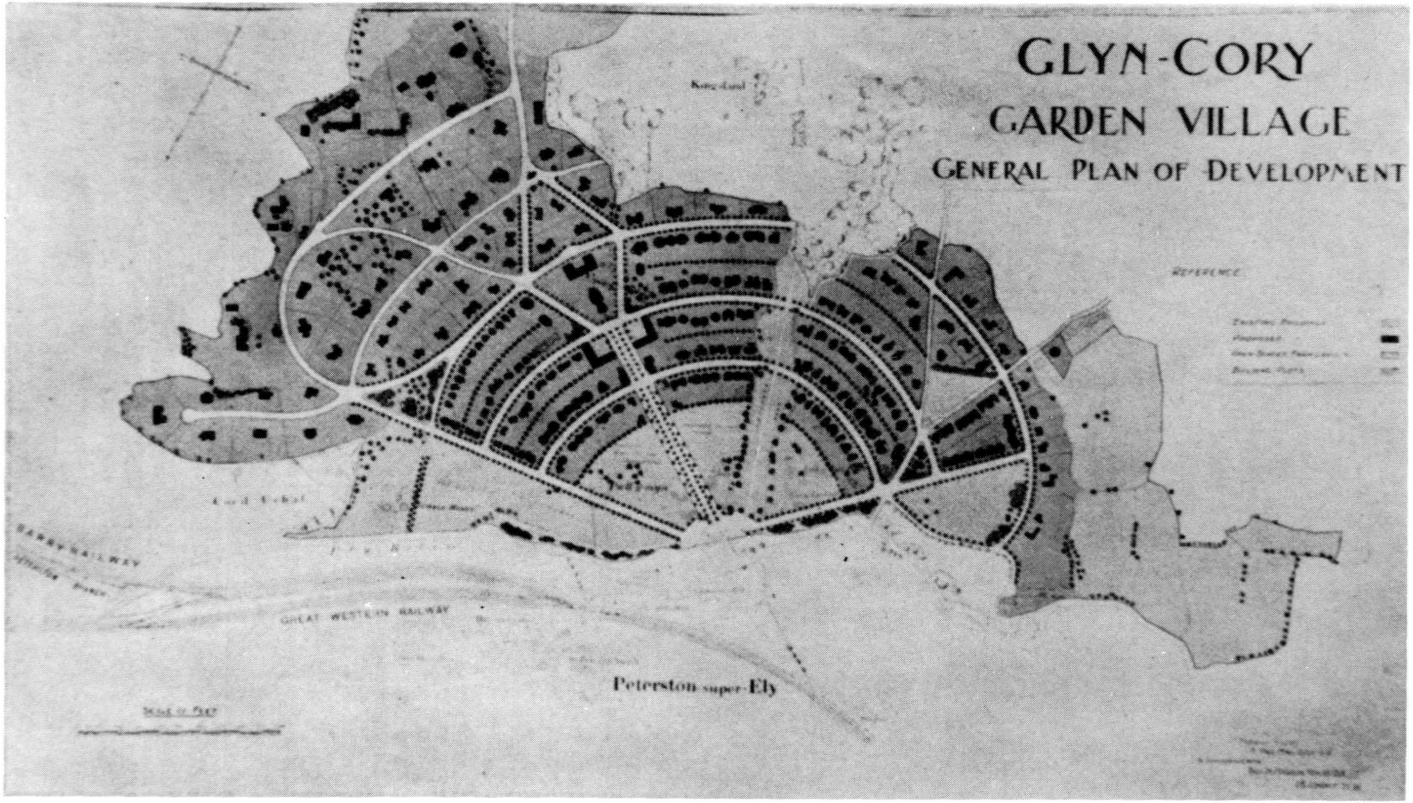

Figure 11. Mawson's plan of Glyn-Cory, near Cardiff, as amended by Adams.

sewer and to connect up to the town by train, and laying out the building plots in such a manner that overcrowding would become impossible, so that 'town workmen can secure the advantages that are to be had in the country.'[65] Indeed, there were few problems in Dunfermline which did not bring him into contact with the evolving field of town planning.

Between 1904 and 1910, Mawson gained further planning experience with the model village of Glyn-Cory, civic design schemes for Southport and the Palace of Peace Gardens at The Hague, a small improvement scheme for Padiham, Black-burn, an estate at Nelson, and a major re-planning scheme for Bolton. Mawson, however, remained a little to one side of the mainstream of developing town-planning thought. He kept aloof from the Garden City Movement like a good many architects – during a Housing Reform Council tour of Germany in 1909, he noted the obsession of some of his colleagues with 12 houses to the acre; he had little to do with the framing of the Town Planning Act, and he commanded little space in jour-nals interested in the new field. He was, of course, a busy landscape gardener and well-known writer on the subject. He had a number of influential clients, including Andrew Carnegie and Lord Leverhulme. The application of swirling park designs to street and city layouts seemed appropriate to the reform of suburban and village estates. In 1911 his monumental book, *Civic Art* was published, a companion volume to the earlier *Art and Craft of Garden Making*. These last attributes were what gained Mawson his later world-wide commissions, on a scale most of his con-temporaries would have envied.

The pioneering work of Adams, Unwin, Geddes, and Mawson had done much by 1909 to establish town planning's right to recognition as a distinct technical practice and discipline, undertaken by particularly enthusiastic professional people. However, the question now arose of how this personal and disparate expertise could be reproduced and institutionalized on the scale that the Town Planning Act seemed to require. How were the new practitioners to be educated and led? In what areas were they to specialize, and how were these areas to be co-ordinated? The work of these four men demonstrated that the new Act was in fact going to demand a new field of work, a new specialism. Both the speed with which these questions had to be answered, and the enthusiasm with which the established professions were joining the debate, suggested that co-operation would provide the main answer.

5   The search for co-operation

At the time that the 1909 Act was passed, the small group of early town planning practitioners foresaw the creation of the requisite army of planners in terms of drawing on the existing professions. It was not their view that future practitioners should go through the same process of self-education through experience that they themselves had done. The problem was to enrich the native skills of the borough engineer's department. However, their own breadth of experience and high stan-dards set a challenge to the professions, none of which had acquired a firm ground-ing in the new field. Moreover, because they were aware that, in their own work, they were using the techniques and experience of a number of professions, they were inclined to see statutory planning as a *co-operative specialism* involving architects, engineers, surveyors, sociologists, and landscape architects.

Although the image of the individual, heroic planner never entirely disappeared from their conception, they increasingly emphasized the need for a combination of skills, either in an exceptional individual or in a more mundane team. Unwin, for example, believed the job of the town planner was to find expression not for preconceived ideas of his own, but for the needs and life of a rising community. 'The details, the exact form, will express his own individuality, but in the main he must in imagination standing on the ground, realise the community that is to come – must instinctively feel the natural lines of traffic and development that such community will take.'[66] Of course, once that role was transferred from an individual to a team, Unwin would want to see the architect in a position of leadership. However, Unwin followed Geddes in extolling the contribution of the sociologist, historian, and local antiquary in performing preliminary site surveys. The engineer then had the important function of providing a framework.

In some respects the work of others is of more importance – I mean that it is more necessary to comply with the requirements of the engineer, the surveyor and the economist and the sociologist – particularly the first three perhaps I may say – as those are the men who must lay down, as it were, the conditions within which we shall work. But when we come to the final stage of putting something down on paper in the way of a definite plan, that is an architectural problem.[67]

There was perhaps a real ambivalence here in the use of 'we' in connection with the final architectural stage, coming after the earlier work of 'others'. However much Unwin broke out of the narrow confines of his profession, he did an equal amount to promote an image of the town planner as a gifted, imaginative architect. It was because Adams and Mawson were far less committed to an established profession that they were inclined to adopt a more synoptic position.

From about 1909, however, three new influences began to bear on the discussion of professional co-operation. The first was mainly a negative one – the failure of the Local Government Board to give much of a lead on the techniques of statutory planning. The second came from the United States – the emergence of the landscape architect as the outstanding professional in urban planning. Third was that of the educational institutions in Britain which began to work on the foundations of a town planning syllabus. All three developments showed the need for a new and partly independent professional body.

Leadership and the civil service

In 1909 Adams was offered, and accepted, the post of town planning inspector to the Local Government Board. His earlier criticism of the Town Planning Bill suggested that the change to the life of the civil servant would not be an easy one for him: 'I think there is far too much red tape and Local Government Board control about the measure.'[68] He also wished to see town planning made compulsory for all urban authorities and felt confident about the recruitment of supporting professions.

In so far as the new Act will result in the establishment of a stronger architectural department at the Local Government Board, and the appointment of local architects to act in co-operation with borough engineers and surveyors, or in the increased architectural knowledge on the part of the surveyors themselves, it will help in developing an improved taste in building design, and a proper sense of proportion and harmony in the development of building areas.[69]

Once Adams became a civil servant, he soon began to feel resentment about the subordination of the technical to the administrative branches of the civil service. He discovered in the Board the same conservatism he was later to find in the real estate interests of Canada. In the examination of countless local enquiries into town planning schemes, he found few constructive outlets for his energy and enthusiasm.[70] Furthermore, nowhere did Adams see the hoped-for increase in architectural employment in central and local government.

In 1909, Ewart Culpin – Adams' successor as secretary to the Garden City Association – had proposed a Central Organisation for the Promotion of the Study of Town Planning. Adams had been cautious, fearing that it might conflict with the Local Government Board.[71] By 1913 Adams, while disappointed in so many respects, had at least learned to discount the danger of such a conflict, should an independent planning organisation be set up.

A new profession: landscape architecture

In the journals and books of the period there is little discussion of the methods of town planning practice in other countries. One country, however, did provide a degree of inspiration – the United States. In 1911, Adams visited America. He noted the landscape architect's position there as a regular consultant to cities and adviser on questions of civic art.

> Whether or not the town planning movement in Britain will produce a corresponding school of experts, either in association with the Royal Institute of British Architects, or independent of them, is interesting matter for speculation, and should be considered by the Institute.[72]

In Britain there was only one recognizable landscape architect, Thomas Mawson. Mawson himself fully recognized the contribution of landscape architecture to town planning, particularly as a mediator between the entrenched, one-sided views of architects and engineers.

> On the one hand we have the architect in general practice whose professional requirements are already so broad as to compel him to specialise more or less and who cannot leave his present task to study all the matters which form the technical training of the Landscape Architect without detriment to his work in his own particular sphere, and on the other hand, we have the engineer who proposes to approach the task with a training which consisting as it does of a knowledge of the exact sciences only, such as sanitation and road engineering, leaves out of account all aesthetic considerations or, worse still, considers the artistic presentment as something superadded to the scheme and not inherent. Besides these we have the sociologist, who neglects all considerations which do not make for the immediate material comfort of the individual citizen.[73]

93

Mawson hoped to establish landscape architecture in England as the master profession of town planning. His widening experience showed him, however, that the landscape architect could not operate on his own.

> Practically all the Town Planning work done in this country so far has been entrusted to and carried out by one man, who has had to combine in himself the functions of Landscape Architect, sanitary and constructional engineer, Town Planner, sociologist, and financial expert; . . . while every scheme of any magnitude provides work for each of these, no one person can undertake the tasks of all, but each must be the work of a specialist and the whole co-related and balanced by the Landscape Architect, whose training has supplied him with sufficient knowledge in the round of the aims and methods of each to sympathise with all and see that every part receives its due place in the *tout ensemble*.[74]

From here Mawson went on to consider the need for a professional Society of Civic Design. The committees of the various institutes were professionally introspective; an 'entirely new profession is required which shall embrace the consideration of Town Planning problems in the mass and from the lofty standpoint over large areas.'[75] He felt that the purpose of such a society should be to create among professions mutual awareness of their various ideals, aims, and positions; to train and educate town planners and landscape architects; and to inculcate civic spirit and educate the public.

The concept of landscape architecture was not well understood in Britain and neither Adams nor Mawson had much material, in terms of trained landscape architects, to support their ideas. Both men, however, began translating the new American profession into English town planning, terms and this inevitably led to their specifying not a new town planning profession, but a new organization of town planning professionals.

Education and the Department of Civic Design

Between 1909 and 1914 three University departments of town planning were set up – at Liverpool, Birmingham, and London – to begin the fundamental task, outlined by the pioneers, of educating future town planners. The Department of Civic Design in the University of Liverpool was outstanding in this respect and both the independently-based studies which it offered and the information and discussion which it reported through its journal, the *Town Planning Review*, played an important part in fostering a spirit of co-operation between professions.

In 1908 W.H. Lever, now Lord Leverhulme, had recovered £91,000 in libel damages from Northcliffe Newspapers, who had been responsible for publishing an article which had accused him of monopolistic practices. Much of the money was used to purchase the Bluecoat School in Liverpool, but the balance was granted to the University as an endowment for new Schools of Tropical Medicine, Russian Studies and Civic Design.[76] In the case of the latter, Leverhulme had been inspired by the work that C.H. Reilly, professor of architecture at Liverpool, had already done to promote the teaching of urban design at the University. 'I can only say', he wrote, 'that Professor Reilly by his enthusiasm in the cause of town planning has been the influence that has brought this matter to a definite shape earlier than would otherwise have been the case. I may say, however, that I have felt for many years that some help is necessary to be given both in educating the public on the matter and also in providing the requisite knowledge available for Towns and Cities . . . in the near future to be able to deal on broad lines with their suburban areas.'[77] The new department thus reflected recognition of town planning as a subject requiring long-term academic study and research as well as detailed technical instruction.

The Department found willing protagonists of the new subject in its first two professors, S.T.Adshead and Patrick Abercrombie. Stanley Adshead was in many ways the architectural profession's ideal – and in particular Professor Reilly's – of a town planner. In addition to Reilly's clear backing, he had the support of many influential architects whom he had assisted in the past in his capacity as a brilliant draughtsman. Reginald Blomfield wrote: 'So far as my knowledge goes, he is the best man for the post, and I believe he would fill it admirably.'[78] Although Adshead recognized that architecture did not necessarily 'cognate' town planning, he naturally shared the beliefs of his supporters.[79] Town planning was about roads, space about buildings, and everything tending to the orderly disposition of a town, but there were other more intangible, elusive issues and their recognition at once raised town planning from the matter of fact to the ideal, from a science to an art – the art of civic design.[80]

The Department offered a certificate course of one year, awarded on the basis of knowledge acquired from lectures, and a diploma course of a further year in which students had to prepare two town planning schemes for definite areas, a study in the reconstruction of an area, and a design for a town planning incident. The certificate course was open to graduates of the Liverpool School of Architecture, to those who had passed Intermediate examinations of the RIBA or the ICE, and to those who had served articles in the office of an architect or engineer for three years. The diploma course was open to those who had gained the certificate or to Members of the RIBA. In 1912 Adshead altered this arrangement, making the certificate course a general introduction to town planning and the diploma course a specialized course in civic design. There were six lecture courses: outlines of town planning; civic engineering; civic law; civic architecture; civic decoration; and landscape architecture. Although the Department had only nine students in the first two years and ten in the third, lectures were opened to local professionals and councillors.

Adshead believed that his Department would train a new expert, a member of a technical profession, or 'a town planner by profession with distinctive qualifications as a member of one of the other professions'.[81] Adshead freely extended his educational theory into the larger world of established professions. The time was right for a 'Society of Town Planners; the members of which drafted from the ranks of the technical professions should be specially qualified by experience or training to take a part in the planning of a town.'[82]

Patrick Abercrombie succeeded to the chair in 1914 when Adshead left to set up the new town planning department at University College, London. He had been a lecturer at the Liverpool School of Architecture since 1907 and was elected research fellow and lecturer in the Department of Civic Design in 1909. A grant from Leverhulme funds enabled him to devote his full time to studying town planning comprehensively and travelling throughout Europe. With these advantages Abercrombie was able to boil down the experience of the past 14 years into a balanced view of the professional town planner.

Town planning was, for Abercrombie, the systematic intention to control the

growth of cities and to remodel their bulk in consonance with modern requirements.[83] This systematic intention was to be expressed in a process of formulating
objectives for the particular town in the context of a general philosophy of town
planning, executing a detailed civic and sociological survey, analysing how the town
fell short of the ideal, and finally drawing up a development and improvement plan.
Planning should stem from a thorough understanding of the whole town as a single
organism. Only 'after profound study, having placed your city and grasped its true
aims, having before you your practical notes, and, above all, having at the back of
your head some mental picture to which you hope to make your town approximate,
you are in a position to prepare a plan for its existing mass and its anticipated
growth.'[84] Abercrombie here articulated Unwin's belief in the social imagination of
the planner, Adams's plea for order and design in future development, Geddes's
survey methodology, and a typically Mawsonian dialogue between ideals and existing conditions. It had a logic and simplicity; the rough, idiosyncratic edges of the
early pioneer's beliefs and work were now smoothed away in a clean, unimpeach-
able abstraction.

So the Department became convinced that neither engineer nor architect should
undertake town planning without a special study of the subject. 'A study of the
movement of populations resulting from altered conditions of communication, of
housing as a definite science apart from the construction of the individual houses, of
habits of recreation and requirements of administration – in a word, sociology, and
from the artistic standpoint, the studied conception of a beautiful city as a whole, are
subjects for analysis and consideration by everyone who contributes to the making
of the "Town Plan".'[85] Town planning, then, was a subject in its own right, making
demands upon a range of subsidiary subjects which did not correspond with the
skills and curricula of those professions which either wished, or were being asked, to
prepare town plans. Adshead and Abercrombie thus did much to provide the
central focus for the coming federation of town planners.

6 The Town Planning Institute

Between 1909 and 1914 two relatively swift developments occurred in the professionalization of town planning. First, the techniques of suburban and town layout
were shown to be related to a coherent but complex subject, outlined originally by
the pioneers, and now fully revealed through a history, philosophy, and method of
its own, through engineering and sociological branch studies, through a legal and
administrative context, and (still) through a central aesthetic preoccupation with
town design. Second, there was a natural growth of practical, town planning opportunities. By 1914 there were some 20 or 30 private architects and surveyors involved
with garden suburbs or garden villages, as well as 80 or more local authority engineers and surveyors at work on the early phases of statutory town planning schemes.
The combination of, and progress within, both developments were bound to lead to
new educational facilities. That they should also have led to a new professional body
is perfectly understandable in the light of the demand for immediate, co-operative,
professional effort which we have been examining.

According to Alfred Potter, for many years secretary of the Town Planning Institute, informal discussions about such a body had been taking place since 1910,
between Adams, Unwin, Adshead, H.V. Lanchester, the noted architect, George

Pepler, a young surveyor who had taken over the supervision of a number of Adams's planning schemes, and J.S. Birkett, a lawyer.[86] In October 1912, the *Town Planning Review* noted:

> A group of Town Planners, all practically engaged in the execution of Town Planning schemes and representing every aspect of the subject, engineers, architects, surveyors, &c. – has organised itself into a body and has held several meetings in London. A combination of experts such as this should do much to advance the interest of Town Planning in this country. We regard this group as the nucleus of a society to which all Town Planners may in time belong.[87]

The first recorded meeting of the Institute was held at the Westminster Palace Hotel on 11 July 1913, attended by Adams, Lucas, Soutar, Lanchester, Adshead, Unwin, Davidge, and Pepler (Lucas and Soutar were architects from Hampstead Garden Suburb).[88] This Provisional Committee nominated 19 architects, 7 surveyors, 12 engineers, and one original member (Patrick Geddes) to join a proposed Institute. A meeting was called for 21 November and at this meeting the Institute was formally founded, 64 members of various categories were suggested, and a Council was elected. In December the Council elected Adams as President, Unwin and J.W. Cockrill (borough engineer of Great Yarmouth) vice-presidents, Geddes as honorary librarian, and Pepler as honorary secretary and treasurer.[89] With the signing of the Memorandum and Articles of Association on 14 September 1914, the Institute was formally constituted as a company, limited by guarantee.

The original idea of a town planning institute had almost certainly been conceived by Thomas Adams. Many years later Alwyn Lloyd recalled a long train journey back from one of the town planning tours of Germany when Adams had first talked about his idea.[90] Unwin, too, wrote: 'This Institute owes its existence largely to our President, as the Town Planning Movement in this country owes its existence no little to his energy in setting the Letchworth Garden City fairly on its way as a public example.'[91] The new institute was the key to Adams' search for a way of harnessing diverse and wayward technical skills, and directing them towards the partially independent service of town planning.

This idea of Adams, however, may have been adumbrated and was certainly later substantiated by professional town planning bodies already in existence by 1910. First there was the Advisory Committee of the National Housing and Town Planning Council, composed mainly of professional people, and formed to advise the Council of planning education, the structure of conferences, and the itineraries for European town planning tours. Six out of the eight professionals who in 1913 attended the first meeting of the new Town Planning Institute were also members of that advisory committee or prominent members of the Council.[92] The Advisory Committee had provided one of the few regular opportunities for representatives of different professions to meet and discuss housing and town planning issues. Second there were the Town Planning Committees of the RIBA, the Surveyors' Institution, and the Institution of Municipal and County Engineers, representing the most enthusiastic and informed planning opinions of those professions. These older institute committees formed the bulk of the nominations for full membership, made at the first meeting of the new Institute.

The purpose of the new Institute was clear. A letter of 11 November 1913, sent out to the nominees, made the following proposal:

to form a Town Planning Institute in order to advance the study of Town Planning and Civic Design, and to promote the artistic and scientific development of Towns and Cities, and to secure the association of those engaged or interested in the practice of Town Planning.[93]

These objects were later confirmed in the Memorandum of Association.

At the centre was a cause. Town planning had emerged as a subject and function in its own right. The Institute drew together what were the common, 'passing' interests of all the reform, propagandist, and professional bodies into a single, coherent interest; it was the sole body devoted to town planning alone. The isolation of this single interest in the context of an apparently professional organization was to have fundamental importance in shaping the semantics of the phrase 'town planner' as a technical professional. The more immediate result was to remove the town planning cutting-edge from the propaganda of reform groups such as the Garden City and Town Planning Association and the National Housing and Town Planning Council, whose interests now tended to contract back to their original interests in garden cities and housing reform.

To each side of this central cause lay two distinctively professional matters, education and professional association. The Institute was the final vindication of town planning and civics as a body of knowledge, worthy of independent investigation; it would promote the mutual exchange of ideas, studies, and practical experience. This object was later elaborated in the Memorandum of Association: teaching any subject related to town planning; devising means of testing the qualifications of candidates for admission to membership of the Institute by examination in theory and practice; and holding conferences and meetings for the discussion and exchange of views on town planning.

The association of professionals was a rather more complex matter. John Burns, at the inaugural dinner, described the organization as 'loose' and 'informal', composed of architects, surveyors, engineers, town planners, artists, and idealists.[94] The Institute was not, however, a study association open to any interested person. The first sketch for membership classes had been based on a definite structuring of the interests: *Members*, prior members of the RIBA and similar institutes, but associated with the practice of town planning; *Associated members*, professionals who had taken an active interest in town planning, mainly solicitors and town clerks; *Associates*, those who had acquired an approved standard of proficiency in town planning; and *Honorary Members*, those distinguished persons who had a special interest in town planning.[95] The structure formalized the reversal of role which had been occurring over the previous 14 years: the reformers and patrons were no longer the town planners. The Institute was placing qualified professionalism at the forefront of reform and local government. The founders saw that their constitution would permit the Institute, through examinations and other criteria for election, to become the qualifying association for those who wished or were being asked to undertake practical town planning work.

The founders of the Institute had not, however, set up a new profession quite like the others. Other professions sought to demonstrate their skills, proficiency, honesty, and status to the public. In planning, however, there was no obvious challenge from any disreputable band of empirics, which needed to be quelled with a 'Hippodamic Oath'. The groundwork for professional status in town planning was already managed by the architectural and other professions. By itself, the Institute did very little to grant status to anyone; rather the professions granted status to town planning – that had been the whole inspiration of Adams. If, however, the professional status of the member was largely assured by other bodies, the Institute was bound to qualify that status. Technical ability and skill were not at issue, but the adequacy of an understanding and commitment to the new subject certainly was. At the heart of the Institute was an ideology not of professionalization but of re-professionalization, a re-baptism of purpose, outlook, education, and co-operative spirit.

The Institute had an appalling start to life with the onset of the First World War. The outward trappings of a professional institute were nevertheless developed in a spirit of hope. Lectures were arranged, a journal and library collection started, an examination syllabus prepared (similar in character to that of the Department of Civic Design at Liverpool, but remaining dormant until 1920), a code of practice and scale of fees adopted, and the coat of arms drawn with Lex Athene balancing the work of the architect and the instruments of the surveyor in her scales.

Until the end of the war, membership of the Institute was dominated by those professionals who had been roused by, or who had taken part in, the town-planning campaign from 1906 onwards. Architects were in a majority and were represented both by senior members of the RIBA like Sir Aston Webb, H.V. Lanchester, and Edwin Lutyens, as well as by less celebrated figures who had been associated with garden suburbs (Hampstead Garden Suburb alone produced five of them). The Institute did form something of a new platform from which architects could influence the direction of town planning. Architects wrote 40 per cent of the papers appearing in the *Journal of the Town Planning Institute* between 1914 and 1918, and they might well have expected the Institute to provide at long last the introduction to statutory town planning for which they had so long been campaigning.

Engineers had more interest in the Institute as a source of education than as a means of professional advancement. Cockrill said: 'My object in joining this institute was to gain knowledge and to extend my experience in the particular work that it was formed to assist, and I would much rather consider myself a student of the professors around me than in any way try to give them a lesson in the work they have so ably carried out.'[96] With the Town Planning Act forced upon engineers, knowledge and wide technical understanding were indispensable for them.

Surveyors were not numerous among the membership yet the profession had produced the most active participants in the founding of the new Institute, namely Thomas Adams, George Pepler, and W.R. Davidge. Adams in fact qualified as a Fellow of the Surveyor's Institution only a few months before the foundation of the new Institute (which may even have been delayed to that effect). The surveyors were in many ways, however, the most completely transformed of the professional members. Davidge was to follow an exemplary career, the model of a professional broadening his horizons under the influence of town planning. From 1901 he had worked as a surveyor in the architects' department of the London County Council and in 1907 he became district surveyor of Lewisham. In time he qualified as surveyor, architect and engineer, and thus indisputably equipped himself to embark on a wide-ranging, international planning career after the First World War.

Amidst the hardships of war, then, the new Institute set out to refresh the jaded outlooks of the individual professions:

Surely our work must contemplate something beyond skeleton plans of highway systems or convenience and amenity in street and playground. It must connote something more than arrangement and dispositions of masses and details in buildings; it must have regard to more than cold-blooded scientific treatment of the problems of land development; it must have in view the building up of a stronger race and a healthier civilisation.[97]

After the war, the major strength of the Institute would lie in extending the scope and nature of these ideals, first to built-up areas, then to regional planning, rural development, and on towards population and industrial planning on a national scale. However, both the immediate and long-term achievement of the Institute in co-ordinating professional town planning effort, and so fulfilling the basic aims of Adams, were negligible.

By 1916, 88 local authorities had 145 town planning schemes in progress, covering 251,266 acres of land. In nearly every case the work was being carried out by the local authorities' own engineers, 82 per cent of whom were members of the Institution of Municipal and County Engineers, and no more than 10 per cent of whom were members of the new Town Planning Institute. Very few authorities were engaging outside advice. Three of them were consulting a number of local architects, seven were consulting so-called town planning experts. The phraseology is enlightening; it varied from 'consultant town planning expert' (referring to Professor Adshead), 'town planning surveyor', and 'architectural adviser', to an 'expert in town planning procedure', and a 'town planning engineer'.[98] A little of the Institute's influence was spreading, but the slow progress was clearly not just the result of narrow-mindedness on the part of municipal engineers. Great Yarmouth officials, for instance, had budgeted £50 for outside consultants' fees but the relevant committee would not hear of the expenditure.[99]

After all those early years of excitement, energy, and outspokenness, town planning was now inevitably settling down into a rather humdrum local authority routine, with little financial encouragement. Town planning was not going to call for great engineering schemes, huge estate developments, grandiose civic designs. Abroad there were certainly a few ambitious schemes under way and after the war many more, served by British town planners, would start in India, Australia, South Africa, and the Americas. But at home, statutory town planning could frequently be confined to developing a simple road network, stopping up footpaths, siting industrial development, reserving open spaces and playgrounds, and preparing for local authority housing schemes. Perhaps few members of those established professions, therefore, felt disappointment if they were not asked to join the new Institute.

Wilenski has written:

Any occupation wishing to exercize professional authority must find a technical basis for it, assert an exclusive jurisdiction, link both skill and jurisdiction to standards of training, and convince the public that its services are uniquely trustworthy.[100]

In 1916 there was hardly an occupation of town planning, let alone one that could claim professional jurisdiction. The Town Planning Institute had been created on the full tide of enthusiasm and recognition of the need for co-operation. However, the test of whether it could really harness professional effort and individual town

planning ideologies never materialized. As general enthusiasm declined and consequently the desire for involvement also faded, the Institute was left focussing on a
frail individuality.

The Town Planning Institute was designed to focus and coordinate the professions
involved with town planning. The demands for expertise, for education, for co-
operation, did not *entail* the creation of a new profession; only the redirection and
re-training of older professions were essential. However, given the frequency with
which new professions were being founded in England during the early part of this
century, and the awareness of the complexity and individuality of the town-planning
subject shown by men such as Adams, Mawson, and Adshead, it is certainly not surprising that the founders of the Town Planning Institute should model their association on professional institutes such as the RIBA, and write into their constitution
the blueprint of a new town planning profession. The founders had no need to
explain or justify. Enthusiasm and co-operation were their own justifications. But
as a result of the stagnation of town planning interest, brought on by war and a
routine statutory duty, the new Institute was left stranded in the borrowed robes of
an independent profession. Paradoxically free but a little lifeless, cut off from the
hot blood of architects and engineers, the Institute had to grow slowly back to
strength by understanding its *raison d'être* in terms of independence rather than co-
operation, and by forging a unique profession of planning out of skills and expertise
rather than ideals and social purposes.

NOTES

1 P.Geddes, *Garden Cities and Town Planning,* n.s. III (July 1908), 69.
2 *Parliamentary Debates,* 4th ser., CLXXXVIII, col.949.
3 *Parliamentary Debates,* 5th ser., III, col.749.
4 J. Cockrill, 'The position of town planning in Great Britain, 1916', *J. Inst. Municipal and County Engineers,* XLII (1916), 453–87.
5 For general discussions on the development of the professions: J.A. Gotch (ed.), *The Growth and Work of the Royal Institute of British Architects 1834–1934* (1934); B. Kaye, *The Development of the Architectural Profession in Britain* (1960); F. Jenkins, *Architect and Patron* (1961); Institution of Civil Engineers, *The Education and Status of Civil Engineers* (1878); L. Angell, 'The origins, constitution, and objects of the Association of Municipal and Sanitary Engineers and Surveyors', *Procs Ass. Municipal and Sanitary Engineers and Surveyors,* XI (1884–5); F.M.L. Thompson, *Chartered Surveyors: the growth of a profession* (1968); G. Cherry, *The Evolution of British Town Planning* (1974).
6 City of Birmingham, *Report of the Housing Committee, 3rd July 1906,* 2.
7 The most comprehensive early statements came from Henry Aldridge, secretary of the National Housing Reform Council: *The Case for Town Planning* (1915); *The National Housing Manual* (1923).
8 Poor Law Commissioners, *Report on an Enquiry into the Sanitary Condition of the Labouring Population of Great Britain* (1842), 371.
9 Local Government Board, *Reports on Public Health and Medical Subjects,* no. 90, 1914 (Public Record Office).
10 Bournville was started in 1878, Port Sunlight in 1887.
11 A.G. Gardiner, *Life of George Cadbury* (1923), 143–4.

12 2nd Viscount Leverhulme, *Viscount Leverhulme by his Son* (1927), 86.

13 W.L. Creese, *The Search for Environment* (New Haven, 1966), 223.

14 H. Barnett, *The Story of the Growth of Hampstead Garden Suburb 1907–1928* (1928), 7–8.

15 E. Howard, *Tomorrow: A Peaceful Path to Real Reform* (1898), 130–1.

16 *Ibid.*, 45.

17 T.C. Horsfall, 'An address on the planning and control of town extensions in Germany', *J. Inst. Municipal and County Engineers*, XXXIII (1906–7), 62. This is a short version of Horsfall's main work on German local government and planning: *The Improvement of the dwellings and surroundings of the people. The example of Germany'* (suppl. to T.E. Marr, *Housing Survey of Manchester and Salford*) (1904).

18 *Ibid.*, 68.

19 J.S. Nettlefold, *Practical Housing* (1908), 48.

20 *Ibid.*, 65.

21 S. Smirke, *Suggestions for the Architectural Improvement of the Western Part of London* (1834), 1–2.

22 J. Belcher, Presidential Address 1904, *JRIBA*, XII (1904–5), 8–9.

23 *Ibid.*, 9.

24 J. Simpson and B. Pite., 'The planning of cities and open spaces', *JRIBA*, XII (1904–5), 342.

25 Chronicle, *JRIBA*, XIV (1906–7), 480.

26 'Architects and town planning', *JRIBA*, XVI (1908–9), 747.

27 *Standard*, 30 August 1909.

28 *Builder*, XCIV (1908), 637.

29 RIBA, *Town Planning Conference 1910, Trans.* (1911).

30 Town Planning Committee, 'Suggestions to promoters of town planning schemes', *JRIBA*, XVIII (1910–11), 668.

31 *Ibid.*, 661.

32 A.E. Collins, Address of President, *Procs Inc. Ass. Municipal and County Engineers*, XXXI (1904–5), 277.

33 Horsfall, 'An address on the planning and control of town extensions in Germany', 70–82.

34 Garden City Association, *The Practical Application of Town Planning Powers, Report of National Town Planning Conference* (1909), 1.

35 *Ibid.*, 47.

36 *Ibid.*, 53.

37 *Engineering*, XC (1910), 863.

38 *Ibid.*, 864.

39 H. Stilgoe, 'Town planning in the light of the Housing and Town Planning Act 1909', *Procs Inc. Ass. Municipal and County Engineers*, XXXVII (1910–11), 44.

40 Greatorix, Address by President, *Report of Conference Held at West Bromwich in July, 1911* (1911), 3.

41 L. Vigers, Opening Address, *Trans. Surveyors' Inst.*, XLIII (1910–11), 12–13.

42 Thompson, *op. cit.*, 300.

43 *Builder*, CIII (1912), 686.

44. Speech to the International Association for the Advancement of Science, Arts and Education, Paris 1900, quoted in P. Boardman, *Patrick Geddes: Maker of the Future* (1944), 227.

45 R. Unwin, Gold Medal Award Speech, *JRIBA*, XLIV (1937), 582.

46 T. Mawson, *The Life and Work of an English Landscape Architect* (1927), ch. 2.

47 T. Adams, *Edinburgh Evening News*, July 1897, quoted in Adams, *Garden City and Agriculture* (1905), 120.

48 Letter from William Thompson to George Cadbury, 23 December 1909, pasted into

Minute Book of the National Housing Reform Council, I.
49 R. Unwin, 'Building and natural beauty' in B. Parker and R. Unwin, *The Art of Building a Home* (1901), 84.
50 *GC*, n.s. I (1906), 165.
51 S. Buder, 'Ebenezer Howard: the genesis of a town planning movement', *J. American Inst. Planners*, xxxv (1969), 395.
52 *GC*, o.s. I (1904), 6.
53 *GC*, o.s. I (1905), 40.
54 C.B. Purdom, *The Letchworth Achievement* (1963), 24.
55 Letter from Sir Richard Paget to the *J. Town Planning Isnt.*, xxvi (1940), 156.
56 T. Adams, 'Some new garden suburb schemes', *Garden Cities and Town Planning*, n.s. IV (1909), 207.
57 R. Unwin, *Co-partnership in Housing* (1910?), 5–6.
58 R. Unwin and M. Baillie Scott, *Town Planning and Modern Architecture at the Hampstead Garden Suburb* (1909).
59 Biographical details from Boardman, *op. cit.*
60 P. Geddes, *City Development: A Study of Parks, Gardens and Culture-Institutes* (1904), 99.
61 *Ibid.*, 211.
62 Report of the Cities Committee of the Sociological Soc. *JRIBA*, xvi (1909), 501.
63 Mawson, *English Landscape Architect*, 41.
64 T. Mawson, *Scheme for Pittencrieff Park Glen and City Improvements* (1904), 3.
65 *Ibid.*, 10.
66 R. Unwin, 'The planning of the residential districts of towns', *RIBA International Congress of Architects. Trans. 16th–21st July 1906* (1906), 420.
67 Unwin in discussion of paper by Beresford Pite at Guildhall Conference 1909, in Garden City Association, *The Practical Application of Town Planning Powers*, 39.
68 T. Adams, 'Some criticisms of the Town Planning Bill', *Garden Cities and Town Planning*, III (1908), 49.
69 T. Adams, 'An analysis of the Act', in Garden City Association, *The Practical Application of Town Planning Powers*, 11.
70 T. Adams, 'Some personal history and impressions'. Unpublished paper in the possession of Mrs Constance Adams.
71 Adams, in discussion of paper by E. Culpin, 'A central consultative body', Garden City Association, *The Practical Application of Town Planning Powers*, 61.
72 T. Adams, *Garden Cities and Town Planning*, n.s. I (1911), 167.
73 T. Mawson, 'The position and prospects of landscape architecture in England', *TPR*, II (1911–12), 227.
74 *Ibid.*, 228.
75 *Ibid.*, pt II, 'The proposed Society', 306.
76 Leverhulme, *op. cit.*, 139.
77 Letter from W.H. Lever to A.W. Dale, 20 November 1908. University of Liverpool, *Documents Relating to the Department of Civic Design*, (1909).
78 R. Blomfield, 'Testimonial for Stanley Adshead', (University of Liverpool, Reports of Faculty of Arts, 1909).
79 Letter from Adshead to Professor Reilly, 11 January 1909. *Documents relating to the Department of Civic Design* (1909).
80 S. Adshead, 'The ideals of civic design', in *Miscellany Presented to John MacDonald Mackay, Ll.D., July 1914* (1914), 14.
81 S. Adshead, 'Town Planning Conference at West Bromwich with some notes on the profession of engineering in its relation to town planning', *TPR*, II (1911), 175.
82 *Ibid.*, 176.
83 P. Abercrombie, 'Study before town planning', *TPR*, VI (1916–17), 171.

84 *Ibid.*, 188.

85 Editorial, 'Town planning and the architect', *TPR*, III (1912), 169.

86 'The history of the Institute', *Year Book of the Town Planning Inst.*, (1966–7), 17.

87 'Chronicle of passing events', *TPR*, III (1912–13), 220.

88 Meeting of the Provisional Committee at the Westminster Palace Hotel, 11 July 1913. Minutes of Council, I, 1.

89 Minutes of Council, I, 5.

90 *J. Town Planning Inst.*, XXVI (1940), 115.

91 R. Unwin, 'The work of the Town Planning Institute', *J. Town Planning Inst.*, I (1914), 131.

92 The Advisory Committee included Pite, Lanchester, MacAllister, Cockrill, Adshead, Thompson, Aldridge, Davidge, Geddes, Horsfall, Pepler, Houfton, and Unwin.

93 Letter pasted into Council Minute Book.

94 J. Burns, Address at the Inaugural Dinner of the Town Planning Institute, *TPR*, V (1914–15), 3–4.

95 Minutes of Council, I, 4. Later in the first year categories were changed to Members, Associate Members, Legal and Legal Associate Members, and Honorary Members.

96 J. Cockrill, Opening Address, *J. Town Planning Inst.*, III (1916–17), 1.

97 T. Adams, 'Town planning in Canada', *J. Town Planning Inst.*, IV (1917), 16–17.

98 J. Cockrill, 'The position of town planning in Great Britain, 1916', *J. Inst. Municipal and County Engineers*, XLII (1916), 453–487.

99 *Ibid.*, 463.

100 H. Wilenski, 'The professionalization of everyone', *American J. Sociology*, LXX (1964), 138.

Housing and town planning in Manchester before 1914

MICHAEL HARRISON

Housing and town planning in Manchester before 1914

MICHAEL HARRISON

1 Introduction

The purpose of this essay is to provide a case study of the development of the housing-reform and town planning movement in Manchester and a review of the planned estates and garden suburbs that resulted from the activities and propaganda of the local advocates of site and town planning. It closely follows the author's dissertation, 'The garden suburbs of Manchester: social aspects of housing and town planning 1894–1914', which was presented to the University of Manchester in June 1974. Virtually the whole of that work has been incorporated in this piece. A certain amount of biographical and statistical material from the appendices of the thesis has been included in the present essay. A fuller description of the use made by the author of local directories is to be found in an appendix to the dissertation. Readers who would like more information on the plans should consult the drawings in the original. Such changes as have been made occur mainly in section 2 and in the treatment of Blackley. The portion of the essay on Burnage Garden Village appeared in substantially the same form in the *Town Planning Review* of July 1976. Thanks are due to the editors of that journal for permission to reproduce that material here.

Of course, a good deal of new work on the subject has appeared since the spring of 1974. This includes a great many dissertations, conference papers and published works. Among the theses that have added to the writer's knowledge those of his fellow contributors stand pre-eminent. A number of valuable papers on the history of planning have in the recent past been presented to the History of Planning and Urban History Groups, whilst the number of published works relating to the subject grows all the time. Eversley, Hall, Cherry, Gauldie, Sutcliffe and Tarn have all published books on housing or planning since the author completed his thesis. It is to be hoped that this local case study will provide material for a comparison with the national and local trends outlined by the above-mentioned individuals and groups.

The town planning movement was, as Cherry has pointed out, a 'reactive development', but the responses of the early advocates of town planning often owed much to the peculiarities of their own locality. In this essay some attempt has been made to show how the Manchester situation conditioned the responses of reformers like Thomas Coglan Horsfall, Thomas Marr and Herbert Philips.

With some justification, the names of Horsfall and Marr have begun to figure more prominently in the literature on housing and town planning. Most writers stress their administrative, sociological and propagandist work. This was undoubtedly important, but a review of the history of the Manchester garden suburb schemes serves to show that they and their colleagues were also concerned with aesthetic and practical matters – with bricks and mortar as well as laws and surveys.

This essay consists of three sections. In the first the local background is explored. As the housing and planning movement in Manchester was the result of the convergence of many reform groups, attention is paid to the differing motives of these varied groups. Although it has been much easier to find out about the views of the 'guiding classes', the author has made some effort to illustrate the views of the labour movement and those at the grass-roots level. The next section consists of detailed studies of some of the planned estates and garden suburbs of Manchester. The estates studied are those of the Corporation of Manchester at Blackley, to the north of the city, the co-partnership ventures of the Manchester and Fairfield Tenants Ltd in the south and east, and the private scheme at Chorltonville, again to the south of the town centre. The financial and organizational arrangements of the different promoters are described, as well as the architecture and the layout of the estates. Within the limits of the source material (in this case directories, rate books and internal descriptions) an attempt has been made to portray the social structure and pattern of life in some of the garden suburbs of Manchester. In the final section an evaluation of these numerically limited but stylistically important ventures is made.

The award of an SSRC Studentship in 1972–3 made this work possible. The City of Birmingham Polytechnic provided funds for the preparation of the essay for publication. Mrs M.H. Grattidge carefully typed the final script. Mr G. MacQueen of Manchester Tenants Ltd, Mr R. Johnson of Fairfield Tenants Ltd, Mr H.F. Dawson and the City Architect and his staff all provided valuable assistance. The author's fellow contributors suggested further sources. The staff at Manchester Central Reference Library helped make this work easier and more pleasant.

2   The pressure for reform

'People who write about social problems in our large towns', wrote R.C.K. Ensor in 1906, 'are much too apt to generalize from London.'[1] In some ways the problems of Manchester were unique, and the London experience was not always relevant to its needs. 'In London the great evil is overcrowding of people per room and per house, in Manchester it is overcrowding and bad arrangement of houses per acre.'[2] In their search for solutions to overcrowding and other urban problems Manchester reformers looked at both English and foreign prototypes for 'an ideal for life in Manchester'.[3] Whatever their source, and whatever their range of application, their schemes owed much to the distinctive nature of the local problems they faced and sought to counter.

For generations a small group of reformers had been trying to analyse and improve the condition of the city. Many were members of the Manchester Statistical Society and the Manchester and Salford Sanitary Association. At first mainly, though never exclusively, concerned with sanitation, these reformers gradually widened their net to include housing, open spaces and pollution. By the early 1900s a more sophisticated form of environmental planning was being advocated, particularly by members of the Citizens Association. The approach of these groups was essentially voluntaristic. Nevertheless, a change in their general political outlook can be detected. The political quietism of the Sanitary Association gave way to the more direct, but non-partisan, political activity of the Citizens Association. A belief in individualistic solutions gave way to a qualified acceptance of 'municipal socialism'. The city council was not unaffected by these developments. On the whole, though, their response was limited, being conditioned by the 'profit-and-loss' attitude of most of the councillors. Consequently, the lead in the housing and town planning movement in Manchester was taken by philanthropists like T.C. Horsfall.

Manchester still suffered from the 'contagion of numbers' at the end of the nineteenth century.[4] Between 1881 and 1911 the population of the city rose from 462,000 to 714,000.[5] While the central areas declined in population, the suburbs were expanding rapidly. The unfortunate corollary of the 'great law of centrifugal expansion' was the presence of a squalid and overcrowded 'industrial collar' around the commercial centre of Manchester.[6]

By 1914 the suburban growth of Manchester had been under way for over a century.[7] The upper middle class had been the principal force in the expansion of the city. By the Edwardian period, however, they were being followed by ever-larger numbers of lower-middle-class residents, moved by the desire to emulate their superiors. Rising real wages, shorter hours of work, the growth of white-collar and service industries, transport improvements and an awareness of the medical advantages of suburban living were among the factors leading to the migration of the middle and lower middle classes to the suburbs. Whilst this 'moving out' process might take some families into Cheshire, to Bowdon or Alderley, most suburban developments took place on the ever-expanding periphery of Manchester.[8] The suburban townships of Gorton, Rusholme and Chorlton-cum-Hardy were in the last decade of the nineteenth century the fastest-growing districts in the city. Chorlton, for instance, which had only 4,741 inhabitants in 1891, had almost doubled that figure by 1901.[9] By 1911 the township contained 24,977 persons.[10] With such a rate of growth it was not surprising that 'the green fields of one summer were the roads and avenues of the next.'[11] The bulk of the property in areas like Chorlton-cum-Hardy was of the cheaper semi-detached kind, being let at from 8s. to 11s. a week. 'These houses are much beloved of newly-married couples,' wrote one correspondent, 'to whose modest style of housekeeping they are no doubt suited.'[12] Though undoubtedly superior to the inner city slums, these suburban areas were not being developed according to any coherent plan. Building controls in some areas were so weak that reformers were beginning to fear that the suburbs were being irreparably damaged. As Horsfall remarked in 1904: 'We all agree that the control of the outskirts is the all important thing.'[13]

Better-paid artisans might also be able to take to the suburbs, but the vast majority of the working classes of Manchester still tended to dwell nearer to the centre of the city. They lived, on the whole, in 'two up and two down' cottage houses set in terraces that usually rose direct from the pavement line. The majority of these houses were plain-fronted, though in the better class of houses bay windows were occasionally to be seen. Gardens and forecourts were exceptional, though the local building bye-laws required increasingly large backyards. Few open spaces were to be found in working-class areas. Working-class houses rarely had bathrooms, and it was only in the Edwardian period that the Health Committee seriously began converting pail closets into water closets. A Board of Trade Enquiry estimated the rents (including rates) of three- to five-roomed dwellings in Manchester in 1905 to be between 4s.6d. and 7s., though two- and three-roomed dwellings could be rented for less. The report went on to say that 'the rents paid by the great majority of the working classes do not generally exceed 7s., though artisans and foremen with large earnings frequently pay as much as 8s. and 8s.6d.'[14]

Most Manchester workmen at this time still lived near their places of work, though a Board of Trade investigation in 1908 detected a growing tendency to live out in the suburbs where better and cheaper houses were to be found. The process was to a limited extent aided by the municipal tramway service. 'This applies,' the report indicated, 'to the artisan class, but still more to clerks, book-keepers, warehousemen, and other employees of small means, large numbers of whom live out of Manchester in houses of about 5s. rental, and use the tramway morning and night at a cost of 2d. per day.'[15] Unskilled workmen were rarely found among the suburbans.[16]

Near the centre of the city the building activities of the railway companies, merchant houses and local authorities often led to the demolition of working-class housing and consequently to overcrowding in adjacent areas like Ancoats, St George's and Hulme.[17] According to the census standard, 34,137 people were living in overcrowded conditions in Manchester in 1901.[18] Compared with other areas this may not seem a high figure, but 'in Manchester the crying evils were out of doors' rather than 'indoors and within the houses' as in London.[19] The connection between overcrowding and high mortality rates, lowered physical efficiency, crime and immorality was noted by many reformers. Manchester men, however, tended to be just as concerned with the surroundings of the workman's house as with the number of residents within it. They were particularly worried about areas like Ancoats Number One Sanitary District, where there was 'an almost entire absence of everything which makes a locality healthy.'[20] T.R. Marr's 1904 study of housing conditions in Manchester and Salford showed, however, that many working-class residents were still attached to these insalubrious districts by old associations and were reluctant to move.[21] This was probably reinforced by the necessity for many of living close to their work-place. As Costelloe pointed out to the Manchester Statistical Society: 'A slum represents the presence of a market for local, casual labour.'[22]

The opening of the Manchester Ship Canal in 1894 and the growth of the central business district led to 'a greater pressure for housing accommodation near the centre to provide for the increasing numbers engaged in casual work.'[23] The Medical Officer of Health, James Niven, was aware of the inelasticity of the housing market:

Prosperity and adversity alike cause overcrowding in the poorest parts of the city. With a wave of industrial prosperity more persons want to have their own house, and more workers are wanted. Every house good or bad, is occupied, and the overflow of workers leads to overcrowding. In adversity poor families take in lodgers, or they occupy different rooms in the same house and overcrowding is caused in both ways. Overcrowding is inevitable among the poorest class at times.[24]

During the depression of 1907 Niven calculated that 20 per cent of the houses in the St John's district were shared. An investigation of the tenants living in a proposed clearance area in the same year showed that over 36 per cent of the families living there earned below 20s. a week, and over 60 per cent of the adults worked within half a mile of their homes. At best only one-half of the working class families living in that area could be expected to migrate to other parts of the city, even if there was enough room for them.[25]

The poverty surveys of Charles Booth and Seebohm Rowntree led many to claim that 'the housing problem is not merely a housing problem, it is a living problem.' At a time when it was claimed that the average wage of an unskilled labourer in Manchester was 16s.8d. a week, it would be difficult to deny the assertion that 'in Manchester, as in London and York, a large proportion of the people were seriously underfed, insufficiently clothed, and unhealthily housed.'[26] In the good year of 1889, Fred Scott, Secretary of the Manchester and Salford Sanitary Association, had calculated that 37.4 per cent of the population of parts of Ancoats and of the Greengates district of Salford were 'very poor' and 13 per cent 'poor'.[27] Writing in 1904, Marr estimated that upwards of 212,000 people in Manchester and Salford were in a state of poverty, and of these more than 75,000 were said to be in a state of severe poverty.[28] Like Charles Booth, Horsfall was concerned to prevent recruitment into 'the residuum' and he felt that by engaging in the war against the slums he could achieve this:

Once let the lowest classes cease to receive the large number of recruits from the higher grades of the working class who fall into vice, crime, pauperism, chiefly through the dullness and miserableness of the life of our towns, and the community would be able to break up its criminal and pauper class.[29]

Whether it was because of their lack of money or because of the unhealthy environment in which they lived the life chances of the poor were limited. In this respect the contrast between the inner city areas and the outer suburbs was quite marked. In 1908 the population density, general death rate, infant death rate and the birth rate were much higher in the St George's district than in suburban Withington, as the following table shows:[30]

Table 1   Comparison of birth rates, death rates and population density in St George's and Withington, 1908

District	Population	Acreage	Persons per acre	Total death rate	Infant death rate	Birth rate
St George's	57,069	498	115	25.07	195	33.26
Withington	5,728	5,728	8	10.67	111	18.75

These differences were of some concern to the small group of middle-class Mancunians who became involved in the housing question. As one leading reformer explained: 'There is a comparatively small set of people who care a good deal about it, but the majority of well-to-do live out of Manchester and they care very little about it.'[31] Members of the Manchester Statistical Society and the Manchester and Salford Sanitary Association were prominent among this close-knit band of reformers.

Ever since its formation in 1833, local men had used the Manchester Statistical Society as a platform for the discussion of the social and economic questions of the day.[32] In the last quarter of the nineteenth century a good deal of attention was given to the social and environmental condition of the working classes. Henry Baker's papers on the growth of the central business district and its consequences,[33] Costelloe's lecture on the housing question[34] and Scott's limited but important survey on the condition of the working classes in parts of Manchester and Salford were the most significant of the Society's deliberations in this field.[35] In the late 1880s the Statistical Society discussed 'Home Colonization'[36] and by the early 1900s was reviewing the progress of the garden village of the Small Holdings Association.[37] Perhaps the most wide-ranging contribution to the debate on the condition of Manchester was Horsfall's paper on local government reform and its relation to future urban development.[38] In this lecture Horsfall went beyond the predominantly statistical or sanitary approach of his contemporaries and put forward a scheme for an ideal Manchester.

The chief exponent of the public health of the public health approach was the Manchester and Salford Sanitary Association for Diffusing a Knowledge of the Laws of Health among the Inhabitants of the Two Boroughs and Neighbourhood.[39] The aims of this important pressure group, which was founded in 1852, were as follows:

1 To promote attention to Temperance, Personal and Domestic Cleanliness, and to the Laws of Health generally;
2 To induce general co-operation with the Boards of Health and other constituted authorities in giving effect to official Regulations for Sanitary Improvement.[40]

Though concerned initially with public health matters, the interests of its members were never narrowly sanitary. It was supported by a small but active group of middle-class reformers, and not surprisingly had a medical bias. The early work of district visitation was not entirely successful and was superseded by scientific and statistical work.

'One of the most remarkable attributes of the Sanitary Association,' wrote Arthur Ransome, a former President, in 1902, 'was its prolific power of creating other bodies like itself, and endowed with a separate vitality.'[41] The Noxious Vapours Abatement Association (1876), the Committee for Securing Open Spaces (1880) – both of which were chaired by Herbert Philips – and the Manchester and Salford Children's Holiday Fund (1884) were among the bodies affiliated to the Sanitary Association.

From the late 1870s working-class housing became a major concern of the Association. With the help of the Manchester Society of Architects, they sought to persuade the City Council to apply the Artisans and Labourers Dwellings Acts, but as Adolphe Samelson sadly recorded in 1883: 'The practical outcome of the movement then set on foot must be allowed to have been infinitesimal.'[42] Samelson was the author of an important pamphlet on *Dwellings and the Death Rate in Manchester* in 1883. This was the first contribution to the literature on 'Squalid and Outcast Manchester and Salford' in the 1880s.[43] The weightiest of the pamphlets on this question was the enquiry into the causes of the excessive mortality in the notorious Ancoats

Number One District in 1889 conducted by J.C. Thresh, another member of the Sanitary Association. Thresh came to the conclusion that it was not the density of the population in the district, but the appalling condition of the houses, the lack of ventilation in the streets and dwellings and the inadequate sanitary system which caused the high death rate in the area.[44]

Local newspapers, some of which had shown an earlier interest in health and housing, took up the issue. The *Manchester City News*, the *Manchester Guardian*, the *Clarion*, and the *Sunday Chronicle* all paid particular attention to the housing problem. It was after doing a survey of the slums of Manchester for the latter paper that Robert Blatchford became a socialist and a propagandist for a return to a more rustic 'Merrie England'.[45] Blatchford's guide round the slums of 'Modern Athens' had been Joe Waddington, the socialist and secretary of the first Hulme Healthy Homes Society.

Several Workmen's Sanitary Associations and Healthy Homes Societies were formed in the wake of these revelations. Most of these societies were set up under the auspices of the Manchester and Salford Sanitary Association. The Ancoats Healthy Homes Society, founded in 1889, was the first and most effective of these working men's sanitary associations.[46] Others were recorded in Salford (1889), Chorlton-upon-Medlock (1890), Hulme (1890), Ardwick and Longsight (1891), Angel Meadow and Red Bank (1892), St John's Ward (1894), Gorton (1903) and East Manchester (1906). Their stated aim was 'to promote healthy lives, healthy homes and healthy surroundings'.[47] Their methods were much the same as those of the Sanitary Association, and their approach tended to be individualistic. 'Such power and influence as the Society may have possessed', explained the Secretary of the Ancoats Healthy Homes Society, 'was never intended ... to coerce, threaten, or harass either the public authorities, or private individuals. The policy of those having the direction of the Society's affairs has rather been that of influencing and stimulating the *individual* to work out his or her own salvation in the way of moral, social and physical reform.'[48] Although most of these societies seem to have been short-lived, they did enjoy genuine working-class support. The meetings of the Ancoats Healthy Homes Society, with their lectures and free entertainments, attracted large numbers.[49] There were some signs that the Society was having an effect even in such an unpromising area as Ancoats.[50] The societies also had their problems. Like most voluntary organizations they suffered from financial difficulties. Though the response to the lecture-entertainments put on by the Ancoats Society was better than might be expected, the Society's first secretary, John Sanders, resigned in January 1893 because 'he had been beaten down by the unsympathetic attitude of many people to whom he had looked for aid and assistance.'[51] Even the larger groups like the Hulme Healthy Homes Society had to be resuscitated several times. The Salford Working Men's Sanitary Association, whose secretary was the prominent Social Democratic Federation and Independent Labour Party member, Alfred Settle, broke up because of 'internal dissensions'.[52] This might well have been the result of conflict between the political activists and those who eschewed such activity. Though often ephemeral, these societies give some idea of the level of grass-roots interest in the environmental problems of late-Victorian and Edwardian Manchester.[53] Such interest, however, was by no means universal among the working classes. Town planning legislation, when it finally came in 1909, 'could hardly be said to be supported by any great wave of popular enthusiasm.'[54] Nevertheless, the popular outcry of the late 1880s led the Corporation to introduce new building bye-laws in 1890 and four years later they built their first municipal dwellings in Ancoats.

By 1894 the housing campaign of the Manchester and Salford Sanitary Association was beginning to lose impetus. Although its members were still considering such issues as pollution, the provision of open spaces and the formation of a garden village, little came of their discussions.[55] Apart from a brief flourish at time of its Jubilee Conference in 1902, the Sanitary Association's role in the Edwardian period was limited.[56]

By the 1890s other approaches to the housing problem were being tried. A certain amount of interest was expressed in the housing management schemes of Octavia Hill, and similar work was undertaken in Manchester by Mrs Skelhorn and later by the Manchester Housing Company Ltd.[57] Under the auspices of the latter, Miss Annie Hankinson and Miss E. Spencer managed property in Ancoats, Collyhurst and Gorton. F.B. Dunkerley, a keen supporter of the Burnage Garden Village scheme, made possible the Company's first experiment in Collyhurst.

Ebenezer Howard's proposals for new garden cities, published in his book *Tomorrow* of 1898, came under close scrutiny. Howard's scheme, whilst evoking a good deal of sympathetic interest, was regarded by many as utopian. Even the secretary of the local Garden City Association believed that 'to transform Manchester into a garden city is an utter impossibility.'[58] Most city-dwellers felt, with the American scholar A.F. Weber, that the suburb furnished 'the solid basis of hope that the evils of city life, so far as they exist from overcrowding, may be in large part removed.'[59]

Middle-class concern about the housing of the working classes in Manchester really came to a head as a result of the recruitment crisis during the Boer War. In Manchester, 8,000 out of 11,000 would-be volunteers had to be turned away, and of the remainder 2,000 were declared only fit for the militia. 'Although coal smoke, drinking and licentiousness are among the factors which produce this physical deterioration', wrote Horsfall, 'bad housing is the chief factor.'[60] The war crisis led to a desire to re-structure national life, and town planning became part of 'the quest for national efficiency'.[61] Horsfall was a leading proponent of these ideas. 'Unless we at once begin at least to protect the health of our people,' wrote Horsfall in 1908, 'by making the towns in which most of them now live, more wholesome for body and mind, we may as well hand over our trade, our colonies, our whole influence in the world, to Germany, without undergoing all the trouble of a struggle in which we condemn ourselves beforehand to certain failure.'[62]

Religion as well as patriotism inspired many a reformer. There were those like Councillor James Johnston, a leading member of the Citizens Association, who argued that it was a primary duty of the clergy to expose the bad housing conditions in the city.[63] Religious interest in the question reached a climax with the Manchester Diocesan Conference on the Housing of the Poor in 1902.[64] Ministers of all denominations became involved in bodies like the Citizens Association, the Social Questions Union (founded in 1892) and the local Healthy Homes Societies.[65] The housing problem also figured prominently in the questions put to local municipal candidates by the Manchester Christian Social Union.[66]

By the early 1900s the housing question and the related problem of the layout of large tracts of suburban land in Manchester was becoming 'the question of questions for the artist, the architect, the philosopher, the engineer, the builder, the teacher, the philanthropist.'[67] The pressure for housing reform and town planning was not simply the result of medical interest, altruism, religious zeal or patriotism. Reformers often emphasized the economic benefits of their schemes: 'When Slumdon is abolished and made impossible there will be fewer hospitals, workhouses and gaols; and that is a dividend well worth working for.'[68] There was also a close connection with the temperance movement which saw 'every step gained towards the solution of the housing problem as something won for sobriety.'[69] Concern was also shown for the lack of social, recreational and aesthetic amenities in the city. Residents at the Manchester University Settlement in Ancoats soon realized the futility of promoting the betterment of the individiual whilst leaving untouched his surroundings.[70]

The Manchester University Settlement, which had been founded in 1894, furnished the housing reform movement with some of its most active workers and in carrying out several valuable social surveys provided a sociological base from which the reformers could work. Patrick Abercrombie, in his important survey of the garden city movement to 1911, recognized the importance of the work of the sociologists. 'The contributions towards the modern town planning movement for which England is responsible up to the present have been largely due to private effort and not municipal enterprise; they have also sprung from the housing and sociological side of the subject. Housing reform rather than a desire for civic art or a study of traffic problems is at the root of the Garden City and Garden Suburb.'[71] The careers of Marr and Horsfall would seem to confirm this statement.

Horsfall and Marr were the key figures in the Citizens Association for the Improvement of the Unwholesome Dwellings and Surroundings of the People which was formally established in May 1902. Through this body 'German' Horsfall and 'Citizen' Marr, as they were locally known, sought to promote 'Municipal and Housing Reform, and ... the furtherance of an active spirit of Citizenship.'[72] Unlike other bodies, whose work they sought to supplement rather than displace, the Citizens Association was willing to put forward its own candidates in municipal elections. The Association's own secretary, Marr, was elected as an independent housing reform candidate in the 1905 local elections. This willingness on the part of the Citizens Association to engage in political activity marks it off from its more quiescent and individualistic predecessors. The Sanitary Association, for instance, whilst approving of the formation of the Citizens Association, did not 'consider it to be in harmony with its traditional policy to take any active part in municipal elections.'[73]

Reformers thus became involved in the politics of housing. Housing legislation was sought by the National Service League as a means of counteracting 'the physical and moral degeneracy brought about by life in crowded cities.'[74] For quite different motives the local Independent Labour Party called for a 'crusade against the slums'.[75] Others saw money spent on working-class housing as being 'in the nature of national insurance.'[76] 'The same reason that made it good statecraft to educate "our masters" when they got the franchise,' the *Manchester Guardian* reminded its readers, 'apply to seeing they have decent homes.'[77]

Although of some importance at both the national and local level, such political pressure was never widespread. Housing (and later town planning) were not major issues at local elections,[78] Housing questions tended to be a serious issue only in some of the older wards, and often their representatives found it difficult to rouse the whole council, especially if their schemes meant an increase in the rates. The council as a whole put financial considerations first and Conservative candidates often drew attention to the costliness of corporation houses and maintained that the building of houses should be left to private enterprise. Both private and municipal reformers had to convince people that their schemes were economically viable before they would be taken seriously. It was often difficult to get money for such ventures unless the promoters could 'absolutely prove a £.s.d. saving by it.'[79]

The Citizens Association not only sought to allay the fears of these 'economists', it also endeavoured to widen the whole debate on the future of the urban environment. It addressed itself to sanitary questions, problems of land tenure, building regulations, improved means of transit, local government reform, and, perhaps most importantly, to town-extension planning. It sought to disseminate information about such exemplary schemes as those at Port Sunlight and Bournville and also the system adopted in certain continental towns.[80] With the publication in 1904 of the wide-ranging reports by Marr on *Housing Conditions in Manchester and Salford* and by Horsfall on *The Improvement of the Dwellings and Surroundings of the People: The Example of Germany*, the Citizens Association put itself in the vanguard of the nascent town planning movement in Britain.

Thomas Coglan Horsfall was the only son of a Manchester card manufacturer. In 1886 he retired from the family business to devote himself to a life of public service and philanthropy. Horsfall's interests were wide and by 1900 he had already achieved some limited fame as the founder of the Manchester Art Museum, an advocate of Working Men's Clubs, a supporter of University Settlements and as an educational and church reformer. Although he is best known as a housing reformer and an early advocate of 'town-extension plans', his ideas on environmental reform were not developed in isolation. As Horsfall himself remarked in one of his many lectures on the housing question: 'The Reform of our Educational System, the Reform of our System of Municipal Government, the Reform of our Public House System, the Reform of the Churches, are all measures needed to make the solutions of the Housing Question or Problem possible.'[81]

Having been brought up on Wordsworth and Ruskin, Horsfall felt 'a sense of shame' when confronted by the slums of Manchester.[82] 'Men in my position', he asserted, 'have almost the same duties towards the people in our towns as officers have towards the soldiers they lead.'[83] Fired by his paternalistic sense of duty and his 'hatred of the slums' Horsfall began his search for like-minded individuals and bodies with whom he could work to improve the environment.[84] Horsfall always sought to apply pressure from without and never himself sought election to the city council. Like Beatrice Webb, he had a low opinion of most Manchester councillors.[85] A council dominated by 'hard headed shopkeepers', Horsfall maintained, could only reflect or follow public opinion. 'Our opinion is better than public opinion', Horsfall exclaimed. He consequently felt that it was his duty, and that of his colleagues, 'to form and lead public opinion.'[86]

It was as a propagandist for German methods of urban control and town layout that Horsfall made his mark. As early as 1880 he was commenting on the lack of paternal solicitude on the part of the Manchester middle classes for the poor of the town, and comparing them unfavourably with their German counterparts.[87] By 1895 Horsfall had become convinced that a revolution in local government was required before his schemes for the purchase and incorporation of large areas of land round built-up areas by town councils, and the adoption of town-extension plans and the zone system, could be achieved. As it stood, Manchester expressed 'only the worst qualities of our race, our disbelief in the need of system, our belief that the most difficult work can be done well by untrained people.'[88] In future, with the equivalent of a German burgomaster, long-term plans could be proposed for the creation of the ideal Manchester. It was to be a city with all the amenities Horsfall's Manchester lacked, a city with wide tree-lined streets, smoke legislation and rings of open spaces beyond which would be found large groups of workmen's houses provided with gardens and playgrounds. It was a city where the packing of the greatest number of houses on each acre of building land would no longer be allowed. Horsfall was convinced by his Manchester experience that 'this crowding together of houses is a far greater evil than is the overcrowding of rooms in houses which stand in wide streets, and all parts of which are well lighted.'[89] With the publication of *The Example of Germany* in 1904 Horsfall's own ideas and those of the Germans reached a wider audience. It was this book that gave wide currency to the concept of town planning – though Horsfall did not use that term himself – and publicity to the work of Adickes, Eberstadt, Sitte and Stübben.

Horsfall's contribution to the early town planning movement was crucial. Ensor describes the movement as a marriage of the 'garden city' idea, preached by Ebenezer Howard, and the 'example of Germany', preached by Horsfall and others.[90] As a prominent member of the National Housing Reform Council, one of the key speakers in the influential deputation that met Campbell-Bannerman and Burns in 1906, and a leading spokesman at the many housing and town-planning conferences held at home and abroad in these years, Horsfall was able to present his ideas to a wide range of social reformers. Indeed, his fellow-workers thought his contribution was of paramount importance. Henry Aldridge, Secretary of the National Housing and Town Planning Council (as it became in 1909) wrote:

> The real and effective work which has produced legislative action (as distinct from private effort) in the town planning clauses of the Bill has been done first, and absolutely foremost of all, by the strenuous educational work of one man – Mr Horsfall. By the publication of his book on 'The Example of Germany', he performed the national service of showing how the creation of slums could be prevented by legislative effort. The great honour belongs to Mr Horsfall. By persistent effort and by personal sacrifice – for his books have always been published at a loss – he has educated us all.[91]

Many felt 'this peaceful war against the slums' to be of great national importance.[92] It was a war to be fought both on the legislative and the practical fronts. As such, Horsfall felt it warranted his support for both parliamentary legislation and local garden suburb ventures. As he remarked when opening the first few cottages at Alkrington Garden Suburb in 1911, 'there was no work that had more urgent claim upon the patriotic Englishman'.[93]

If Horsfall's was a Ruskinian reaction to the physical and moral chaos of Manchester, the response of Marr was conditioned by his knowledge of the sociological work of Patrick Geddes. Marr had been engaged in educational work before he took over the joint running of the Outlook Tower in Edinburgh for Geddes.[94] Although Marr and his colleague supported most of Geddes's schemes they found it difficult actually to work with him, and in 1901 they finally resigned their posts. 'We are in complete sympathy with your ideas,' wrote Marr to Geddes. 'It is in the practical carrying out and sustaining of them that we lose confidence in you.'[95] The running of the Outlook Tower had also involved Marr in serious financial difficulties. He was probably relieved to take up the congenial, if strenuous, post of warden at the Manchester University Settlement.

By the time Marr reached Manchester he was already immersing himself in the literature of the housing question.[96] Within a few years he was an acknowledged expert on the problem. His knowledge was not just that of an armchair scholar; living in Ancoats he had first-hand experience of slum conditions. Like his mentor, Patrick Geddes, Marr felt the need for thorough preparatory surveys before attempting to solve the problems of town life. 'Time has persuaded me', he wrote in 1903, 'that one can only build a useful plan of social work after careful and lengthy study of the problem at first hand.'[97] Marr's survey of housing conditions in Manchester and Salford for the Citizens Association was just such an attempt to throw some light on a difficult problem. The report came to the conclusion that there was a 'deficiency in house accommodation within the reach of the working classes.'[98] In order to remedy this deficiency it recommended:

> that a comprehensive housing policy be formed for the whole of the Manchester–Salford area including the suburban and intermediate districts as well as those in the centre. . . ,[99] that both our Town Councils and private builders in the district should strive to attain in their building schemes – in the general laying out of the sites as well as in the construction of the houses – the admirable conditions obtaining in Bournville, Port Sunlight, and other places . . .[100] [and that] care should be taken in any scheme of any kind to encourage the movement to the outer districts of all classes of the community.[101]

On election to the city council in 1905 Marr sought to implement some of these policies. He found many of his fellow councillors opposed to municipal housing and town planning schemes. 'We are at the moment in the grip of reactionaries,' Marr complained in 1912, 'and it is well-nigh impossible to get them to even talk about town planning, and less possible to get them to think of spending money on a town planning exhibition.'[102] Although he was unable to persuade the council to undertake any large-scale housing or planning schemes, Marr, as chairman of the Unhealthy Dwellings Committee, was able to launch an ambitious reconditioning scheme. This was, as Lady Simon noted, 'the brightest spot in the history of Manchester housing' in the period before the First World War.[103] Apart from his work with the Citizens Association, the council, and the University Settlement, Marr helped to found the local branch of the Garden City Association and was chairman of the two co-partnership tenant societies that developed garden suburbs in Manchester.

To reformers like Marr, who were confronted by the slums of Ancoats on the one hand, and unplanned suburbs that were potentially no better on the other, the planned garden suburb was a promising and practical solution to some of their problems.[104] As E.G. Culpin noted in 1913: 'The Garden Suburb has not to create new conditions, but simply to direct an existing flow, and therefore since we as a people are inclined to take the line of least resistance the Garden Suburb succeeds the more quickly.'[105] Support for the garden suburb came from supporters of the ideas of John Ruskin and William Morris. Like Raymond Unwin, they accepted Ruskin's ideal of a house: 'Not a compartment of a model lodging house, not the number so and so Paradise Row, but a cottage all of our own, with its little garden, its healthy air, its clean kitchen, parlour and bedrooms.'[106] The local platforms for the transmission of the ideas of Ruskin and Morris were Horsfall's Art Museum, Charles Rowley's Ancoats Recreation Movement and the Northern Art Workers' Guild.

The seminal 'Cottages Near a Town' exhibition, organized by the Northern Art Workers' Guild in 1903, was probably a major stimulus to the garden suburb movement in Manchester. Here the formidable talents of Parker and Unwin, and of Edgar Wood, were to be seen together. The emphasis on siting, amenity and low density in the Parker and Unwin exhibit was to influence all the ensuing Manchester developments.[107] There were, however, other influences. There was already a sizeable body of technical literature publicizing the planning ventures of the period.[108] In retrospect, it would seem virtually impossible for any architect, developer or builder not to have known about the schemes at Bournville, Port Sunlight, New Earswick, Hampstead Garden Suburb or Letchworth Garden City. There was also a local planning precedent in the residential park. The best known of these was Victoria Park, founded in 1837. The garden suburb can be seen as a variant on this model – a manifestation of the desire of the middle and working classes to share some of the environmental advantages of the rich.[109]

That such developments were possible (even when produced by local builders) was due to the 'domestic revival' in architecture at the end of the nineteenth century. Architects like Baillie-Scott, Parker, Unwin and Edgar Wood were applying themselves to the design of working-class housing. 'To design a comfortable and beautiful house for a limited sum of money', wrote Baillie-Scott in 1910, 'is perhaps one of the most difficult problems the modern architect has to solve. It is also the most important – for the housing question as applied to the great majority of the people is still a question which remains unanswered in an intelligent way.'[110]

The vast mass of houses put up in Manchester in the Edwardian period continued to be of the traditional terraced variety, built by ordinary speculative builders.[111] The pressure of the reformers did, however, lead to the creation of a small group of exemplary garden suburbs on the fringes of the city. The schemes were varied. The first experiment was the municipal cottage estate at Blackley. Others were the result of private promotions like the Chorltonville and Alderdale Estates. There were co-partnership schemes at Burnage and Fairfield. That at Alkrington was a mixed venture, incorporating private and co-partnership schemes, whilst the Didsbury suburb was the result of a co-operative scheme in which the people who built the houses became the owners of them within a determined period.[112] All were purely residential, and all were concerned with the attempt to move stylistically away from the much-maligned urban tenement and terrace. They were examples of site planning rather than town planning, yet even such small-scale ventures illustrated the benefits of planned development when compared with the chaos and monotony of the older parts of the city, and even those parts built since 1868, under the bye-laws.

3 The garden suburbs

i The Manchester Corporation Blackley estate

Late-Victorian Manchester had a large stock of old and insanitary houses. 'The old houses are rotten from age and neglect. The new houses often commence where the old houses leave off and are rotten from the first,' commented the city's Medical

Officer in 1886.[113] Growing concern about the state of Manchester's housing stock led to the publication of new building bye-laws in 1890. The houses built under these bye-laws were an improvement, but they still conformed to the narrow-fronted terrace type. Most lacked gardens and few had bathrooms.

By the 1890s more and more people were advocating municipal housing for the working classes. Others saw such schemes as a manifestation of rabid socialism. But as the Medical Officer of Health argued in 1884; 'If helping the poor in this way – doing for them what they cannot accomplish alone – be socialism or communism, the more we have of it the better, when wisely and judiciously administered.'[114] Such reports, the continued pressure from bodies like the Sanitary Association, and the new legislative situation created by the 1890 Housing Act, led to the first experiments in municipal housing in Manchester.

By the turn of the century Manchester Corporation had provided homes for persons displaced by their own activities in a series of tenement buildings in Oldham Street, Pollard Street, Chester Street, Pott Street and Harrison Street. They had not, however, attempted to rehouse those tenants whose homes had been closed under the peremptory nuisance provisions contained in Section 41 of the Manchester Corporation Waterworks and Improvement Act of 1867. In 1904 it was estimated that upwards of 5,965 houses had been closed under that section since 1885, and that only 2,782 houses had been substituted by the owners on or near those sites.[115] It is possible that the want of dwellings was partially met by private enterprise, but some reformers had begun to doubt the efficiency of free market forces in providing dwellings for the poor. These included the city's medical officer and the relieving officer of the Chorlton Poor Law Union.[116] Realizing there was a need for working-class housing the Sanitary Committee suggested that 'the Corporation should accept the responsibility of providing from time to time, and as the needs and circumstances might seem to denote, such a reasonable number of dwelling houses as would provide for those who had been or might be dispossessed under the Act of 1867.'[117]

The corporation's first block dwellings and tenement houses had been built on expensive central sites. None of these early schemes were financially self-supporting and the block dwellings were heartily disliked.[118] The council, therefore, turned their attention to the suburbs where land was cheaper, and where it was hoped that working-class houses could be let at lower rents. As a result a decision was made to buy the Blackley Estate in north Manchester, and the purchase was completed in February 1901. In all, approximately 243 acres of land were bought, at a cost of about £36,500. The cost per square yard of the land at Blackley was a mere 7½d. The price of land on the corporation's other building sites had been considerably higher. It was estimated that the land in Oldham Road had cost as much as £5 6s.0d. per square yard, whilst at Chester Street it cost £2 13s.5d. per square yard and at Pollard Street £1 14s.10½d.[119] The economic benefits of a suburban site were obvious.

The Sanitary Committee's first scheme for Blackley came under heavy attack from Horsfall and the Citizens Association.[120] As a result of their suggestions the plans were altered, and instead of all the houses being two up and two down, the majority were planned as three-bedroomed houses with baths. The layout also was amended to allow more light into the houses. In its previous ventures into the housing field the corporation had agreed to 'the practice of the most rigid economy in planning and fittings.'[121] Although Horsfall persuaded them to accept a higher standard of design and layout, the city council still tended to put financial considerations first. They were reluctant to initiate a scheme that 'might prove a financial failure and discourage future action.'[122]

Only nine acres of the site were developed at first. The plans for these municipal cottages were drawn up by the first city architect, Henry Price. They were intended to be 'more in accord with those which may be seen in model villages, of which Bournville and Port Sunlight may be taken as examples.'[123] Price took up his post in 1902, and was immediately required to produce plans for the first 150 houses. As a result of a difference of £5,680 between the lowest tender and his original estimate, Price was 'instructed to revise the plans of the houses to be erected on the Blackley estate ... with the object of reducing their cost to the amount of the estimate', which was £19,458.[124] Price achieved this result by reducing the height of the houses by about two feet. This involved the construction of partly-sloping bedroom ceilings, the bedrooms graduating in height from five feet to nine feet. Apparently this was permissible under the bye-laws, and met with the approval of the Housing Sub-Committee and the medical officer of health, Niven.[125] The tactic led at least one commentator to criticize the houses because of their lack of space. In these 'hatbox houses', he maintained, 'there is precious little house and air space for your 6s.4d. and 7s.'[126] Despite such criticisms the neatly-designed houses with their wider frontages represented an advance towards the housing reformers' ideals of light, air and amenity. In plan, the estate was spacious but unoriginal. At 17 houses per acre, the housing density at Blackley was much lower than in central working-class areas.

The houses themselves were built of brick and rough-cast plaster. When compared with earlier working-class housing types they seem quite picturesque. On the ground floor these houses were provided with either a parlour and kitchen, a

Figure 12. The first houses at Blackley (courtesy of Manchester Public Libraries).

kitchen and large scullery, or a living room and kitchen-scullery. Upstairs, most houses had three bedrooms, and all three-bedroomed houses had bathrooms, either on the lower or upper floor.[127] The rents charged by the council for the houses at Blackley put them in the upper reaches of the working-class housing market, and led to complaints that the corporation was providing houses for an entirely different class than the one they were legally required to rehouse. 'You might as well apply a sticking plaster to a cancer as try the Blackley scheme [on a slum] district.' wrote one critic. 'It is a most extra-ordinary mix-up of impracticable ideas ... somebody has been trying to blend, say, Fallowfield and Didsbury with Collyhurst and Red Bank, which is an impossibility at the prices named.'[128] Manifestly houses built in a distant and comparatively inaccessible suburb like Blackley, involving an expenditure of up to 2d. fare for each tramway journey into the city, could not meet the needs of people of the unskilled labouring class displaced by the Corporation's demolition programme.[129]

Even though the cost of moving to the estate no doubt acted as a deterrent to many, there were those who felt that the new tenants would make slums of the houses in the near future.[130] Others maintained that the gardens would never be used.[131] Even enlightened reformers like Horsfall argued that the new tenants should be educated to make the best use of their new environment. An earlier experience with 'careless' tenants in the Manchester and Salford Workmen's Dwellings Company's tenements in Holt Town led him to express the view that 'we must look to education as well as to improvement in the houses for any improvement of life.'[132]

Certain basic amenities were provided on the estate, though perhaps not enough to satisfy most of the early tenants. There is some record of a co-operative store and of houses serving as shops. A school was soon provided, and even at this stage 13 acres of land had been set aside for open spaces, and 50 acres for small-holdings and allotments.[133] The dream of self-sufficiency, or even profit-making gardening schemes, fired the imagination of many a housing reformer. Not everyone who came to live on the estate held such a sanguine view of the horticultural potential of the area. There were those who felt that by the time the men arrived home from work it was too late to work in the garden or return to the city for entertainment. 'Where are they to go when they want to meet with their friends, to hear a little music, to read the news or to improve their minds by reading or discussion?' was the plaintive, but warranted, cry of one such tenant.[134] Despite such complaints the cottage estate at Blackley proved more popular than the corporation's block dwellings.

One noticeable feature of the Blackley estate was the width of the roads. The main roads were 60 feet wide and lined with trees, whilst the minor roads were not less than 42 feet wide. Though this was a welcome change from the narrow, congested and often foetid streets in the older parts of the city, it did mean that the estate cost more to develop than it need have done. Marr, Unwin and Nettlefold maintained that not all residential roads needed to be constructed like arterial highways. 'The effect of reducing the cost of street-making is to reduce the rents of the houses considerably.'[135]

The hillside situation and the spacious layout of the estate no doubt contributed to the healthy atmosphere of the area. By 1913 it was estimated that the resident population of the estate was 600. The general death rate for the area was 13.7 per 1000, whilst the infant mortality rate was 102.[136] These were relatively low figures compared with those of the central districts and must have given heart to the local healthy homes enthusiasts.

There were no further additions to the estate until after the First World War, although plans were afoot before 1914 for further extensions along garden-city lines. 'The [Sanitary] Committee have in view', wrote the *British Architect*, 'a fine garden city with trees, playgrounds, churches, schools and other amenities of a full life. There is room for 4,000 more houses on the estate. How best to arrange these houses and keep up the idea of a city beautiful is the problem.'[137] To this end, in 1910, the corporation announced an architectural competition. There were innumerable delays before the final adjudication of the scheme. The competition was won by W. Rupert Davison of London. His scheme was very much in the domestic revival/garden suburb tradition, the house with its low eaves and horizontal window openings fronted by a garden, pavement and tree-planted grass verges. Unfortunately these plans were made public only in 1914 and the war interrupted any possible execution of them.[138]

Conceived in 1899, the Blackley scheme was too early to be influenced by the full wave of propaganda that affected the later garden suburbs of Manchester. The somewhat limited Blackley development can hardly be said to have made a significant contribution to the housing problem in Manchester before 1914. Nor can it be said to have proved as popular as its supporters would have hoped. Indeed, like the corporation's previous housing ventures, Blackley posed as many problems as it solved. The main problem was that the municipal estates did not pay. As the British Association reported in 1915; 'There is a loss on these houses of about £11,000 per annum, and the Council is very loath to permit the Sanitary Committee to extend its works on these lines owing to the heavy cost of doing so.'[139] Almost everywhere in the council the cry was 'no burden on the rates', and as there were competing claims for municipal funds it is not surprising that the proposals of the Sanitary Committee were viewed with a jaundiced eye.[140] One proposed scheme was vetoed 'because it was estimated to cost 1/300th part of a penny in the pound on the rates.'[141] Small wonder that the *Manchester City News* in 1908 complained of the 'lethargy that has stolen over the municipality in the past four or five years.'[142]

In the years before the First World War there was a growing feeling, both in Manchester and elsewhere, that 'the question of the housing of the poor should be taken out of the realm of £.s.d.'.[143] Councillor Jackson, a prominent member of the Sanitary Committee, pointed out that many municipal services 'did not pay' in the ordinary sense, but the results of the expenditure on education, public cleansing, parks and libraries justified the money spent on them.[144] His colleague, Alderman M'Cabe, argued that 'the city would not secure a financial return from housing but it would recoup itself by the better health and better morals of the people.'[145] Philip Snowden, speaking in Manchester in October 1913, showed the way forward: 'He did not believe that private enterprise could ever deal properly with the housing question. To regard good housing as part of their public health policy was the only economical system, and he was in favour of the state coming to the assistance of some of their municipalities in dealing with the housing question.'[146] Like many others he was moving towards Exchequer subsidies for housing.[147] Such financial assistance was not available before the First World War. The best the garden suburb developers could hope for was a loan from the Public Works Loan Commissioners, or after 1907 from the Co-Partnership Tenants Ltd. Some of the later garden suburb promoters did draw on these sources, just as they drew on the wider range of exemplary models available to them as the garden city movement developed. Limited as it was, Blackley can be seen as a stage on 'the peaceful path to real reform', a portent of things to come.[148]

ii Burnage Garden Village

Thanks to the work of George Cadbury and John Nettlefold, Birmingham's contribution to the environmental reform movement is obvious. Manchester, however, also had its contribution to make. The development of a series of garden suburbs in Manchester makes clear the *practical* as well as the educational role of Manchester men in the early town planning movement in Britain. As one local sceptic remarked: 'We have had no end of books, pamphlets, lectures, addresses, discussions. An object lesson is worth them all.'[149] Burnage Garden Village was intended to be just such an object lesson.

At a public meeting held in the Co-operative Wholesale Society committee rooms in Balloon Street on 26 June 1906, Manchester Tenants Ltd was formed. The society was a co-partnership public utility company registered under the Industrial and Provident Society Act of 1903. The original stimulus for this scheme seems to have been an address by Ebenezer Howard on 'Garden Cities' to a group of Manchester clerks. The subject was taken up by a group of Co-operative Wholesale Society employees at a Ruskin Hall class held in Balloon Street in 1901. Further meetings followed and a committee was formed to investigate the possibility of building a garden suburb in Manchester. The outcome was the inaugural meeting of Manchester Tenants Ltd.[150]

Co-partnership housing was not taken up very quickly in Lancashire, the recognized home of the co-operative movement. The idea was not tried in Manchester until it had been tested successfully elsewhere.[151] 'Garden villages are much to be desired', commented Percy Redfern of the Co-operative Wholesale Society, 'but if they are to be democratically co-operative it is necessary they should originate with employees or other tenants themselves, or with local co-operative societies.'[152] Though having strong connections with the co-operative movement, Manchester Tenants Ltd remained an independent body. Similarly, the Tenants had no direct political affiliations, though the Village (as the residents have always called it) included among its early residents a number of prominent Labour men.[153] In these early days, political neutrality was, as we have seen, necessary.

James Rowbottom, in a letter to the *Manchester Guardian*, noted the favourable response to 'the idea of creating a garden village similar in style to Bournville and Port Sunlight, for the benefit of Manchester clerks and artisans.'[154] Striking a more ambitious note, an early prospectus declared the aim of the Society (and of the garden suburb movement generally) as being 'to provide those healthier homes and surroundings and to point the way to a much needed general social reform.' The prospectus further amplified and clarified the aims of the Manchester Tenants:

We desire to do something to meet the housing problem by placing within the reach of working people, clerks, etc., the opportunity of taking a house or a cottage with a garden at a moderate rent. We believe that in cleaner air, with an open space near to their doors, the people would develop a sense of home life and an interest in nature.

Future generations must have healthier homes and more cheerful surroundings and we assert that for the success of the scheme, the independence of the tenants should be preserved and fostered so that they may individually take an interest in keeping the estate in good order, and so base their lives on economically sound principles of collective ownership.[155]

The advocates of housing co-partnership schemes of this nature sought to achieve the benefits of a marriage between art, health and economy. It was more feasible for them to plan a modest garden village, rather than an entirely new garden city, yet even such small-scale ventures as that of the Manchester Tenants were able to combine advantages derived from two sources – 'from the workman having an interest in his house and that house fitting in with an ordered plan for the development of an estate.'[156]

Manchester Tenants Ltd was formed under the auspices of the Co-Partnership Tenants Housing Council and later registered with the Co-Partnership Tenants Ltd.[157] The latter was the central body, formed in 1907, to provide expert advice, raise money and pool orders for the member societies. Manchester Tenants Ltd raised capital by the issue of shares and loan stock. The shares were £10 each, and the dividend on share capital was not to exceed five per cent, like those Victorian housing trusts that offered 'philanthropy and five per cent'.[158] The loan stock, which had priority, was to bear only 4 per cent interest. No individual shareholder could hold more than £200 in shares. All tenants were required to hold at least two shares, and they had to pay £5 on the first share before they could take up residence. Even though the balance on the first share and subsequent shares could be paid for by instalments, the £5 deposit was an insurmountable financial barrier to residence in a garden suburb for many working-class Edwardians.

The co-partnership system made the tenants joint owners with outside capitalists of the houses they occupied. The tenant co-operators had advantages not shared by private owners; after giving a week's notice they could leave their house, which would then be taken over by the Society. As an early Manchester Tenants' prospectus pointed out; 'In these days, when workers of all grades find themselves often at a few days notice compelled to move to another district, this freedom is of value.'[159] The former tenant could either retain or return his shares.

The rules of the Manchester Society also provided for a sinking fund of half of 1 per cent on the cost of the houses. It was estimated that the cost of the houses, at 3½ per cent interest, would be written off in 60 years. Any surplus profits, over and above the 5 per cent paid on share capital, were to go partly to a reserve fund, partly to a social and educational fund and partly as a dividend to the tenants. Some of this money was used for estate maintenance.

Many of the stockholders came from important Manchester families. The names of Renold, Broadhurst, Ryland, Simon, Fitszimmons and Eckhard were among the first loanholders, as were those of Professors Herford, Schuster, Weiss and Toller. Reformers and philanthropists like Margaret Ashton, E.A. Gaddum, Harold Shawcross and Horsfall gave generously. The largest individual loan-holders were Rose Hyland, a local Poor Law Guardian, and the Dunkerley brothers, Frank, an architect, and Roylance, an agriculturalist. The Manchester and Salford Equitable Co-operative Society made a loan of £400, but by far the largest amount, some £5,500, came from the Co-Partnership Tenants Ltd.[160] The management of the society was in the hands of a committed elected by the shareholders, and chaired initially by Marr. The rules of the society stipulated that a certain (unspecified) proportion of the committee should be tenants.

Such were the financial arrangements for the Burnage scheme. They were meant to combine the advantage of easy movement with tenant involvement, and of economic housing with a safe field for investment. Further savings were made at the building stage as a result of the Tenants' decision to erect the houses by direct labour under their own works department. Thus there were no contractor's profits to increase the society's indebtedness. The purchase of materials through the Co-Partnership Tenants Ltd meant further economies. Both the chairman, H. Vivian, and the secretary, F. Litchfield, of the latter company, were on hand to address meetings in the town and to help the Manchester Tenants with their scheme. Their involvement and that of Marr and Horsfall put the Burnage venture in the main-stream of the housing reform and town planning movement of these years. As the *Manchester City News* commented: 'In these days public attention to the housing problem is mainly directed to those phases of it represented by the Garden City movement and co-operative enterprises like the Ealing Tenants.'[161] The Burnage estate was the first Manchester contribution to this new tradition.

Built on an 11-acre site on Burnage Lane, the estate was five miles from the centre of Manchester and about a mile from Levenshulme station. Closer to the garden village was the Mauldeth Road station on the new London & North Western Railway's branch line which was opened for passenger traffic in May 1909. It is worth noting that the latter company was more concerned about the Manchester–London traffic than with suburban services. Municipal tramcars did not reach Burnage either, the nearest service stopping at West Point. The railway and the trams made no great contribution to the growth of Burnage Garden Village.[162] The physical appeal of Burnage was undoubtedly a stronger attraction than the question of transport. Writing in the 1890s, W.A. Shaw stressed the rustic appeal of the area: 'It is held to be the prettiest village near Manchester, still untouched in its cottage existence and rusticity, as it is endless in foliage. Its lingering life and loveliness are all the more acceptable for the progress of growth, devouring space, which is going on all around.'[163]

Several houses had been built on the site when it was purchased from Earl Egerton of Tatton in 1907. The fine trees were happily still there, and in keeping with the new spirit in estate development they were incorporated into the plan. The building plot consisted of a fairly level field with a considerable oblong pond in the centre. Beyond lay open fields. It was intended that 'the estate be laid out as a whole compact orderly plan, so that every road may have its own characteristic, that small open spaces may be within reach of every child and old person, that no house may darken or offend a neighbour's house, and that all parts of the estate be grouped round central features.'[164]

The first suggestions for the layout of the estate came from J. Horner Hargreaves, ARIBA. His plan had three avenues running north to south, with curved connecting avenues to the west and east of these. Semi-detached villas were intended to line these avenues. The main entrance lay off Burnage Lane, behind an artistic crescent of grass and foliage. The most interesting aspect of this abortive acheme was the two rows of eight cheap cottages at the far end of the estate. Reporting on these pro-posed cottages, *Co-partnership*'s correspondent remarked that 'as artistic treatment and general convenience are not to be left out of account, it will prove a real object lesson of what houses for the workers should cost.'[165] Hargreaves's plan, which seems to ignore the large hollow at the centre of the site, was not used, but the emphasis on the need for cheap but pleasant houses was not lost on the Tenants.

The plan used was not signed. An early prospectus does however list a distinguished group of advisers, including Hargreaves, C.G. Agate, F.B. Dunkerley, FRIBA, and Raymond Unwin. Though there is no evidence of his direct involvement, Unwin's general influence can be seen in the low-density layout, the removal of back-projections in the house designs and the through living rooms. The chief purpose of the new plan was 'to provide that each house should be so placed as to have the maximum amount of light and air and pleasantness of outlook, and also to secure some open space for recreation.'[166] As built, Main Avenue ran westward from Burnage Lane and connected that main highway with North, South, East, and West Avenues and West Place. The houses were placed on each side of these grass-verged and tree-lined avenues. 'The estate', wrote Abercombie, 'is laid out simply with no attempt at creating a centre of local life; it is frankly a group of houses situated in a suburb of Manchester, forming part of the general life of the district.'[167] In terms of general amenities this was true, but the Tenants did have at the centre of their estate, like a London square, their own tennis courts and bowling green. With the addition of the clubhouse to the plan and the allocation of space for allotments and a children's playground, the recreational aspects of tenant life were catered for in a way that contrasted quite markedly with the lack of amenities on the corporation estate at Blackley.

Further adjustments to the original plan were made when the largest houses proved difficult to let. Smaller houses were built instead on Burnage Lane, whilst an additional group of terraced houses was built in West Place, the access road to the recreation ground.

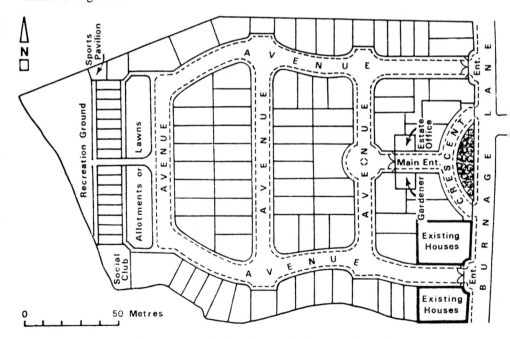

Figure 13. Burnage: the proposed plan by J. Horner Hargreaves 1907 (courtesy of *Town Planning Review*).

Some 136 houses were built in all, at about 12 houses to the acre – approximating to what was rapidly becoming the normal housing density for planned estates. The houses varied in size from two-bedroomed cottages with a living room and a scullery to four-bedroomed semi-detached with a hall, parlour, living room, kitchen and scullery. In true Unwinian fashion, the Tenants recorded that 'an effort has been made to increase the size of the rooms rather than add to the number of the rooms.'[168]

Most of the houses were semi-detached, but two detached houses and several rows of cottages were built. In style, most were simplified examples of the cottage houses then being produced by architects like Voysey, Baillie-Scott, and Parker and Unwin. Master plans were sent to the Manchester Society by the Co-Partnership Tenants Ltd and by C. Gustave Agate, a local architect, and it would seem the Tenants used simplified versions of these plans in their scheme.[169] Such changes as were made by the Society did not affect the quality of the detailing on the dwellings.

Considerable use was made in these buildings of the local common brick, which in ordinary suburban developments of the time was considered good enough only for rear elevations. In the opinion of the *Town Planning Review*, 'the effect of the grey brick alone in conjunction with rough-cast is exceedingly quiet and restful and the example of these homes should do much to explode an expensive and unsightly material.'[170] Inside, each house contained a bathroom and was provided with hot and cold water and electric lighting. This marked a real advance, especially for those paying the lower rents. Many tenants also dispensed with cooking ranges and used instead gas cookers provided by the Manchester Corporation Gas Department.

In spite of having been executed under the ordinary bye-laws, which stipulated 24

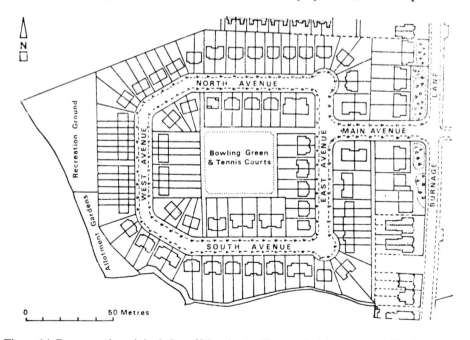

Figure 14. Burnage: the original plan of Manchester Tenants Ltd (courtesy of Manchester Tentants Ltd).

feet of granite metalling and flagged pavements of 9 feet, the roads on the Burnage estate were constructed with only an 18-foot strip of macadam down the centre, and bordered on each side by tree-planted grass verges and 5-foot-wide flagged pavements. Despite some opposition from the Withington Committee of Manchester Corporation, the Tenants were never forced to change their pleasant avenues, which, as reformers like Marr pointed out, had no heavy traffic to bear.[171] By building their roads in such a manner, Manchester Tenants were able once again to make savings.[172]

The combination at Burnage of carefully designed houses, well-kept gardens and tree-lined avenues produced a 'street picture' that was rightly eulogized by the early supporters of the garden suburbs. The Tenants saw the Village as an experiment. They hoped it would illustrate the advantages of low-density development and point to the value of town-extension planning. By 1911 Burnage Garden Village was already being held up as a successful prototype for the larger development at Alkrington.[173]

Burnage Garden Village was meant to be a social as well as an architectural experiment. As the secretary of a later garden suburb explained; 'Living in a co-

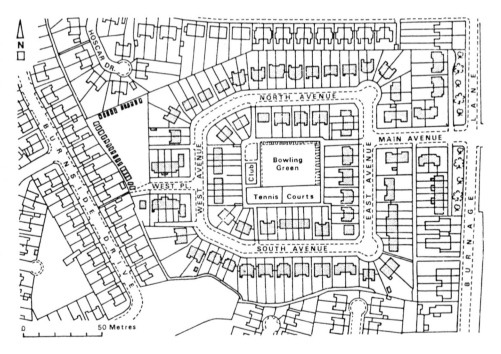

Figure 15. Burnage: the completed estate, showing the small houses on Burnage Lane, the new group of houses in West Place, and the club house.

Figure 16. This illustration from a prospectus for the Alkrington Estate gives a clear view of the social and environmental advantages enjoyed by the tenants at Burnage (courtesy of Rochdale Public Libraries).

BURNAGE GARDEN VILLAGE.

A SIMPLE SUM: IF SO MUCH CAN BE ACHIEVED WITH ELEVEN ACRES, WHAT CAN BE DONE WITH SEVEN HUNDRED?

partnership suburb did not mean being isolated tenants, but that the whole of the social and recreative life of the estate would be managed by the tenants themselves.'[174] A clubhouse was built by the society, to promote a keen social life among the tenants. A Village Association, designed to cater for the social, educational and recreational needs of its members, soon emerged. In addition a Village Dramatic Society was formed. Its commemorative programme, published in 1933, gives a picture of the birth of the society and of life in the Village prior to World War One:

> In the early days before the War 'the Village' was a novel venture. Its early residents were 'inmates' and regarded as cranks. Picture theatres were just penetrating the suburbs, radios were either unknown or luxuries beyond our means, as were motors. We 'villagers' boasted that we made our own pleasures and amusements. The bowling green, the tennis courts, annual sports, rambling clubs, etc., were our recognized social activities, and supplied the simple needs of our neighbours. We were mostly young married couples, enjoying the novel experiment of a co-operative garden suburb. The dark nights found us dancing and 'whisting', and the increasing need for a decent meeting place was met by the parent body, the Manchester Tenants Limited, by the erection of our dearly loved Village Hall. . . . Setting forth one sunny afternoon in the summer of 1911 . . . one of the aforesaid young, and in this case vivacious, married ladies, sought to gather signatures of those who imagined they might be able to act, and thus add to the already many troubles of a suburban residential experiment. The response was an immediate success, for were not many of us already acting, i.e. the part of trying to keep up positions that suburbia called for on a meagre town wage?[175]

Such were the Burnage Garden Villagers, whose boast it was 'never to leave the village for anything if we could obtain it therein.'[176]

The rents charged varied from 5s.3d. to 11s.6d. per week exclusive of rates. (The Tenants held that the separate collection of rates stimulated an interest in municipal affairs among the Village residents). The great majority of Manchester's working-class tenants were not paying more than 7s. per week, inclusive of rates, though skilled craftsmen and foremen often paid as much as 8s.6d.[177] Many of the houses at Burnage must have been beyond the means of large sections of the working class.

To attempt to gauge the social class of the early residents in a rigorous manner is difficult.[178] Lacking the census enumerator's books for 1911, one is bound to rely on the inadequate local directories. Nevertheless, the occupations of the Burnage residents were checked in the directories. As table 2, shows the largest identifiable groups were those of the clerks and the salesmen and travellers. (The designation 'householder', is singularly unhelpful in the present context. However, considering the fact that the Tenants found if difficult to let the larger houses on the estate, it would probably be safe to assume that most of the residents classified as householders were not persons of independent means.) Apart from the group of artisans and craftsmen, most of whom could be characterized as 'labour aristocrats', the residents can safely be described as being middle or lower-middle class.

An attempt was also made to locate the former place of residence of the tenants at Burnage in the local directories. Almost a half of the residents were traced, and of these the largest numbers came from the nearby suburbs of Longsight, Levenshulme, Fallowfield and Gorton. Some of the worst areas of the city, like Ancoats and Hulme, were represented, but it can hardly be claimed that the deni-

Table 2   The occupations of household heads in Burnage Garden Village

Occupation	Number on estate	Occupation	Number on estate
Journalist	2	Secretary	1
Insurance inspector	1	Clerk	24
Manufacturer	1	Telegraphist	2
Contractor	1	Foreman	1
General dealer	1	Meter inspector	1
Police inspector	1	Engineer	6
Artist	1	Fitter	1
Professor of music	1	Mechanic	1
Organizer	1	Electrician	2
Patent agent	1	Tailor	1
Buyer	1	Engraver	3
Teacher	4	Printer	2
Draughtsman	1	Signwriter	1
Sub-postmaster	1	Cabinet maker	1
Cashier	2	Lino operator	2
Manager	2	Machinist	1
Wood engraver	1	Gardener	1
Warden	1	Drysalter	1
Salesman/traveller	11	Householders	45

Source: *Slater's Manchester, Salford and Suburban Directory*, 1913

zens of the slums were being decanted into the garden village.

In order to try to ascertain the amount paid in rent by the tenants before they moved to Burnage a search was made for some of the Manchester ratepayers.[179] Of the 36 residents traced in the Manchester rate books, 22 paid more rent at Burnage than in their previous abode, 9 tenants paid less, and 1 the same as before. The increases were large in some instances, especially where low rents had been paid previously, whilst most paid well over £1 *per annum* more. It was also noticeable that those paying less did not live in the cheaper houses on the estate.

We are thus left with a picture of an estate tenanted by white-collar workers and 'labour aristocrats'. Residence in the garden suburb was probably, for many of them, the summit of their social aspirations. The residents of such garden suburbs were often 'a little self-conscious', even eccentric. 'We cannot pass through a garden suburb', wrote a *Manchester Guardian* correspondent in 1912, 'without apprehension of ladies in djibahs or men with large, loosely-tied bows.'[180] It could be conjectured that this vision of the garden suburbs as introvert, faddist havens did much to delay the working-class recognition of such experiments. More important, however, was the fact that many of them either did not want to move out to the suburbs, or they simply just could not afford to do so.[181] As the editor of the *Manchester City News* explained: 'The Garden City and other laudable schemes do not touch the main question, but only deal with side issues and affect a different class. The casual labourer and the pound-a-week man can derive no more substantial advantage from

Table 3   Former places of residence of Burnage Garden Village residents

Not known	67	Ancoats	2
Longsight	11	Besses o'th'Barn	1
Levenshulme	6	Chorlton-cum-Hardy	1
Fallowfield	5	Chorlton-upon-Medlock	1
Gorton	5	Moston	1
Hulme	3	Old Trafford	1
Moss Side	3	Pendleton	1
Whalley Range	3	Seedley	1
Rusholme	2	Victoria Park	1
Manchester Township	2	Lower Broughton	1
Miles Platting	2	Sale	1
Salford	2	Heaton Moor	1
		Irlam O'th'Height	1
		Flixton	1

Sources: *Slater's Manchester, Salford and Suburban Directory*, 1906–12; *Kelly's Directory of Lancashire exclusive of Manchester and Liverpool*, 1908–9

these beneficent enterprises than he could from the establishment of an Utopia.'[182] The garden suburb and the garden city reflected the social aspirations and the market situation of a higher 'housing class'.[183]

Burnage was the first proper garden suburb in Manchester. It was officially opened in September 1910 by the lord mayor, Councillor Charles Behrens. At the opening Marr admitted that 'the Burnage village was a modest contribution towards the solving of the housing problem in the Manchester district'.[184] The Tenants had set a high standard for their fellow citizens to follow. The developers at Chorltonville set out to emulate their achievement.

iii   Chorltonville

The private estate developed at Chorltonville by J.H. Dawson and W.J. Vowles was somewhat isolated from the other Manchester housing and town planning schemes of this period. These latter were mainly the work of people like Marr, the Manchester Society of Architects, the local members of the Citizen's Association or Tenant Co-Partnership companies. Dawson and Vowles seem to have had little contact with such figures. Nevertheless the Chorltonville scheme has an interesting history.[185]

James H. Dawson and William J. Vowles were originally in trade in the Hulme district of Manchester. Dawson was a draper and undertaker and Vowles was a boot manufacturer. Their passion for public service stemmed from the social work they had undertaken with Rev. Dr Charles Leach at Cavendish Street Congregational Chapel, Chorlton-upon-Medlock. General concern for the people in that area and in the adjacent township of Hulme led them to take an active part in the Hulme Healthy Homes Society. An attempt had been made to start a Healthy Homes

Society in Hulme in 1890,[186] but little seems to have come of this first effort. It was not until late in 1893 that the society really got under way. Rev. Dr Leach presided at the first meeting on 17 November of that year.[187] The object of the association was 'to diffuse amongst all classes a knowledge of sanitary matters and hygiene by means of short lectures and addresses. With a view to popularizing and making the meetings attractive, each will open and terminate with a musical programme.'[188] The fortunes of the society seemed to fluctuate, but it gives some indication of local concern about the housing question in the area. In later years members of the Independent College Settlement in Hulme helped to keep the society going.[189]

As the new century opened Dawson and Vowles turned their attention more directly to the housing question. In 1904, as equal partners, they established an estate agents' business in the expanding suburb of Chorlton-cum-Hardy in south-west Manchester. They had close connections in the building trade, for Thomas Whitely, Dawson's brother-in-law, had already done much work in fast-growing suburb of Chorlton-cum-Hardy.

Their first joint venture was on the Darley Hall estate. For this development they set up a private company and engaged Edward Hewitt, FRIBA, as architect.

> The object of this Company was that of building on the site and gardens of the old hall, seventy-five houses of modern design and as far as possible upon semi-garden village lines, together with fourteen shops, forming a terrace, turreted at either end, gracefully conceived and unique in planning presentation, replete with spacious show windows and floor areas, and affording generous living accommodation.[190]

If we allow for the element of self-advertisement, we can see that the estate, with its grass verges, variegated trees and functional buildings, was a serious attempt to move in the direction of a garden village scheme.

The desire to produce a garden suburb led Dawson, Vowles and Whiteley to visit Bournville and Harborne. Such a trip shows the three were aware of national developments in town planning, even if there is little evidence of their connection with local planning circles. Although apparently not completely satisfied with the house designs on these two estates in Birmingham, their general influence seems to have affected the plans of the Chorltonville designer, Albert Cuneo.[191]

The original conception of trying to provide homes for workers' families from Chorlton-upon-Medlock and Hulme fell through as Dawson and Vowles realized that few of these people wanted, or could afford, to move out to Chorlton-cum-Hardy.[192] Whenever the question of slum clearance came to the fore in Hulme many of the inhabitants expressed a desire to be rehoused in the same neighbourhood rather than be forced out into the suburbs.[193] Questions of association and access to the food and labour markets no doubt also influenced the decision of these people. Thus when Chorltonville Ltd was floated as a company, it was with the intention of creating a more obviously middle-class garden suburb. The slums were left behind, but the interest in health and amenity was retained.

The stated objects of the company indicate the influences upon, and intentions of, the founders:

1 To provide beautiful, healthy, conveniently planned homes, with plenty of light and abundance of fresh air, at reasonable rents.

2 To assist health by the provision of wide open spaces – giving ample accommodation for healthy outdoor recreation.

3 By laying out a Bowling Green, Tennis Courts, and otherwise providing for the Social well-being of the Tenants.

4 To prove that this can be done so as to yield a satisfactory return on the Capital invested.[194]

Such unexceptionable proposals were no doubt welcomed by all local housing reformers.

Chorltonville was larger in scale, but similar in conception, to the co-partnership scheme at Burnage. As Chorltonville Ltd was not a public utility society the scheme did not qualify for a loan from the Public Works Commissioners. Fortunately Dawson managed to get financial support from the Bradford (Manchester) Third Building Society.[195] The capital for Chorltonville came, therefore, in the usual way from loan-holders and building societies.

The 40-acre estate was situated on high land on the south side of Chorlton-cum-Hardy. The estate was within walking distance of the railway station (1880) and provided easy access to the tram terminus. The only drawback to the site was the proximate presence of the Withington Sewage Works. Dawson made several unavailing attempts to get the corporation to remove the sewage works.[196] Fortunately, the prevailing winds were favourable.

Great concern was devoted to the layout of the estate. Similar care was shown in the design of the houses, 'in which up-to-date Convenience and Comfort should be united with Artistic Beauty and surrounded by a generous supply of land available for gardens and open spaces.'[197] The houses' designs, 15 of them, were provided by a young Manchester architect, Albert Cuneo.[198] There is thus a wide variety of housing types on the estate. It was hoped that the houses would 'combine the maximum of comfort with the minimum of work and cost of upkeep.'[199] These houses did indeed contain such useful features as wash-houses and plentiful cupboard space. As one woman contemporary wrote of such houses: 'They offer not only beauty of line and harmony of light and shade, but an ample supply of cupboards in the right positions.'[200] Electric lighting (or gas if preferred) was available in the living rooms, and gas was laid on for stoves and boilers. Dawson came into conflict with the Gas Committee over some of his proposals. They refused to run mains pipe for gas cookers unless gas lighting was adopted in every kitchen, scullery and wash-house.[201] Great attention was also paid to the drainage arrangements of these houses.

The houses at Chorltonville were generally larger and more self-consciously imposing than those on the other estates so far discussed.[202] They had three, four or even five bedrooms. The larger size of the houses indicates the higher social status of the estate and its residents. Even the smaller houses at Chorltonville had, instead of a small dining room and kitchen, an ample-sized living room, a good drawing room and a large scullery with tiled walls. One of the chief characteristics of these houses was that each had a fine, airy, wood-panelled entrance hall. Externally, these houses were faced in the traditional manner in best Accrington stock brick or Ravenhead rustic brick. Common bricks were used for the side and rear elevations. As in most garden suburbs, rough cast plaster work was used on many of the houses. Burslem tiles were used on the roofs. The appeal of the local vernacular (and probably the example of Port Sunlight) led Cuneo to introduce applied half-timbering to the façades of some of his houses, but the impact of this was never overpowering.[203]

The estate was carefully planned, and it presented a pleasing contrast to the nearby red-brick terraces. The grassed areas of the Meade and South Drive were particularly attractive. The number of houses to the acre was low (below seven if one takes into account the whole site) and the emphasis on wide frontage to the dwellings and the provision of gardens ensured the maximum of light and air to the front and back. The winding roads on the estate had grass verges planted with trees. Such elements were almost obligatory in any planned venture at this time, but they could present problems. Dawson, like the Manchester Tenants, clashed with the Withington Committee of the city council because these pleasant drives did not comply with the local bye-laws. Some of the bye-law requirements were eventually waived because of the private nature of the estate and because as such, it did not carry any through-traffic. Isolation from the main traffic flow of the area meant that the estate could flourish in an atmosphere of semi-rural calm. The recreation area, with its well-used tennis courts, bowling green and children's corner, provided for the more active of the residents. The estate was opened by Henry Nuttall, M.P., and Dr Charles Leach, M.P., on 7 October 1911. Dr Leach suggested that the City Council might 'take a lesson from what had been admirably done by private enterprise at Chorlton', whilst Henry Nuttall expressed the hope that in time 'we might see workmen's cottages built and laid out as had been done at Chorltonville' – at least, 'that was the idea to aim at'.[204] The city press also responded favourably to the venture. The *Manchester Evening Chronicle* writer found 'the effect of the winding streets, with their broad grass verges, and the broken outline of the villas, with their prominent black and white gables and expansive bay windows is very pleasing.'[205]

These prepossessing houses were not for sale. Yearly tenancies were available from £24 and upwards. As with the co-partnership schemes tenants had to hold at least two shares, although unlike the co-partnership tenants the householders of Chorltonville could hold shares to more than the value of their house. The company paid 5½ per cent on cumulative preference shares and ordinary shares. Like earlier housing reformers, the promoters of Chorltonville Ltd were keen to stress the fact that the company was a sound commercial investment.[206] In all, 273 houses were built on the Chorltonville estate. The company owned 43 other, easily recognizable, houses in the area. Besides the houses, 5½ acres of land in the south-west corner of the estate were laid aside for recreation. A pavilion was also provided by the directors.

The entire estate was built by the company's own direct works team under Thomas Whiteley. The estimated cost of the whole venture was over £100,000. An early brochure explained that 'the expectations of the Directors have been fully realised as regards Capital, Site, Architecture, Builder and Tenants.'[207] Unfortunately the local directories tell us little about the latter, although the rents charged at Chorltonville were an obvious barrier to those lacking a reasonable income.

In the early 1920s the company found itself in financial difficulties and under pressure from developers. The company went into liquidation in 1921, giving first option in the sale of the houses to the sitting tenants. The success of the Chorltonville venture prior to the First World War had led Dawson and his associates to plan a further estate at Polefield Hall in north Manchester. Because of the uncertain economic climate after the First World War this larger venture was never completed.[208]

The originators of the Chorltonville scheme showed that combination of

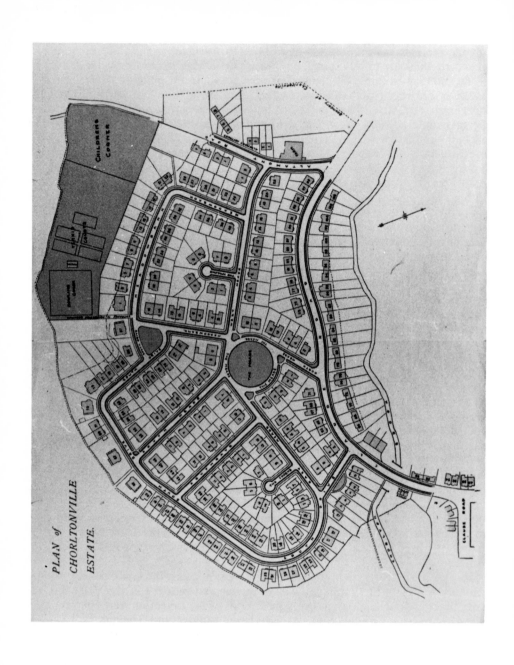

Figure 17. Plan of Chorltonville Estate (courtesy of F. Dawson and Sons).

religious-social zeal, sanitary concern, economic wariness, architectural interest and desire for amenity that pervaded the local and national housing reform and town planning movements. We have evidence of their direct links with Bournville and Harborne, and the drawings of Albert Cuneo show a keen awareness of the 'domestic revival' in English architecture. If the financial arrangements of the scheme looked back to nineteenth-century precedents, the estate itself, with its well-designed houses and low-density layout, was to provide one of the models for the private developers of the inter-war years.

iv Fairfield Tenants Ltd

Fairfield Tenants Ltd were the second co-partnership society to plan a suburban estate in the Manchester area. Registered later than Manchester Tenants Ltd, the Fairfield Tenants' venture was interrupted by the First World War and thwarted in its full development by the inflationary situation that developed in 1919–20.[209]

Fairfield garden suburb was the outcome of a successful allotment scheme started about 1907 on a 2½-acre plot let to a group of working men by the Fairfield Moravian Church.[210] The notion of creating a garden suburb crystallized in October 1909 when, at the suggestion of Hedley Smith, a party went over to see the Burnage scheme which was then being built. The party consisted of Revs. N.S. Libbey, M.A., Hubert Libbery, B.Sc., and G.H. Shawe, B.A., and Messrs A. Grimshaw, G.B. Leishman, R. Rowbotham and Hedley Smith.

After collecting information concerning other similar projects and several informal meetings, it was decided that a formal offer would be made to the Moravian Church for land near Fairfield Avenue. Marr was asked to be chairman of the society. He accepted and steps were taken to form Fairfield Tenants Limited.[211] The aims of the Fairfield Tenants were as follows:

> The objects of the Society shall be to carry on the industry, business or trade of providing housing for persons mainly of the working classes in Droylsden, and of establishing and carrying on social and recreative and educational work and institutions, subject to the provision that no intoxicating drink shall be sold on any of the Society's premises.[212]

A temperance bias was quite normal among the garden suburb enthusiasts of the period. Hedley Smith was rather more direct in his appeal to the local press for better living conditions for the working classes: 'we want to make Droylsden a better place to live in ... In addition to providing gardens for each house it was hoped in the new housing scheme to provide a bowling green for the use of the tenants. Rich people had gardens on three sides of their houses, and there was no reason why the working classes should not have them.'[213]

The company was floated in 1912, and obtained some 22 acres of land in 1912–13 on a 999-year lease from Unitas Estates Ltd.[214] The site was situated about four miles east of the centre of Manchester, just off the Ashton Old Road and just inside the Droylsden border. The estate lay near to the Manchester-to-Ashton tramway route, and five minutes walk away from the Fairfield station of the Great Central Railway Company. Nearer to the industrial areas of Manchester than Burnage or Chorltonville, the Fairfield garden suburb achieved the normal air of suburban calm by its proximity to the fine and peaceful eighteenth-century Moravian settlement.[215]

It was intended that the rentals of the houses on the estate should range from 6s.0d. to 10s.0d. per week. The Tenants hoped to keep the housing density as low as ten or eleven houses per acre, in order to ensure ample light, space and air for each house. It was also hoped that labour-saving appliances would be introduced so as to save unnecessary work for the housewife. Adequate garden space was also allowed, which is not surprising considering the origins of the society.[216] The almost obligatory bowling green, tennis courts and recreation area were included in the original plan.

The financial arrangements at Fairfield were similar to those of the Manchester Tenants. Along with Marr, who was the chairman of both ventures, other familiar figures became involved in the Fairfield scheme. Prominent among the loanholders were Sir John Purser Griffiths, E. D. Simon, G.H. and A. Kenyon, Alfred Haworth and Horsfall. The bulk of the money for the development came from the Public Works Loan Commissioners, who agreed to lend the Tenants approximately £15,000.[217] Building commenced in 1913 and it was expected that the estate would be developed over a period of three years.

Fairfield Tenants Ltd were fortunate in their choice of architects. The estate was designed for them by Edgar Wood and James Henry Sellers. Wood, the leading Manchester architect of the time and president of the Manchester Society of Architects in 1911, was deeply involved in the housing reform and planning movement. He had taken part in the 1903 Northern Art Workers' Guild exhibition, had produced designs for Hampstead Garden Suburb, and had designed the Manchester Society of Architects' proposals for the Platt Fields area of Manchester.[218] These talents were needed if the new estate was to live in harmony with the adjacent Moravian settlement. The result of their work was the construction of 39 houses for the Tenants between 1913 and 1922. The vast majority of these (33) were built between 1913 and 1914, the other six being built in a less generous manner in the inflationary years of the early 1920s.

According to J.H.G. Archer, the expert on Wood and Sellers, 'The precise authorship of the scheme is uncertain, but the imaginative exploitation of levels and texture suggest that Wood was responsible for the layout, but the chaste neo-Georgian character of the houses undoubtedly reflects the taste of Sellers.'[219] This hypothesis would seem to be confirmed by the minutes of the society which indicate that layout plans were requested of Wood, and record payments made to Sellers for house designs.[220] The style certainly reflects the neo-Georgian revival of the years prior to the First World War, but the fine detailing and the careful handling of the whole made this the finest of the Manchester garden suburbs, even in its incomplete state. It did indeed combine well with the nearby Moravian settlement.

The grouping of the houses on this slightly sloping site was both charming and ingenious. It included a fine three-sided court with a green, an impressive raised corner block that incorporated a typical concave Wood motif, and a series of well-designed, finely-detailed dwelling. The frontage lines varied, as did the house designs, which incorporated features advocated by reformers like Unwin, such as through living-rooms.[221] The houses themselves were built of brick, though sandstone walling on parts of the site provided an interesting textural contrast.

The houses varied in size. Some were detached, others were semi-detached or terraced. In terms of sleeping accommodation the houses ranged from small units with two bedrooms and a boxroom through to a single five-bedroom detached house. All

Figure 18. Chorltonville: illustrations from the programme for the official opening, 1911 (courtesy of F. Dawson and Sons).

had fine porches, neo-Georgian fanlights and windows. Similar internal provisions were made to those at Burnage, and externally a liberal amount of grass was allowed. Like other garden suburb developers the Fairfield Tenants had a certain amount of trouble with the local authority concerning the roads on the estate.[222]

As Fairfield was to the industrial east of Manchester, it might have been expected to have attracted more working-class members to its fold. It seems to have attracted a few artisans, but foremen and managers were to be found there in almost equal numbers. As table 4 shows, Fairfield had its white-collar workers, but more surprising was the trading element among the householders. What had happened to the working classes of Droylsden?

Fairfield thus attracted a knowledgeable group of designers and reformers. Some, like Horsfall, were coming to the end of their active careers; others, like E.D. Simon, the future advocate of the Wythenshawe satellite town, were on the threshold of full and famous careers. Architectually Wood and Sellers provided a fitting climax to this phase in the history of housing and town planning in Manchester. The influence of the garden suburbs spread, yet the stylistic hold never seemed quite so certain again.

4 Conclusion

The motives of the garden suburb developers were mixed. The Ruskinian appeal for

Figure 19. Fairfield: the three-sided court on Broadway (photograph: M. Harrison)

Table 4   Occupation of household heads in Fairfield Garden Suburb

Occupation	Number on estate	Occupation	Number on estate
Householder	11	Managers	2
Managing director	1	Station master	1
Cardboard box manufacturer	1	Cashier	1
Works manager	1	House furnisher	1
Wholesale grocer	1	Agent	1
Wine merchant	1	Secretary	1
Chemist	1	Foreman	1
Hardware dealer	1	Engineers	2
Butcher	1	Electrician	1
		Calico printer	1

Source: *Slater's Manchester, Salford and Suburban Directory*, 1918. Volume 2, Manchester Surburban.

beauty was paralleled by the sanitarian's call for a more healthy environment. Whether the appeal for healthy and artistic homes came from the economist, imperialist, philanthropist or Christian mattered little to this small group of reformers, for they tended to see housing and town planning as essentially a non-partisan issue. Nevertheless, most Manchester housing reformers were supporters of free enterprise and voluntary effort, and still viewed 'municipal socialism' with suspicion. Even Marr and Horsfall, who were not averse to the corporation providing houses for the working classes, felt that the council's main task was to stimulate and regulate the schemes put forward by philanthropists and professional builders.[223] 'I believe', wrote Horsfall, 'that if Town Councils obtained power to incorporate large areas round towns, and, by adoption of good building plans and the Zone system, made it certain that good dwellings would not be spoilt by bad surroundings, philanthropic societies and persons and professional builders would soon provide Manchester with ample supply of wholesome cheap dwellings.'[224]

Apart from the municipal estate at Blackley, the garden suburbs of Manchester were examples of private enterprise or collective self-help.[225] They were all purely residential, and as Marr put it, 'examples of site planning rather than town planning.'[226] Built in close proximity to pre-existing local communities, the garden suburbs did not require their full quota of social amenities, such as churches, schools and shops.[227] The desire for some sort of community identity did, however, lead their developers to provide (or plan) recreational facilities for the estates. Yet taking into account the vast number of insanitary houses and streets in central Manchester, it cannot be said that these ventures were much more than experimental contributions to the Edwardian housing problem.[228] More was required, as Horsfall explained: 'The admirable work of all these associations needs to be supplemented by Town-planning, as each ensures only that a small area is well-used.'[229]

Town planning in this wider sense made only slow progress in Manchester. After a promising start in 1906, when the mayor of Manchester took the lead in pressing the Association of Municipal Corporations to consider drafting a town planning bill, the city council merely proceeded to 'make haste slowly' in the following years.[230]

Whilst making allowances for the cumbersome nature of the procedures under the 1909 Housing and Town Planning Act, Manchester Corporation could hardly claim to have been in the forefront of the planning movement before 1914. At a time when the Manchester Society of Architects, the Municipal School of Technology, Manchester University and the Lancashire and Cheshire Federation of Trades Councils were all discussing town planning, the council showed no great enthusiasm for the subject.[231] Planning schemes for the north and south of the city were eventually put forward, but even then it was claimed that 'the Corporation had no intention of spending any money on their scheme.'[232] The Town Planning Special Committee spent a mere £2 13s.6d. in 1901–11 and only £17 7s.10d. in the following year.[233] The council's lack of commitment to town planning was also reflected in staffing levels. The Town Planning Special Committee had the assistance of only a very diminutive staff.[234] Negotiations with the local landowners also made slow progress. The *Manchester Guardian* was sceptical of the outcome of these talks 'because no definite plans can be determined.'[235] One of the problems was that the responsibility for executing schemes under the 1909 Act had been 'practically thrown into the general duties of the city surveyor and his staff.'[236] In Manchester no official was given the specific duty of overlooking the work of town planning.

It is hardly surprising, therefore, that the council's recommendations were limited. The corporation showed some concern about road linkage with neighbouring authorities, and proposed a limit of 20 houses per acre, but would not consider the purchase of suburban land.[237] Early in 1912 a member of the Planning Committee told the press that he 'was not hopeful as to results' from their work.[238] Their work was not quite at a standstill for in the summer of 1914 the Local Government Board authorized the *preparation* of the City's northern scheme and two smaller ventures.[239] This work was, however, definitely interrupted by the First World War.

In the years before the War, reformers tended to link their proposals for a solution to the housing question to the provision of 'cheap and rapid transit'.[240] Manchester men were no different in this respect. Despite the fact that Manchester's municipal trams were numerous and relatively cheap, they were regarded, as one American critic put it, 'not as an agency for the promotion of the decentralization of the population but as an agency that can be made to turn money into the public treasury.'[241] In 1913 the city council still demanded that the Tramways Department hand over 5 per cent of its capital expenditure for the relief of the rates.[242]

The minor reduction in fares on the electric tramway made by the corporation in the Edwardian period contributed to the large increase in the volume of traffic in the city. By 1913 the penny fare charged in Manchester gave a longer ride than any other tramway system in the country.[243] Unfortunately, the rate per mile rose considerably in the higher fares and this discouraged the wider dispersal of the population.[244] The council admitted in 1912 that tramcar fares and travelling time were still important limitations to the outward movement of the working classes.[245]

The local railway companies also carried an increased number of passengers in the years before the War. Their main concern, however, was with main-line traffic.[246] When it came to suburban traffic they preferred middle-class passengers whose trains were fully loaded before they reached the heavily trafficked track nearer the city centre. The timing of the trains gave little encouragement to the working classes.[247] The pricing policies of the companies benefited the contract and excursion ticket holder rather than the working man.[248]

The tram and the railway obviously made it possible for sections of Manchester society to move out, but on the whole large numbers of the working class were not able to take advantage of this facility. Despite their obvious usefulness, there is no evidence of their direct influence on any of the garden suburbs of Manchester.

It was not the slum-dwellers therefore who were decanted into the suburbs. Like earlier semi-philanthropic bodies, such as the Peabody Trust, if the garden suburbs attracted workmen at all, they tended to be of the more affluent, skilled variety. Indeed, it would seem more accurate to class most of the residents of these garden suburbs as middle or lower-middle class. The middle-class supporters of the garden suburb movement rationalized this failure to house the poor by claiming that the centrifugal tendencies of the 'labour aristocracy' and the middle class would enable the rest of the working class to occupy the houses they had vacated.[249] As Henry Nuttall, M.P., said of the theory at the opening of a co-operative housing scheme in Didsbury: 'There was something in that, but it was not altogether satisfactory.'[250] A handful of garden suburb ventures were hardly sufficient to achieve a 'levelling up' of the housing classes in the years before the First World War,[251] at a time when it was estimated that nearly half the population of Manchester and Salford lived in dwellings with less than five rooms.[252]

Just as some reformers over-estimated the immediate effects of these garden suburb developments, so others failed to see the forces, both social and economic, that kept the working classes in the 'industrial collar'. Some planners, like Raymond Unwin, did recognize 'a certain picturesqueness and excitement about the slum life near the busy centre of the town.'[253] The inhabitants of such a neighbourhood might fear the loss of those patterns of interdependence and support that were a part of their own sub-culture.[254] Travel costs, the higher price of goods in suburban shops, and the lack of secondary employment opportunities in the suburbs, were among the financial disincentives to the suburban movement. A major problem for the working classes was that industrial decentralization was not proceeding at the same pace as suburban development.

Though a review of the 1901 census figures might show that there were more than enough houses for the population, and that in some parts of the town there were unoccupied houses, the Citizens Association in 1904 had been 'forced to the conclusion that there is a deficiency in house accommodation at rents within the reach of the working classes.' Their report went on:

> To provide houses simply for those who are at present overcrowded would necessitate the building of thousands of houses. But . . . many of the existing houses are unfit for human habitation. The two Town Councils (of Manchester and Salford) are fully aware of this, and they are continually weeding out the worst houses. So long as there is a deficiency in house room, however, they cannot do much.[255]

If Manchester Corporation's own cottage estate was of little numerical significance, the vigorous 'reconditioning' programme pursued by Councillor Marr in the period after 1906 did counter some of the worst evils of the housing problem.[256]

In the deteriorating situation after 1909, the garden suburbs could not hope to have more than a marginal effect on the housing problem. Lloyd George's Finance Act, the condition of the money market, the rise in the cost of building materials and the greater number of closures under the 1909 Housing and Town Planning Act were seen as the reasons for the decline in the number of new houses erected in the years before 1914.[257] Contemporaries began to talk about a 'housing famine'. A survey conducted in 1913 estimated that in the whole of the City of Manchester (excluding Withington) there were only 517 houses at 8s.6d. or less per week which were empty. This represented only about ½ per cent of the housing stock. The gravity of the situation can be measured by the fact that in normal times estate agents considered themselves fortunate if they had no more than 3 or 4 per cent of their property in this class vacant.[258]

The War only accentuated these problems, though it did sharpen Labour interest in the housing problem.[259] Unwin's villages at Gretna and Queensferry for the Ministry of Munitions were a measure of the official recognition given to the garden city/garden suburb model. Reconstruction plans for 'homes fit for heroes' followed in the wake of this international bloodbath. In calling for a housing programme Lloyd George stressed that 'you cannot maintain an A–1 empire with a C–3 population.'[260] This appeal, which echoed the concern shown about physical deterioration after the Boer War, was made in a speech at Manchester in September 1918.

Though the garden suburb ventures were generally well received, a few contemporaries were critical of even the architectural merits of such schemes. Prominent among the critics was A. Trystan Edwards. In two articles in the *Town Planning Review* he made a series of telling attacks on the garden city movement. Although admitting the value of its role as a propagandist, he felt that by 1913 this 'sectarian movement' had served its purpose. He felt the garden city to be a denial of the architectural values of the town, and yet, at the same time, a threat to nature. He especially disapproved of the garden suburb:

> But of all suburbs, perhaps the most shoddy and depressing is the typical garden suburb. It has neither the crowded interest of the town nor the quiet charm of the country. It gives the advantages neither of solitude nor society. And the great inconvenience of this manner of living must also be noticed. The working man does not want to traverse long distances to see his friends after his day's work is done. Some of these suburbs are so big that trams are needed for the inhabitants, but cannot be employed without sacrificing the rustic aspect which is so much desired.[261]

Edwards, like C.F.G. Masterman, had little to say for the inhabitants of these garden suburbs: 'The very word "suburban" implies something that is second rate, some narrow and pharisaical attitude of mind.' Unlike Masterman, however, Edwards was not willing to believe that the suburbs, for all this, would lead to 'a clean and virile life'.[262]

Despite such criticisms, there could be no doubt as to the environmental and sanitary advantages of the garden suburbs. Death rates were indeed lower in the garden suburbs.[263] It was also difficult to convince contemporaries that the architecture of the garden suburbs was worse than that of the bye-law terrace. Yet at times the garden suburbs could come near to producing a surfeit of the picturesque. As Charles Reilly was to remark: 'Our Gothic inheritance of picturesqueness has prevented our desire for simplicity from taking the form of simple rooms simply put together.'[264] By about 1909, however, many architects were addressing themselves to this problem, and though varied in their layout, such schemes as those at Burnage or Fairfield, for instance, could scarcely be dismissed as being fussy.

Pleasing as these schemes were, the overt emphasis on the architectural at the expense of other aspects of the housing problem could lead to a narrowing of the housing reformers' field of vision. 'This outlook,' as Ashworth has pointed out, 'which treated town planning as a predominantly architectural function, was bound to result in a concentration on the outward appearance of things, not on the satisfaction of social needs, although it was growing awareness of social shortcomings that had created a demand for statutory town planning.'[265] Even so, it was as architectural and planning examples that the garden suburbs were so influential. The garden suburb idea could be said to have been given constitutional form in the Housing and Town Planning Act of 1909, practical expression in the Ministry of Munitions wartime housing estates and full governmental approval in the post-war Tudor Walters and Women's Housing Sub-Committee reports.[266] At a less formal level the garden suburbs provided local models for innumerable similar developments, both private and municipal, as the process of emulation got under way. 'Mr Jerry Builder is creeping up', remarked John Burns, president of the Local Government Board, in 1910. 'You have only to see the way in which a garden suburb is surrounded wherever one is started, by builders who try to live up to the model and exemplar which has been planted in their midst... Garden cities and garden suburbs are magnificent in themselves, but they are a hundred times more useful because of the inspiration they create and the example they are to others to copy.'[267] Estates like those at Burnage represented not a distant ideal, but a local and practical example of what could be done by local craftsmen. Thus, however, peripheral the garden suburbs may seem to the housing problem of Edwardian Manchester, they proved to be compelling prototypes for the low-density estate developments that became the planning norm in the inter-war years.

NOTES

1 R.C.K. Ensor, 'Workmen's homes in London and Manchester' *Independent Review*, VII (1906), 170.
2 *Ibid.*, 179.
3 See T.C. Horsfall, *The Improvement of the Dwellings and Surroundings of the People: the example of Germany* (1904); T.C. Horsfall, *An Ideal for Life in Manchester Realizable If –* (1900) and H. Philips 'Open spaces in American cities', *Health J.*, January 1886, 125–6.
4 See H.J. Dyos and M. Wolff (eds), *The Victorian City: Images and Realities* (1973), I. ch. 4.
5 B.R. Mitchell and P. Deane, *Abstract of British Historical Statistics*. The figures are for the whole city, including such suburbs as were incorporated in the period 1881–1911.
6 S. Low, 'The rise of the suburbs', *Contemporary Rev.* (1891), 550. See also the map in T.R. Marr, *Housing Conditions in Manchester and Salford* (1904).
7 H.B. Rodgers, 'The suburban growth of Victorian Manchester', *J. Manchester Geog. Soc.*, LVIII (1961–2), 5.
8 See K. Chorley, *Manchester Made Them* (1950), 13, 147.
9 *MG*, 11 July 1901.
10 1911 Census.
11 *MG*, 20 September 1901.
12 *MCN*, 23 December 1905.

13 *Report of the Interdepartmental Committee on Physical Deterioration*, vol. 2, List of Witnesses and Evidence (T.C. Horsfall), British Parliamentary Papers (1904) Cd. 2210, XXXII, 145, para. 5727.

14 *Report of an Enquiry by the Board of Trade into Working Class Rents, Housing and Retail Prices*, British Parliamentary Papers (1908), Cd.3864, CVII, 299. See also Marr, *op.cit.*, ch. 4.

15 *Report of an Enquiry by the Board of Trade, op. cit.*, 301–2.

16 *Ibid.*

17 This argument had been made as early as 1866. See A. Ransome and W. Royston, 'Report upon the health of Manchester and Salford during the last fifteen years,' *Trans. NAPSS* (1866), 463–4. See also E.R. Dewsnup, *The Housing Problem in England: its statistics, legislation and policy* (1907), Appendix A; MCP, 4 January 1899.

18 Marr, *op. cit.*, 30.

19 Ensor 'Workmen's homes', 172.

20 J.C. Thresh, *An Enquiry into the Causes of the Excessive Mortality in No. 1 District Ancoats* (1889), 38.

21 Marr, *op. cit.*, 59.

22 B.F.C. Costelloe, 'The housing problem', *Trans. MSS* (1898–9), 48.

23 *MOH* Report, 1902, 174.

24 *Report of Interdepartmental Committee on Physical Deterioration*.

25 *MOH Report*, 1907, 178ff.

26 *MCN*, 5 April 1902 (Priestley Prime). See also John M. McLachlan, 'The prevention of slums: a policy of reform', a cutting in the Mattley Collection, RPL. Martin Gaskell guided me to this source.

27 F. Scott, 'The condition and occupations of the people of Manchester and Salford', *Trans. MSS* (1888–9), 114. Very poor – those who are always face to face with want. Poor – those who have a hand to mouth existence. Scott defined poverty as 'the inadequacy of income to supply the minimum of food necessary for the proper nourishment of the body and for the provision of other necessaries, such as clothing and shelter.'

28 Marr, *op. cit.*, 59

29 T.C. Horsfall, *Means Needed for Improving the Condition of the Lowest Classes in Towns* (1884), 29.

30 McLachlan, *op. cit.*, quoting *MOH* (1908).

31 Horsfall, in *Report of the Interdepartmental Committee on Physical Deterioration*, para. 5610.

32 See T.S. Ashton, *Economic and Social Investigation in Manchester 1833–1933* (1934).

33 *Trans. MSS*, 1871–2 and 1881–2.

34 *Trans. MSS*, 1898–9.

35 *Trans. MSS*, 1888–9.

36 *Trans. MSS*, 1889–90 (Rev. H.V. Mills).

37 *Trans. MSS*, 1903–4 (J. Long).

38 *Trans. MSS*, 1895–6.

39 For the MSSA see the excellent dissertation by P.A. Ryan, *Public Health and Voluntary Effort in Nineteenth Century Manchester* (M.A. thesis, University of Manchester, 1973).

40 MSSA Rules, MPL Archives.

41 A. Ransome, *The History of the Manchester and Salford Sanitary Association, or Half-a-Century's Progress in Sanitary Reform* (1902), 12.

42 A. Samelson, *Dwellings and the Death Rate of Manchester* (1883), 11ff.

43 See series of articles in *Health J.* of 1884 on 'Squalid and outcast Manchester and Salford', another series by 'a Lady' in *Health J.*, (1886) on 'Afternoons in the Manchester slums'; J.H. Crossfield, *The Bitter Cry of Ancoats and Impoverished Manchester* (1887).

44 Thresh, *op. cit.* The death rate in the area was 55.2 per 1000 in 1887 and 48.7 in 1888. In the courts, however, the death rate exceeded 80 and in one street it actually reached 90.
45 *SC*, 5 May 1889–23 June 1889. See also *Clarion*, 11 March 1893: 'I showed Blatchford round the slums, and that made Blatchford – made a Socialist of him.' (Joe Waddington).
46 HHS (Ancoats) Healthy Homes Society, Cuttings and Reports in MPL Archives.
47 *Ibid.*, 4. HHS, *Rules*.
48 (Ancoats) *Healthy Homes Society, Annual Report*, 1898–9.
49 The average attendance in 1890–91 was 514 (18 meetings) in 1891–2, 613 (28 meetings), in 1892–3, 850 (23 meetings) and in 1893–4, 700 (31 meetings). In the early 1900s the *Annual Reports* claimed that the meetings were 'still crowded'.
50 See, for example *Annual Report*, 1891–2.
51 *MG*, 6 January 1893.
52 MSSA Minutes, 29 November 1899, in MPL Archives.
53 See *Workman's Times*, 17 October 1890. 'The Hulme Working Men's Sanitary Association have elected their officers and amongst their names are those of several trade unionists who will not allow "grass to grow under their feet" before taking spirited action and trying to remedy the disgusting state of affairs which today exists in Hulme.'
54 *MCN*, 15 May 1911. Henry Aldridge of the National Housing and Town Planning Council, speaking to a conference of trade unionists and co-operators on housing.
55 See Ryan, *op. cit.*, 79, and MSSA *Annual Reports* for 1894–7.
56 See *MG*, 25–6 April 1902. Among the speakers were A. Ransome, T.C. Horsfall, Dr A. Newsholme, T. Adams, Dr J. Niven and the Earl of Meath.
57 *MCN*, 12 and 19 July 1913. See also article on Manchester Housing Company Ltd in RPL, Mattley Cuttings (1913).
58 *MCN*, 22 March 1902 (C.H. Spencer).
59 A.F. Weber, *The Growth of Cities in the Nineteenth Century* (new edn, 1967), 475.
60 T.C. Horsfall, *The Housing of the Labouring Classes* (1900), 3.
61 See G.R. Searle, *The Quest for National Efficiency* (1971), especially 60–7.
62 T.C. Horsfall, *The Relation of Town Planning to the National Life* (1908), 13–14.
63 Manchester Diocesan Conference, *Report of the Committee Appointed to Consider the Question of the Housing of the Poor* (1902), 19.
64 *Ibid.*
65 Social Questions Union for Manchester, Salford and District. Established 26 September 1892 as a result of two meetings addressed by W.T. Stead. The union, which elected T.C. Horsfall as president in 1893–4, had a Conditions of Home Life Committee. Records in MPL Archives.
66 *MCN*, 15 October 1904.
67 *MCN*, 12 April 1902.
68 *MCN*, 29 February 1908.
69 *Report of the Interdepartmental Committee on Physical Deterioration*, vol. 1, para. 174.
70 M. Stocks, *Fifty Years in Every Street* (1945), 18.
71 P. Abercrombie, 'Modern town planning in England: a comparative review of "Garden City" schemes in England', *TPR*, I (1910–11), 18.
72 Marr, *op. cit.*, 108.
73 MSSA, *Minutes*, 25 September 1901: MPL Archives.
74 *Rules* of National Service League in T.C. Horsfall, *The Relation of National Service to the Welfare of the Community* (1904).
75 *MCN*, 26 October 1895 (Fred Brocklehurst).
76 M. Kaufman, *The Housing of the Working Class and of the Poor* (1907, repr. 1975), 57.
77 *MG*, 29 June 1889.
78 See S.M. Gaskell's 'A landscape of small houses', in *Multi-Storey Living*, ed. A. Sutcliffe (1974), 120.

79 T.R. Marr to P. Geddes, 14 November 1908: NLS Geddes Papers.
80 See Marr, *op. cit.*, and Horsfall, *The Example of Germany*.
81 T.C. Horsfall, *The Housing Question* (n.d.), 3.
82 T.C. Horsfall to Frances Reeves, 21 October 1877: Horsfall Family Papers in possession of Mrs D.M.H. Betts.
83 *Ibid.*
84 T.C. Horsfall, *The Place of Admiration, Hope and Love In Town Life* (1910), 5.
85 See A. Briggs, *Victorian Cities* (new edn, 1968), 235.
86 T. C. Horsfall to Frances Reeves, 31 December 1877, Horsfall Family Papers.
87 T.C. Horsfall to Alfred Venning, 29 September 1880, Horsfall Family Papers.
88 T.C. Horsfall, 'The government of Manchester', *Trans. MSS* (1895–6), 6–7.
89 Horsfall, *The Housing Question*, 3.
90 R.C.K. Ensor, *England 1870–1914* (1936), 518. The best analysis of Horsfall's work for town planning is to be found in M.G. Hawtree, 'The origins of the modern town planner: a study in professional ideology' (Ph.D. thesis, University of Liverpool, 1975). See also J.P. Reynolds, 'Thomas Coglan Horsfall and the town planning movement in England', *TPR*, xxiii (1952), 52–60.
91 H.R. Aldridge to G. Cadbury, 20 December 1909. Letter in Minute Books, vol. 2., National Housing and Town Planning Council.
92 The phrase is Aldridge's. See Campaign Circular of National Housing and Town Planning Reform Council, 29 November 1909.
93 *MG*, 31 July 1911.
94 For Marr see biographical cuttings in MPL Local History Department.
95 T.R. Marr to P. Geddes, 5 February 1901, NLS Geddes Papers.
96 T.R. Marr to McGegan, 25 April 1901, NLS MS10568/180.
97 T.R. Marr to P. Geddes, 8 December 1903, NLS Geddes Papers.
98 Marr, *op. cit.*, 6.
99 *Ibid.*, 4–5.
100 *Ibid.*, 8.
101 *Ibid.*, 85.
102 T.R. Marr to P. Geddes, 7 June 1912, NLS Geddes Papers.
103 S. Simon, *A Century of City Government* (1938), 297.
104 Marr, *op. cit.*, 85.
105 E.G. Culpin, *The Garden City Movement Up-to-Date* (1913), 12.
106 Quoted in W.L. Creese, *The Search for Environment* (1966), 276.
107 Northern Art Workers' Guild, *Exhibition Catalogue* (1903).
108 *Studio, Country Life* and the Manchester-based *BA* all gave a good deal of attention to the subject.
109 Rodgers, *op. cit.*, 8–9.
110 M.H. Baillie Scott *et al.*, *Garden Suburbs, Town Planning and Modern Architecture* (1910), 83.
111 For numbers of houses built 1891–1920 see J. Niven, *Observations on the History of Public Health Effort in Manchester* (1923), 175–6.
112 For Alkrington see *BA*, 26 October 1906, *MG*, 31 July 1911 and 26 June 1912. Although the most grandiose of the Manchester schemes, little was done on this estate, which was planned by Thomas Adams and Pepler and Allen, before 1914. For Didsbury Provident Co-operative Society Ltd, see Culpin, *op.cit.*, 23; *MG*, 26 June 1912 and 4 October 1909. For the Alderdale Hall Estate see *MG*, 25 September 1911 and 26 June 1912. Maps of these estates are incorporated in M. Harrison, 'The garden suburbs of Manchester: social aspects of housing and town planning 1894–1914' (M.A. thesis, University of Manchester, 1974).
113 *MOH Report*, 1886, quoted in S. Simon, *A Century of City Government* (1938), 294.
114 *MOH Report*, 1884, quoted in Simon, *op.cit.*, 293.

115 Manchester Corporation Sanitary Committee, *Housing of the Working Classes: A History of the Schemes etc. of Corporation Dwellings* (1904), 9.

116 See *MOH Report* 1896, 139ff, and the 'Report upon the Relation between the Demolition of House Property and the Living Conditions of the Poorer Classes in the Township of Manchester' by Joseph Dewsnup, in E.R. Dewsnup, *op.cit.*, 309–11.

117 Sanitary Committee, *op.cit.*, 9.

118 See Gaskell, 'A landscape of small houses', 99ff.; *MCN*, 12 April 1902.

119 Marr, *op.cit.*, 84–5.

120 Simon, *op,cit.*, 295; MSSA Minutes, 25 January 1901, 3 January 1902, 23 December 1902, 24 February 1903: MPL Archives.

121 H. Spalding, 'Block dwellings: the associated and self-contained systems', *JRIBA*, 3rd ser. VII (1900), 255, quoted in Gaskell, *op.cit.*, 104.

122 MCP, 22 December 1899.

123 *Ibid.*

124 Sanitary Committee, *op.cit.*, 18.

125 *Ibid.*, 19.

126 *MCN*, 7 March 19? (cutting in Mattley Collection, RPL).

127 See plans in Harrison *op.cit.*,

128 *MCN*, 7 March 19? *loc.cit.* See also *MCN*, 9 May 1908 and 4 May 1889; *MOH Report*, 1902.

129 *Report of an Enquiry by the Board of Trade* 301.

130 *MCN*, 23 April 1904.

131 *MCN*, 22 October 1904, 25 October 1905.

132 Horsfall, in *Report of Interdepartmental Committee on Physical Deterioration*, vol. 2., para. 5662.

133 *Report of an Enquiry by the Board of Trade*, 301.

134 *MCN*, 15 March 1902.

135 J. Nettlefold, *Slum Reform and Town Planning: the garden city idea applied to existing cities and their suburbs* (n.d.), 2. See *MCN*, 22 October 1904 and 26 October 1907 for criticism of the Corporation's 'scandalous waste'.

136 Culpin, *op.cit.*, 20.

137 *BA*, 23 December 1910, 434.

138 *Ibid.*, 11 December 1914.

139 British Association, *Manchester in 1915* (1915), 25.

140 *MG*, 15 December 1910 and 16 July 1912.

141 'A municipal program', by 'Mamecestre', in Mattley Cuttings (October 1911), RPL.

142 *MCN*, 29 February 1908. 'Mamecestre', *loc.cit.*, was still complaining in 1911 of 'the carefully studied procrastination which characterises our municipal efforts in coping with the housing evils in Manchester'.

143 'Housing conditions; seething criticisms of Manchester's slums. A call to the City Council', a cutting of 1911 in the Mattley Collection, RPL (C. Egan).

144 Councillor Jackson (cutting in Mattley Collection, RPL 1913).

145 'Housing conditions: seething criticism of Manchester's slums. A call to the City Council'.

146 *MG*, 7 October 1913.

147 See P. Wilding, 'Towards Exchequer subsidies for housing 1906–1914', *Social and Economic Administration*, VI (1972).

148 'A Peaceful Path to Real Reform' was the sub-title of Howard's *Tomorrow* (1898).

149 *MCN*, 29 March 1902.

150 *Burnage Garden Village Jubilee 1906–1956*, 4.

151 *Co-partnership*, XIII (1907), 192.

152 P. Redfern, *The Story of the C.W.S.* (1913), 366. For the housebuilding activities of local co-operative societies see S.M. Gaskell, 'Housing estate development 1840–1918'

(Ph.D. thesis, University of Sheffield, 1974), 147–79, 304.

153 These included Marr and the journalist R.C. Wallhead. For a brief picture of the estate after the First World War see C.S. Davies, *North Country Bred* (1963).
154 *MG*, 19 September 1906.
155 *Burnage Garden Village Jubilee*, 5, quoting the original prospectus.
156 *Co-partnership, loc.cit.*, 192, See also *GC*, o.s. I (1905), 65 (Henry Vivian).
157 *Co-partnership*, xiii (1907), 129.
158 J.N. Tarn, *Five Per Cent Philanthropy* (1973).
159 *Burnage Garden Village*, Prospectus I(n.d.), 3.
160 MT, Minute Books.
161 *MCN*, 7 March 1908.
162 M.D. Greville and G.D. Holt, 'Railway development in Manchester – 3', *Railway Magazine* (November 1957), 766; Gaskell, *op.cit.*, 259; B.W. Beacroft, 'The streets and street traffic of Manchester 1890–1914', (M.A. thesis, University of Leicester, 1964); A.A. Todd, 'The development of railway passenger traffic in Late Victorian and Edwardian Manchester', (M.A. thesis. University of Manchester, 1975). Cf. M. Simpson, 'Urban transport and the development of Glasgow's West End 1830–1914', *J. Transport Hist.*, n.s.I (1973), 149–59.
163 W.A. Shaw, *Manchester Old and New*, III, (1894), 138.
164 *Burnage Garden Village Jubilee*, 5.
165 *Co-partnership*, xiii (August 1907), 129.
166 *Burnage Garden Village*, Prospectus I, 4–5.
167 Abercrombie, *op.cit.*, 120.
168 *Burnage Garden Village*, Prospectus II (n.d.), 14.
169 I thank Stuart Evans of Sunderland Polytechnic and Jonathan Hall and Philip Atkins of the Civic Trust for the North-West for bringing these plans to my attention. Unwin was the Co-Partnership Tenants' consultant architect. Drawings of the cottages then being erected at Burnage were shown at the Exhibition of Cottage Designs held at the City Art Gallery, the Queens Park Gallery and the Manchester Art Museum between June and November 1909. The designs for the Burnage Tenants were said to have been the work of C.G. Agate, T.H. Sutton and others: Manchester University Settlement Scrapbook.
170 Abercrombie, *op.cit.*, 121.
171 Withington Committee was a temporary committee consisting of councillors from that area, set up to control the health services of that district for ten years after its incorporation in the city: Marr, *op.cit.*, 93–4.
172 R. Unwin, *Nothing Gained by Overcrowding*, (1912), in W.L. Creese (ed.) *The Legacy of Raymond Unwin*, (1973).
173 *Alkrington Garden Village*, Prospectus (n.d.), RPL.
174 *TPR*, II (1911), 128.
175 Burnage Garden Village Dramatic Society, *Our Majority* (1933), 1.
176 *Ibid.*, 2.
177 *Report of an Enquiry by the Board of Trade*, *op.cit.*, 229.
178 See Appendix 1 in Harrison, *op.cit.*,
179 Using the local directories, some of the Manchester residents were traced (no attempt was made to trace those tenants who came from outside the city). The rate books of the City of Manchester (MPL Archives) were then used to check the amount paid per year by the Manchester Tenants before and after they moved to Burnage. 32 out of the 126 residents were thus traced.
180 *MG*, 6 July 1912. cf. O. Lancaster, *Here of All Places* (1959), 114–15.
181 Marr, *op.cit.*, 59 pointed to the residents of St John's Ward who stressed their attachment to the area, and who stated that they would be reluctant to move.
182 *MCN*, 29 February 1908.
183 See J. Rex, 'Sociology of a zone of transition', in *Readings in Urban Sociology*, ed. R.E.

Pahl (1968), and S.M. Gaskell 'Housing and the lower middle class 1870–1914', in *The Lower Middle Class*, ed. G. Crossick (1977), 159.

184 *MG*, 26 September 1910. cf. Marr, *op.cit.*, 5.

185 See H.F. Dawson, 'Pioneers of the garden village movement in England (Chorltonville)' (B.A. thesis, Geneva Theological College and St Mark's Institute, Wisconsin, U.S.A.; copy in MPL. Local History Section).

186 *MCN*, 15 April 1890.

187 *MCN*, 18 November 1893.

188 *MCN*, 21 October 1893.

189 MSSA, Minutes, 1 November 1899: MPL Archives.

190 Dawson, *op.cit.*, 10.

191 See plans 29–38 in Harrison, *op.cit.*

192 Gaskell, thesis, 357.

193 *MG*, 9 September 1896.

194 *Chorltonville Limited* (programme of official opening, n,d,), 6.

195 Dawson, *op.cit.*, 17.

196 *MCN*, 14 October 1911.

197 *Chorltonville Limited*, 7.

198 Cuneo's office was in Brown Street, Manchester.

199 *Chorltonville Limited*, 11.

200 Sybella Gurney in Baillie Scott *et al., op.cit.*, 25–6. Such female interest in the housing question anticipates that of the Women's Housing Sub-Committee of the Ministry of Reconstruction: see British Parliamentary Papers, 1918, x, 629 (cd. 9166). It was part of the quest for the ideal 'servantless house'.

201 MCP, vol. 27, 23 February 1910 and 11 March 1910.

202 Compare the plans in Harrison, *op.cit.*, where copies of the plans of Blackley, Burnage and Chorltonville will be found.

203 Cuneo may also have been influenced by the Jubilee Exhibition in Manchester. See Creese, *op.cit.*, 138–9 and 273.

204 *MCN*, 14 October 1911.

205 *Manchester Evening Chronicle*, 7 October 1911.

206 *Chorltonville Limited*, 14. See Tarn, *op.cit.*, and J.S. Nettlefold, *Practical Town Planning* (1914), xii: 'A strong economic incentive in the right direction is far more effective for reform than all the rules and regulations that were ever framed.'

207 *Chorltonville Limited*, *op.cit.*, 17.

208 Dawson, *op.cit.*, 30. On post-war problems generally see P. Abrams, 'The failure of social reform 1918–1920', *Past and Present*, xxiv, (1963), 43–64.

209 Tameside Metropolitan Borough Council Planning Department seem to have either lost, or misplaced, the plans for this development. On post-war problems see Abrams, *op.cit.*, especially 56–7.

210 Fairfield Tenants Ltd, Minute Book I, 1; Fairfield Congregation Diaries, 15–16 December 1907. (Fairfield Moravian Church).

211 Fairfield Tenants Ltd, *loc.cit.* The Committee of Management consisted of Marr, Shawe, Smith, Leishman, Councillor G.H. Kenyon and Dr Elkington Smith.

212 Fairfield Tenants Ltd, *Rules*.

213 *MG*, 23 September 1912.

214 Although many of the promoters of the scheme were connected with the Moravian Church a comparison of the names of the Tenants with those on the Moravian Church's Marriage Register for the period 1897–1918 shows virtually no overlap. This was probably because the management of Moravian property was passing to the national executive (Property Executive Committee) and neither they, nor the Fairfield Tenants, it would seem, practised a policy of letting property only to church members. Unitas Estates Ltd was the body set up by the national executive of the Moravian Church to

administer this property. See Fairfield Congregation Diaries, 1911, Addenda, for the fact that Fairfield Estate had passed into the hands of Unitas Estates Co. Ltd, and that this tended to loosen the connection between the Congregation and the Estate. They had received 'information from P.E.C. that henceforth the Committee will not be consulted as to new tenants'. See also *MG*, 23 April 1913.

215 For the Moravian settlement see Creese, *op. cit.*, 6–9.

216 Cf. R. Unwin, *Town Planning in Practice* (1909), 320, on profitability of gardens.

217 Fairfield Tenants Ltd, Minute Book I, esp. 7 March 1913, 3 April 1913, 29 October 1913 and 4 November 1914.

218 J.H.G. Archer, 'Edgar Wood, a notable Manchester architect', *Trans. Lancs. and Ches. Antiq. Soc.* (1963–4), and *AR*, xxviii (1910), 145–9.

219 *Ibid.*, 181–2.

220 Fairfield Tenants Ltd, Minute Book I, 7 March and 7 June 1912, 30 December 1913, 24 November 1914, 11 May 1917. The debt to Sellers was finally liquidated by the issue of £300 loan stock to Mrs Sarah Sellers on 16 October 1919.

221 See plates in Harrison, *op. cit.*,

222 Fairfield Tenants Ltd, Minute Book I.

223 Marr, *op. cit.*, 5–6. The main aim of the corporation's dwellings 'which should be self-supporting' was 'to raise the working man's ideal of a dwelling and . . . to set a higher standard for those who are building or may build workmen's dwellings', T.C. Horsfall, *The Place of Admiration, Hope and Love in Town Life* (1910), 7.

224 T.C. Horsfall, *The Housing Question in Manchester* (n.d.), 11.

225 The Didsbury Garden Suburb Provident Co-operative Society Ltd was rather different. It operated a kind of rental-purchase scheme.

226 *BA*, lxxiv (30 September 1910), 218.

227 The relative isolation of Blackley made it necessary to provide at least a few of these amenities, even though they were regarded as inadequate by some.

228 Approximately 670 dwellings had been erected at Alkrington, Blackley, Burnage, Chorltonville, Didsbury and Fairfield Garden Suburbs by 1913–14. Even in 1914, a very bad year for building in Manchester, 748 new dwellings had been erected. In the peak years of 1898 and 1906 over 2,500 houses were built in the city. As fewer houses were being closed as 'unfit for human habitation' in the years before the war, because of the MOH's desire not to increase overcrowding, it can be seen that these scheme's did not make a great quantitative impact. Cf. S.M. Gaskell, 'Housing estate development', 303, who writes 'Out of the 2955 houses erected by societies connected with the Co-partnership Tenants Limited by 1913, only 640 rented for below 6s. a week, 1,912 for between 6s. and 20s. and 155 for over 20s. a week. The Societies appealed to middle class tenants, as they did to middle class values.'

229 T.C. Horsfall, *Town Planning and National Life* (1908), 17.

230 *Municipal J.*, 14 June 1907, 507; *MG.*, 18 February 1913.

231 *MCN*, 20 May 1911; *MG*, 15 May 1911; *AR*, xxviii (1910), 145–9. The Warburton Lectures at the University of Manchester: R. Neville, *Garden Cities* (1904); P. Waterhouse, *Old Towns and New Needs* (1912); R. Unwin, *The Town Extension Plan* (1912); B.S. Rowntree and A.C. Pigou, *Lectures on Housing* (1914).

232 *MG*, 18 February 1914.

233 MCP, 2 August 1911 and 7 August 1912.

234 MCP, *Epitome*, 29 January 1914.

235 *MG*, 16 July 1912.

236 *Ibid.*

237 *Ibid.*

238 *Ibid.*

239 MCP, 10 June 1914.

240 Manchester Corporation Sanitary Committee, *Housing of the Working Classes*, *op. cit.*,

10; Marr, *op.cit.*, 10.

241 Quoted in Manchester Corporation Tramways, *Report by the Special Sub-Committee on Fares and Stages*, 27 August 1907, 14.

242 Manchester Corporation Tramways Committee, *The Passenger Transportation Problem* (1914) 136.

243 *Ibid.*

244 Manchester Corporation Tramways, *op.cit.*, (1907), 6. The report pointed out that in Manchester all cars run before 7 a.m. were regarded as workmen's trams. In the evening, however, only one workmen's car was run on each route, ordinary fares being charged on all other tramcars. The report recommended that the 2d., 3d. and 4d. stages be lowered before any consideration was given to workmen's return tickets. In 1907 the average ordinary fare per mile was 0.472d., whilst the workmen's fare was 0.292d.

245 MCP, 21 February 1912.

246 Greville and Holt, 'Railway development in Manchester – 3', 766.

247 See Todd, *op.cit.*, 75.

248 MCP, 4 January 1899.

249 For criticism of this concept see G. Stedman Jones, *Outcast London* (1971), 198–9 and 213–14.

250 *MG*, 4 October 1909.

251 'Housing classes' are distinguished from one another by their strength in the housing market. See J. Rex 'Sociology of a zone of transition', in Pahl, *op.cit.*, 212–14.

252 Marr, *op.cit.*, 15.

253 Quoted in Creese, *op.cit.*, 288.

254 Rex, *op.cit.*, 213. See *MOH Report*, 1907.

255 Marr, *op.cit.*, 81.

256 E.D. Simon and J. Inman, *The Rebuilding of Manchester* (1935), 152–3.

257 B.S. Rowntree and A.C. Pigou, *Lectures on Housing* (1914), 8–9. See also *MG*, 8 April 1913, which points out that builders were more profitably employed constructing or reconstructing factories.

258 *MG*, 30 September 1913. See *MG*, 16 March 1914, for Manchester and Salford House Famine Committee.

259 Labour pressure led to the introduction of rent controls in 1915. For Manchester see L. Bather, 'A history of Manchester and Salford Trades Council', (Ph. D. thesis, University of Manchester, 1956), 176–8.

260 Quoted in B.B. Gilbert, *British Social Policy 1914–1939* (1970), 15.

261 A. Trystan Edwards, 'A criticism of the garden city movement', *TPR*, IV (1913), 150–7.

262 C.F.G. Masterman, *The Condition of England* (1960 edn), 76.

263 See, for instance, H.R. Aldridge, *The Case for Town Planning* (1915), 130–1. The general death rate at Bournville was 5.7 per 1000, in Manchester it was 19.98. The death rate at Blackley was 13.7 per 1000.

264 *RIBA Town Planning Conference* (1911), 341.

265 W. Ashworth, *The Genesis of Modern British Town Planning* (1954), 194.

266 Local Government Board, *Report of the Committee on Building Construction in Connection with the Provision of Dwellings for the Working Classes in England and Wales and Scotland* (Tudor Walters Committee), British Parliamentary Papers, 1918, VII (Cd. 9191); Ministry of Reconstruction Advisory Committee, *Report of the Women's Housing Sub-Committee, First Interim Report*, British Parliamentary Papers, 1918 x, 629 (Cd. 9166); *Final Report*, British Parliamentary Papers, 1918 x, 637 (Cd. 9232).

267 *RIBA* Town Planning Conference, *op.cit.*, 67.

The contribution of Sir Raymond Unwin (1863–1940) and R. Barry Parker (1867–1947) to the development of site planning theory and practice c. 1890–1918

MICHAEL G. DAY

The contribution of Sir Raymond Unwin (1863–1940) and R. Barry Parker (1867–1947) to the development of site planning theory and practice c. 1890–1918

MICHAEL G. DAY

1 Introduction

This essay, which is a summary of an M.A. thesis of the same title presented to the University of Manchester in 1973, describes and analyses only one aspect of the wide-ranging careers of these internationally distinguished pioneers of modern British town planning – the part they played in the development of site planning theory and practice. Their place in the history of the town planning movement is astride the old order and the new. They formed the practical link between the Victorian social and housing reformers and the central government housing programmes of the twentieth century.

To assess the contribution and influence of Parker and Unwin this section traces the development of their site-planning ideas and analyses a selection of their executed works. Their contribution as writers is evaluated as is Unwin's government work.

The main influences in the careers of Parker and Unwin were twofold: firstly, the very strong climate of social reform which stemmed philosophically from the Oxford socialist group – Ruskin, Maurice, Green and Toynbee; secondly, the artistic revolt against drudgery and the machine age, exemplified in Carpenter, Morris and the arts and crafts movement. These strands instilled in them a concern for human welfare and led them to a particular field of social action – architecture and town planning.

Parker and Unwin were in revolt against everything which was ugly and poor in life around them. Thus they believed that town planning was a complex craft rather than a free art; it was the art of the possible and the well doing of what needed doing. It was also common sense. It is not without significance that Unwin especially was gifted with 'judgement as to what was practicable'.[1]

The early work of Parker and Unwin, at New Earswick, Letchworth and Hampstead Garden Suburb, afforded valuable pioneer experience of the possibilities of raising the national standard of housing and indeed marked a new approach towards the creation of a better environment for the whole community. This work contributed to the recognition by government of what could and should be achieved in the rehousing of the working classes and thus helped to commit the nation to the principle of subsidizing public housing.

The aims of Parker and Unwin as practitioners were to help the community to promote health, welfare and amenity – particularly for the working classes. No other architects or planners had hitherto wholeheartedly devoted themselves to improving the lot of this section of the community. Their designs changed traditional relationships of dwelling and environment. They replaced the bye-law terrace with the low-density, 12-to-the-acre, house and garden. Hitherto, low-density dwellings, although not untried, had rarely been provided for the working classes. The influence of this development can be seen in estates built today. Parker and Unwin developed the concept in accordance with their ideals of community and co-operation. Their layouts were designed to produce landscaped communal open spaces with recreation areas as well as large individual gardens, and to accommodate other facilities including shops, schools and halls. Their site planning concepts, inspired in part by the village and the village green, evolved from communal areas, through courtyards, to the cul-de-sac, and eventually led to the superblock or neighbourhood. Clarence Perry cites the work of Parker and Unwin at Hampstead Garden Suburb, 'in which neighbourhood institutions have been happily grouped, shops conveniently and yet unobtrusively located, and the beauties of the original landscape have been preserved,'[2] suggesting that much of the finer residential planning in America had been 'influenced by the craftsmanship of English town planners as exemplified in Hampstead Garden Suburb.'[3] 'The town planners' function', said Unwin in 1910, 'is to provide a form of expression for the expanding life of the town which shall minister to the convenience of that life, shall be thoroughly incorporated with the site over which development is to spread.'[4] To Parker and Unwin their function was to make provision for the needs, and afford satisfaction for the aspirations, of an organized community. They believed in an ordered society. They believed, too, that town planning – or 'civic art', as they had previously called it – was also a 'democratic art', and that the public should participate in the plan-making process. Fifty years before Skeffington,[5] Unwin stated that 'as citizens . . . you should study and discuss plans . . . the city plan should express the ideals and provide for the needs of the citizens; in order to do this effectively the plans and reports should be published on the widest possible basis and exhibitions and general discussions held.'[6]

Their belief that well-planned physical conditions promoted social welfare never faltered. They held that with proper planning 'the increased opportunities and amenities which may be provided in connection with work and play, education and culture, may reasonably be expected to exert a similar beneficial influence on the social life and corporate spirit of the community.'[7] No less strong was the belief of Parker and Unwin that 'the evidence as to the marked beneficial effects of good dwellings upon human occupants is decisive.'[8] Indeed, their contribution to the evolution of modern domestic architecture has not been fully recognized to date. In Osborn's opinion, for sheer aesthetic craftsmanship Parker was probably the more gifted but it was to Unwin that Parker owed the clear thinking-out of the function of the dwelling and its garden and surroundings as a home for the human family.[9] Much of their creative energy was spent developing and improving the internal design and space standards of the individual dwelling and its relation to garden space. They democratized the stylistic achievement of their time, making great advances in the planning of the smallest dwelling, in economy of construction and road layout, and in aesthetic landscaping and grouping of dwellings. They pioneered the provision of internal bathrooms and toilets, adequate space standards, and proper sunlighting standards for the working-class dwelling. Their work in this field, especially that of Unwin for the Tudor Walters Committee (1918) and at the Ministry of Health, transformed popular housing standards at home and abroad.

Parker and Unwin believed in order, community, co-operation and a degree of physical determinism; these were strong messages in their writings. Unwin's achievements as a writer were particularly outstanding. He penned the first modern comprehensive study of the principles of town planning, civic design and site planning, *Town Planning in Practice* (1909). This was both a scholarly study and a manual of techniques, and it became a standard text in both Europe and America. Earlier Parker and Unwin had published a collection of papers and speeches under the title of *The Art of Building a Home* (1901). In effect, the early articles of Parker and Unwin were illustrated instructions on how to design. For example, 'Cottage plans and common sense' (1902) and 'Cottages near a town' (1903) provide the methodological base for an eager and pioneering planning movement. *Nothing Gained by Overcrowding* (1912) was a major landmark in planning literature and can perhaps be considered the most influential of all Unwin's publications. It provided the economic and aesthetic arguments for low-density development which, whether fully understood or not, influenced most housing layout up to 1939. The impact in America was significant. Buttressed by personal association between Parker and Unwin and Stein and Wright, it led to Radburn, New Jersey, which, in turn, was the model that was to most influence site planning thought in this country after 1945.

Whilst never being as prolific a writer as Unwin, Parker published many practical and instructive articles. Between 1911 and 1914 he wrote a series of 28 articles on town planning, architecture and landscape design for an American publication, the *Craftsman*. These articles constitute a remarkable record of how the environmental-design disciplines of town planning, architecture and landscape design are interrelated and show the wide range and depth of Parker's understanding of the nature of design. They remain worthy of study today. Although the impact of Parker's writing was clearly less than that of Unwin, his part in helping Unwin to formulate his ideas must not be overlooked.

As teachers, the contribution of Parker and Unwin was no less significant. Both lectured at the Architectural Association (1911), and at Birmingham University Unwin was the first lecturer in town planning (1911–14). Later Unwin lectured extensively in America, particularly at Columbia University, New York (1936–8). His style of lecturing, first developed during his early propagandist days, was meticulous and effective and those who listened testify that the teaching was inspirational.[10]

That Parker and Unwin were reformers, there is no doubt. Their socialist background (both were members of the Fabian Society[11] and both firm believers in land nationalization[12]) speaks for their radical opinions. Unwin claimed that in 1931 the slums of London still brought out the 'latent revolutionary' in him.[13]

In 1921, Adshead attested to Unwin's contribution as a technician by claiming that: 'Unwin fully justified his right to be regarded as the foremost pioneer in the technicalities of town planning. Unwin had opened up vast fields of research.'[14] *Nothing Gained by Overcrowding* was the synthesis of the ideas of Parker and Unwin on residential density, developed as they were through a long process of trial and error. Unwin was not doctrinaire, rather a man of practical and scientific habit. Parker's strengths in these areas are exemplified by such matters as his proposals for dealing with motor traffic in town planning (e.g. his introduction of service roads, roundabouts, the parkway, etc., at Wythenshawe, 1927–41). Unwin, especially in his government work, was able to assimilate and codify many kinds of information in order to produce reports and manuals for the instruction and guidance of others, such as the Tudor Walters report and Ministry of Health housing manuals.

As the first modern town planners, Parker and Unwin pioneered many new practices. They were the first to practise the planning methodology of their friend, Patrick Geddes, 'Survey – Analysis – Plan'.[15] They also devised and implemented development control techniques at Letchworth and Hampstead which provided the models for government legislation and the basis of many of our methods today.

2   The early life and work of Raymond Unwin and Barry Parker

Raymond Unwin was born at Whiston, near Rotherham, Yorkshire, on 2 November 1863, the second son of William Unwin and Elizabeth Sully. Unwin's father was in the cloth trade but whilst Raymond was still a child the business failed, because, according to his son, 'my father was always more interested in study than commerce and I am afraid that sometimes the customers had to wait downstairs because he was immersed in a book upstairs.'[16] William Unwin was one of the generation who had to confront the shock of modern biological and geological science with its proofs that much of the Old Testament was myth and not history. By way of his friendship with T.H. Green, William Unwin was in touch with the school of Oxford reformers associated with the names of Ruskin, Green and Toynbee. To pursue William Unwin's interests, the family moved to Oxford in 1873 or 1874, and Raymond's father took his degree there at the age of 50.[17] Brought up among 'liberal ideas in religion and politics',[18] the young Unwin proceeded with his education at Magdalen College School where, by his own admission, he conferred no lustre on the school and won no prizes.[19] During the latter part of his education Raymond became interested in social questions. This interest derived from his father, who by then had graduated from Balliol College and was working as a poorly paid extra-collegiate coach to supplement a private income from property in Sheffield.[20]

Upon leaving school there followed four years of uncertainty for Raymond Unwin and he seems to have spent his time travelling around the country. It was during this period that he met Edward Carpenter, the socialist poet, when Carpenter was giving university extension lectures at Chesterfield in the winter of 1880–1.[21] Unwin acknowledged that Carpenter, and his book *Towards Democracy*, published in 1884, became a great influence in his life.[22] But it was only in April 1884 that Unwin developed a lasting friendship with Carpenter. In 1939 Unwin observed retrospectively that 'among the men, evangelists, artists, poets whom the socialist movement inspired or captivated, Edward Carpenter holds a unique place ... for he was at once most penetrating in thought, most delicate in feeling, most lucid in expression, most intimate in his personal relations and affections. These qualities, with many others, constituted a personality, and led to a life, as complete and beautiful as they were rare.'[23] Much earlier, and more simply, Unwin had described Carpenter as being 'thoroughly simple and boyish ... thoroughly genuine'.[24]

Carpenter believed that there was something in the idea of trying to make religion meet socialism – so proving that it was capable of meeting the needs of the people. This strengthened Unwin's own feeling that he was not inclined merely to teach socialism and keep Christianity to himself, arguing that the two must go together although the matter of social justice was of first importance.[25] Unlike his brother William, who eagerly took up the opportunity of a university education with a view to joining the Anglican Church, Unwin was prepared only to submit to a university education and then decide upon the question of an ecclesiastical career. According to family legend,[26] at this crucial time in his development he received advice from Canon Barnett who founded Toynbee Hall and was later to be connected with Hampstead Garden Suburb. He directed Unwin onto a practical if not too certain path by asking him, 'Raymond, are you more interested in making people good or making them happy?' Unwin's reply was to resolve against university and thence the Church. Feeling the overwhelming complexity and urgency of the social problem when 'intercourse with working people and close contact with their lives'[27] brought home to him the contrast with all that he had known in his Oxford home, Unwin turned again to Edward Carpenter.

This path led Unwin, in February 1885, to Queens Park, Manchester, as a draughtsman-fitter in a 'dreary office',[28] probably attached to a cotton mill. Unwin did not feel himself suited to the work and applied himself to his engineering theory with little enthusiasm. As his letters show, he did not consider this his real 'work'; his more important role, he felt, was his work for socialism.

At this time Unwin was corresponding with Ethel Parker, much against the wishes of her father. It is clear from the letters that by far the most important influence on the direction of Unwin's life during this period was a book by James Hinton, the surgeon and socialist philosopher, entitled *The Lawbreaker*, which Unwin took as his 'gospel'; to the extent that he was convinced that 'there is only one law by which a Christian is bound and that is the service of man . . . service of man is all.'[29]

Even though Unwin had found his 'gospel' – and it was not to leave him – he was frustrated in its practical application. Not until a year later was he to find his ultimate direction; for if Carpenter and Hinton gave the larger frame to his thoughts, it was William Morris who influenced their final shape. Unwin generously credits Morris with developing his interest in the 'inter-relation of planning, design and social reform'.[30] It was the robust personality of Morris and his crusade for the restoration of beauty to daily life and more gladness in work that gave Unwin 'inspiration'.[31] Unwin regarded Morris as one of the first to recognize that the haphazard muddle of urban life 'must give way to design and planning'.[32] It is not difficult to understand why the ideas of Morris, the architect, poet and socialist, struck the young Unwin so indelibly and forcibly, for they appealed by combining art and socialism. Morris translated socialism practically and artistically, believing architecture to be an all-embracing art; this was just the interpretation towards which Unwin was striving. Much of the teaching of Morris, implanted at that time, manifests itself in Unwin's later work. It clearly influenced his concern for suitability of building materials, preservation of trees and natural features, craftsmanship and less ornamentation. In 1884 Morris said decency of surroundings included 'good lodging, ample space, general order and beauty. That is our houses must be well built, clean and healthy. There must be abundant garden space in our towns and our towns must not eat up our fields and natural features of the country.'[33] This could equally well have been said by Unwin 20 years later when health, light and air were Unwin's watchwords. Similarly, Unwin was influenced by Morris in terms of principles of architectural style. 'Let us be humble and begin once more with the style of well constructed, fairly proportioned brick homes ... which look snug and comfortable,'[34] states Morris. Unwin was to write in much the same terms.

In 1885, whilst working in Manchester, Unwin met Morris and his friend, Ford Maddox Brown, who was painting the frescoes in the town hall there.[35] Unwin was already an activist member of a Manchester socialist society with a membership of 43.[36] He wished to be identified with the working classes and loathed his own 'respectability'. 'I walk about', he said, 'and alternatively loathe the people and long to be one with them.'[37] It was to take Unwin some time to overcome this feeling. He 'preached, agitated or educated'[38] on Manchester's street corners to groups of up to 200, on topics ranging from temperance and women's rights to freedom and independence, at a time when socialist groups in Manchester were being harassed by the local police.[39] To aid the cause Morris came to lecture on 'Socialism: the ends and the means' at the Ancoats Brotherhood,[40] of which Unwin was a member,[41] and 'Socialist tactics and organization' at the County Forum. From this time onwards, it seems Unwin became more involved in socialist activities and when Morris founded the Manchester branch of his Socialist League, in 1886, Unwin was its first secretary.[42]

Little else is known of Unwin's activities at this time but from his correspondence it is clear that he was troubled by his 'failure' in Manchester, presumably his failure in his socialist work, and it is apparent that his membership of the Manchester branch of the Socialist League ceased with his removal to Staveley, Derbyshire, in May 1887. Nevertheless he carried on with his socialist preaching upon arrival in Derbyshire, and from March 1887 he began to write regularly for the socialist press, chiefly *Today* and *The Commonweal*, expounding his ideas more formally, claiming that 'nothing short of revolution will do'.[43] Workers' co-operation rather than competition was the future way, he believed, and patching up evil effects instead of removing their causes would not do. Although recognizing the worth of eminent social experiments such as those of Robert Owen and other philanthropists, he believed that 'society smells no smells that aren't forced up its nose'.[44] Clearly, Unwin's socialism was that of a discontented man. Hinting that his discontent was already partly directed to the physical environment, he said, 'to be a socialist nowadays a man must first have enough discontent with his surroundings to look for something better.'[45]

Here then are the roots of Unwin's skills as pamphleteer, propagandist, orator, organizer and persuader, attributes which were to prove potent in his later life. He had learned that 'an argument is no use unless it is based upon some ground which your opponent will admit',[46] a contrast, by his own admission, to the attitude of the 'self-opinionated, cocksure' boy of his schooldays.[47]

At this time Unwin was also developing his design skills. His new job, which he had begun on 2 May 1887 and which lasted until he joined Parker in partnership at Buxton in 1896, was as head draughtsman and subsequently as 'engineer and architect'[48] for the Staveley Coal and Iron Company. Indeed, he considered himself a designer,[49] having previously had only two skills, 'drawing and fitting'.[50] He was still not content with engineering, partly because of his 'double life'[51] with socialism and partly because of his lack of enthusiasm for his work. However, with pay rises and more interesting work he continued at Staveley,[52] asserting that he could stick to anything he had really made up his mind about.[53]

Staveley was the seat of a vast iron works, with associated coal mines, owned by the Staveley Coal and Iron Company. The company had been formed in 1863 and by 1891 employed 4,000 men.[54] Each company on the coalfield built cottages for its workers. Therefore small settlements, of about 200–300 cottages each, grew up around the pit heads. Those built by the Staveley Company included Barrow Hill (1864), Barlborough (1875), Hartington (1877), Markham (1888), Arkright Town (1890–5), Poolsbrook(1891) and Warsop Vale (1893–4).[55] Unwin's early work for the company involved designing pit-face and pit-head machinery such as cranes and gantries, but about 1890 he became involved with cottage design. The company's cottages were in long terraces to minimum standards, although the terraces were spaced widely. The cottages had a small parlour and back kitchen, a pantry beneath the stairs, two or three bedrooms upstairs with no bathroom, and an outside toilet and coal house. Although the individual cottage design shows little development over time, in the later settlements it is noticeable that more land is given over to community facilities and recreational activity. This may have been due to Unwin's influence, for only he and George Bond, the general manager, seem to have worked on the designs. A church, shop, public house, allotments, cricket field and football pitch appear at Warsop Vale. The company always required that the cottages should be built at the minimum cost. The cottages at Poolsbrook were built for £118 each and at Warsop Vale for £123 each.[56]

The conditions in the mines were very bad and if mining accidents did not kill or cripple, then there was always the possibility that typhoid fever in the pit villages would. Cleanliness was a necessity and Parker credits Unwin with the idea of introducing pithead baths.[57] This may have been a reference to fitting bathrooms in each cottage, which was certainly Unwin's aim by 1901. Williams suggests that pithead baths, as we know them today, were not introduced into the area until Emerson Bainbridge built them at Bolsover in 1904,[58] near Creswell model village designed by Percy Houfton in 1898. The idea, however, had been mooted a great deal earlier and the Staveley Company did construct what they called 'baths at the works' in August 1892.[59] But this only entailed leaving open for bathing one section of an old canal which was being infilled at the works.

The various activities of the Staveley Coal and Iron Company provided Parker and Unwin with their first opportunities for joint work. Richard Barry Parker, the eldest son of Robert Parker, a Chesterfield bank manager, had a more conservative upbringing than his half-cousin. Barry Parker was born in Chesterfield on 18 November 1867, but, owing to his father's ill health and the family's consequent removal to Ashover, then back to Chesterfield and finally on to Buxton, his education was frequently interrupted. This was doubly unfortunate for he did not shine at school work. Unlike the Unwins, the Parker family were financially independent and Barry's future was his own choice. John Parker, Robert's late brother and a tanner of Mansfield, had settled his money on his brother's children. It was part of this money which purchased the Track Ring at Buxton from the Duke of Devonshire, where Barry was to design and build his first houses. Barry Parker's formal artistic training began in 1886 upon leaving Ashover school at the age of 19.[60] He enrolled at Thomas Charles Simmons' studios, Derby, later to become known as the 'Ateliers of Art', and seems to have been there for almost two years.[61] 'One entire year', Parker tells us, 'was devoted to work among draughtsmen engaged exclusively in pattern design such as is usually applied to carpets and wallpaper. Other considerable terms were spent in gaining technical knowledge of design and workmanship of different crafts.'[62] From Simmons, a landscape painter, Parker probably gained his love for that art form and the basic skills of draughtsmanship and compositional design.

Wishing to acquire a solid background of general knowledge on artistic matters, Parker enrolled as a student at the South Kensington School of Art in the summer of 1888. Much of his time was spent in the British Museum sketching the work of other ages including Egyptian and medieval designs. He studied nature, anatomy, geometry, perspective, principles of design and history of art – too exacting for an indolent student, for his notebook shows that he spent more time at lectures sketching the other students than making notes. He left the school after only three months but seems to have become an external student until 1890.

Following his London adventure, Parker made his first step towards an architectural career when he returned north to Altrincham, near Manchester, and became articled to G. Faulkner Armitage, the artist, interior designer and restorer of buildings. Armitage had long held a prominent place in the public, social and religious life of the district. At the 1887 Manchester Jubilee exhibition, Armitage was commissioned to decorate the central nave and dome of the main building. He also 'showed some excellent rooms – kitchen, parlour, bedroom, designed by him for the use of the working man in which the furniture was very good and substantial.'[63] Creese notes that a sketch of the Armitage kitchen suggests the later warmth and utility of Parker's domestic interiors, particularly in its focus on the brick fire-place, high-backed settle, and built-in cupboards.[64] The search for an ideal cottage design was already discernible in the work of Armitage, along with the ancillary problem that was destined to plague Parker and Unwin far into the future – how to arrive at a superior and tasteful effect, 'at a price such as a thrifty artizan could be supposed capable of paying.'[65] Unwin too would have known Armitage's work, for he visited the exhibition on 15 July 1887.[66]

Of this period in Manchester, Parker tells us that the more he learned the more he felt his own limitations with regard to the practical side of the work in which he meant to engage. 'Being determined not to remain content with office and academic training', he states, 'I spent three more years working upon buildings of one sort or another in the process of construction, acting as clerk of works . . . and assistant or pupil to clerk of works.'[67] This gave him the opportunity to discuss and work out at first hand each difficulty by working over it with the man in whose department it happened to be. This restoration and construction work was carried out in Carleon, Monmouthshire and Ross, Herefordshire.[68] As clerk of works to Armitage he helped remodel Brockhampton Court Hotel, Brockhampton-by-Ross. The core of the house was a late 'eighteenth century' rectory, 'the tower is dated 1793 and the whole is a big composition in a neo-Tudor style, decidedly pre-Lethaby . . . the lodge . . . is in a florid imitation Jacobean black and white.'[69] Mrs Parker remarked that her husband would have gladly spent his whole life restoring such buildings.[70]

Parker indicates that when it was time for him to start in practice he went to live with the Unwins at Chapel-en-le-Frith. This was probably about Christmas 1893, shortly after Unwin had married Barry's sister, Ethel. Parker tells us that it was about the time when Unwin was 'planning many miners' cottages, houses for managers and others, schools and other buildings in mining villages.'[71] Among these was St Andrew's church, Barrow Hill, designed in February 1894, for which Parker designed the fixtures and fittings. The church had been proposed and financed by the Staveley Company in April 1892.[72] This was probably their very first joint project, for the partners meticulously preserved the drawings of the designs. The towerless church is 'red brick with short pairs of lancet windows and a friendly interior with open timber roof starting low down on corbels.'[73] Parker's designs show an understanding eye for use of materials and colour, whilst Unwin's more simple design of the church as a whole still shows an engineer's hand tempered with a developing understanding of space and proportion.

Earlier, in September 1891, on a site next to the church, the company had proposed that a new infant school should be built at a cost of £1,300 on land given by the Duke of Devonshire.[74] This brick-built school is probably amongst the buildings mentioned by Parker as being of Unwin's design. The school has a charm recaptured later by the partners in their designs for the New Earswick school in 1912. Unwin's preoccupation with light and fresh air is reflected in the use of large windows and good orientation.

The informal nature of the partnership between Parker and Unwin, which was to continue as it had begun, reflects the implicit trust and respect that existed between the two men. No partnership agreement was ever drawn up in legal form or even committed to writing. It was not necessary, although Parker tells us that there was an agreement as to whose decision should be final, but leaves us to ponder which partner had that responsibility.[75]

They had first come to know each other well just before Unwin left Magdalen College School in 1880, when Unwin was 17 and Parker 'a sensitive, imaginative boy of thirteen'.[76] Parker also tells us that they had 'quite decided . . . to go into partnership some day',[77] and that during his training and assistantships, whenever proposals were made to him which bore on his future, he always replied that it was settled. Mrs Parker recalls that it was Parker's sister, Ethel, who prompted the move, having resigned herself to the fact that her brother was not to be a second William Morris, and noting that her husband, Unwin, had compensating qualities that her brother lacked.[78] However, it seems clear that Parker and Unwin had already formally decided upon their future by 1891, when Unwin wrote in a letter to Ethel Parker that her brother wanted Unwin and himself to set up as architects, he doing 'the artistic' and Unwin 'the practical'.[79] In the same letter, Unwin described his future partner as 'a nice lad, tho' he has a few faults rather aggravating. It is not nice to see him giving so much trouble to those about him through indolence or easiness.' He ends with a more kindly summing up, declaring that Parker's 'share of faults is not large and they are not deep ones.' Much later Unwin described his deep gratitude to Parker for his tolerance in teaching him the ways of architecture and his lifelong help in their partnership.[80] Parker, in his turn, described his partner's outstanding characteristics in an obituary notice as 'singleness of purpose and the strength of that purpose, selflessness, the absence of personal ambition, hopefulness, buoyancy and courage.'[81] Parker continued that in Unwin's singleness of purpose were included everything for 'justice, humanity, friendship, sympathy, and equality of opportunity among the whole of mankind.'[82]

The essence of the partnership was the blend of technical skills and personal characteristics. Unwin had the ability to conceptualize accurately the nature of a whole problem and the skill to create a design to help solve it, whilst Parker had the finesse to enable him to devise ways of achieving the small-scale intricacies necessary to implement the concept. Similarly, the shy, retiring, ruminative and sensitive Parker was complemented by the unflagging, mentally alert and energetic Unwin. Unwin could bring harmony into the most discordant gathering and find wise and hopeful solutions to almost any difficulties. Their individual characteristics shine through their photographs – the reposeful Parker and the keen, hawk-like Unwin.

3 Principles of domestic architecture, 1895–1901

In this period the partners, confident in their own skills, began to publish their ideas on architecture in a series of articles which culminated in the publication in 1901 of their first book, *The Art of Building a Home*. From this period onward the partners were amongst the most prolific and original writers on planning and architecture in modern times.

An analysis of the early writing shows two major lines of influence. The first was plainly architectural. Parker's articles deal with interior design and principles of architecture. The second was social. Unwin's contributions increasingly show, through his involvement in mining village planning and his co-operative socialist convictions, an extension of his partner's ideas into the field of planning and layout of housing areas. This development culminated with the partners' exhibit and associated article, 'Cottages near a town', for the 1903 exhibition of Walter Crane's Northern Art Workers' Guild in Manchester.[83] It can be said that at this exhibition the partners pioneered the concept of residential site planning (that is the consideration of the planning and layout of a settlement as a whole community) as an art in itself separate from the skills of engineering, architecture or surveying. The link between these two strong, influential strands was the partners' joint acceptance, from their different approaches, of the ideas of the arts and crafts movement.

Parker left the Unwins for Buxton in 1895 because of his father's illness and set up an office there, where Unwin joined him the following year; 1896 was also the year of Unwin's registration as a member of the Society of Architects. Their office was in the fashionable Quadrant, adjacent to the Crescent and Paxton's town park. The partnership was almost extended in 1899 to include Unwin's socialist friend and neighbour, John Bruce Glasier, who himself had trained as an architect, but Glasier declined, preferring to pursue his socialist activities.[84] A clear underlying factor in the partners' architectural and planning ideas at this time was their aspiration to improve the physical environment, especially that of the working classes. This was reinforced by their adherence to the commonly-held belief that physical surroundings influenced people's character and behaviour. Already in 1895 Parker believed this factor to be underrated,[85] a point he was still trying to drive home 12 years later. 'It is difficult', he said, 'to over-estimate the importance, or ... the enormous influence for good of beautiful surroundings and the degrading influence of ugly surroundings.'[86] Further, the partners believed that, apart from the skill of the designer, the only way to improve the environment was to educate the public to demand better surroundings.[87] 'Unity, completeness, comfort and repose'[88] were Parker's simple Ruskinian architectural tenets, which Unwin interpreted at the broad scale in his planning.

'Unity' meant unity and harmony in design, involving sympathetic treatment of proportion and scale and the understanding use of materials. 'See that building is done', said Parker, 'as simply, easily and straightforwardly as possible ... composed naturally ... thoroughly effective, practical and artistic.'[89] Further, Parker believed that 'the most potent factor in artistic success or failure in the designing of small houses was the relation of solids and voids'[90] and that 'the right use of

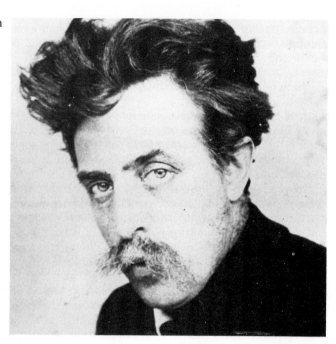

Figure 20. Raymond Unwin as a young man.

Figure 21. Barry Parker as a young man.

materials is really the whole art of architecture, and the selection of the right material to use is certainly not the least part of this.'[91] The partners believed that local materials were best, for they tended, quietly and unostentatiously, to create a style characteristic of the neighbourhood.[92] Unlike others in the arts and crafts movement, however, Parker was not opposed to new materials or methods of work: 'we should welcome', he said, 'all new materials and processes on their true merits, without prejudice'; and he observed perceptively that 'concrete blocks have a great future before them', and that 'standardising' was a means of reducing the cost of building which could not and must not be neglected.[93]

'Completeness' meant completeness and continuity of style, the creation of a whole design, embracing the house, its furniture, its garden. 'It is essential to any good result', Parker insisted, 'that one man should design the house as a whole, not necessarily that he should design everything in it, or draw with his own hand every detail; but he must exercise a controlling power, selecting where he does not design, and ensuring that the work of all may be done in a spirit of co-operation towards a complete whole which he planned.'[94] One of Parker's earliest opportunities to demonstrate this principle was 'Moorlands', the house he built for his father in Buxton during 1893–4,[95] whilst still under the eye of Armitage. It was a large, stone, three-storey house set in one corner of the plot, somewhat ungainly in its proportions but nevertheless a bold design. The interior of the house is bright, a product of the designer's insistence on good orientation for an abundance of sunlight. But the design is contrived to obtain this effect, which leads to some awkward angles and corners. It was perhaps a saving grace that the furniture was designed for the house, thus enabling the architect to fill the difficult angles with specially designed fittings. The wooden furniture, in a simple vernacular style is – like the house – bold and well executed. Parker designed every fixture, even including the door knobs. The ingle nook, which later became a recurring feature in the partners' work, also appears. The garden, including a rock garden, is simple; and adjacent large trees, which were probably there at the time the house was built, emphasize the large scale of the house. Although Parker and later the partnership were commissioned to design many such houses, the real development of their cottage architecture, for which they are most remembered, did not mature until their work at New Earswick. Their cottage architecture followed the then contemporary style of Voysey and others, and, indeed, the partners' links with Voysey were close. Stanley, Barry's brother, a furniture designer who made most of his brother's furniture, had been a pupil of Voysey and much later Voysey's son, Cowles, was a pupil in Barry Parker's Letchworth office.[96]

'Comfort' was the comfort of convenience and comeliness, ensuring that the user was at ease with the design. This was reflected in simple interiors, the proper functional arrangements of fires, doors and windows, and the use of such features as the ingle nook which provided a feeling of protection and security as well as a physically secluded, draught-free, intimate area. The partners considered that 'a room must always derive its dignity or meanness from and reflect somewhat the character and kind of occupation carried on in it.'[97] They further recommended that to understand a client's family life, and his personality, it would be a good thing if the designer could always spend a few days in the client's old home before designing him a new one.[98] This factor highlights one reason why the partners were so successful in designing small houses and cottages. Unwin had lived and worked in working-class communities and understood their wants and needs. Few other contemporary architects could claim such intimate, first-hand knowledge.

'Repose' was the repose of an object designed for its place. Parker, reaffirming his arts and crafts beliefs, stated that 'the first essential in the form and design of any decorative object (and everything in a room should be a decorative object) is reposefulness',[99] for 'most things to look right and happy in their places must be designed for their places'.[100] On no account should there be 'over-decoration'. Unwin was fond of relating a story about William Morris, who upon visiting the Glasiers at Chapel-en-le-Frith, was commissioned by a wealthy but not very intelligent woman of the district to design some stone cottages for her estate. Morris designed these cottages with very stark interiors. The woman was rather disappointed at their austerity and asked Morris how she should decorate them, and was astonished by his curt reply, 'with flitches of bacon, madam!'[101] Certainly, the partners concurred with these sentiments. Unwin designed his own cutlery, linens and curtains, and was never seen wearing anything but Ruskin tweeds. In the house, in which his family lived a simple, frugal life, he always wore Carpenter sandals.[102]

These tenets of unity, completeness, comfort and repose thus formed the basis of the partners' design discipline. Parker, at the outset of their work, pointed the way in which they were to seek to extend the application of these ideas, claiming that 'insofar as we do these we shall rise above the mere planners of houses, and take our place in the work of planning and moulding the future life of the people.'[103] Here Unwin's influence came to the fore with an interpretation of these principles as planning concepts. Unity, completeness, comfort and repose were not only physical concepts, they were social concepts. 'It is the crystallization of the elements in the village', he said, 'in accordance with a definitely organized life of mutual relations, respect or service, which gives the appearance of being an organic whole, the home of a community, to what would otherwise be a mere conglomeration of buildings.'[104] As the object was designed for its place, so the house should be designed for its setting, the village in the countryside, the town in the region. In 1901, being familiar with Ebenezer Howard's book, *Tomorrow: A Peaceful Path to Real Reform*, Unwin was already advocating the relief of overcrowded towns 'by developing hamlets and villages in outlying districts',[105] for 'there is nothing' he declared, 'which it seems more hopeless to harmonize with natural scenery than the modern town suburb.'[106] Unwin considered that 'a successful plan might be to gather the houses and other buildings on three sides of an open space adopting the village green as a model'.[107] He was able to develop this idea in practice at New Earswick and in parts of Letchworth before Hampstead Garden Suburb allowed him to grapple with the problem of suburban development.

4 New Earswick, 1901–4

On 13 December 1904 Joseph Rowntree, the Quaker philanthropist and cocoa manufacturer of York, founded the Joseph Rowntree Village Trust to administer the New Earswick village estate which had come into being in 1901 on the basis of his gift of land and money.[108] By the terms of the trust deed, all income derived from the estate was to be devoted to the improvement and extension of the village.

One of the main aims of the Trust was 'the improvement of the conditions of the working classes ... by provision of improved dwellings with open spaces ... gardens ... and the organisation of village communities with such facilities for the enjoyment of full and healthy lives';[109] another was that the cottages should be 'well-built, convenient, healthy and artistic in design',[110] 'an object lesson to be followed by others'.[111]

In turning to housing and community development, Joseph Rowntree followed the course of action of other earlier and contemporary industrialists, including Owen, Salt, Arkwright, Lever, and his friend George Cadbury to whom he initially turned for practical advice. Additionally, Seebohm Rowntree attended the Garden City Association's 1901 conference at Bournville and probably greatly encouraged his father in his proposed venture.

Cadbury sent one of his architects, Alfred Walker, to York to help Rowntree choose a site for the development.[112] The development was not to be for Rowntree workers alone – a significant difference, this, from almost all other previous 'model' experiments with the exception of Bournville. In 1901, Joseph Rowntree purchased 123 acres of farm land which bordered land already owned by the Rowntree Company, 2½ miles north of York.[113] The purchase of the land was against the advice of Walker. The site was low-lying, flat, sloping to the north and susceptible to flooding which would make drainage and the disposal of sewage difficult. Flooding was in fact a really serious danger, for the River Foss formed the curving eastern boundary to the otherwise rectangularly shaped site, and caused major complications later. The site was bisected by the Haxby Road which ran north from York. The York-Hull railway line of the London & North Eastern Railway, which passed through Earswick station, formed the southern boundary. Thus it came about that the new community adopted the name of New Earswick, which in 1934 was to be constituted as a separate parish.[114]

Parker, recalling the partners' first visit to Earswick, stated that on being commissioned in 1902, on Seebohm Rowntree's advice, they were informed that the object of the development was to 'demonstrate what could be done to improve village and cottage design without exceeding the limits of sound finance.'[115] The development of New Earswick falls into three clearly defined periods, each with its own characteristics. The first period (1901–4), upon which we concentrate here, is prior to the formation of the Trust, when major decisions were made by the founder and his immediate colleagues. The land was purchased and the site plan for almost half the village was largely settled at this time on the basis of proposals made by Parker and Unwin. During the second period (1905–18) it was possible, after an uncertain start, to achieve many of the original objectives of the Trust. During this period the village matured into a community, which found particular expression in elements such as the folk hall, the school and the shops. The third period (1919–46), when Parker alone was the architect, covers that stage of the development when almost all the houses built by the Trust, received State subsidies, and house design was dominated by the need to keep down costs. The possibility of achieving greater economy whilst designing houses within the standards set by the Trust was soon exhausted and the houses inevitably became almost uniform in internal layout and accommodation. The scope for further economy lay in site planning and it is for this aspect that this period is notable.

In the first period (1901–4) the estate developed in an anti-clockwise direction about the centrally-placed village green. Building started in the south-east corner, probably because it was the closest to York and the Rowntree Company works, although that portion of the estate was perhaps the most difficult to develop because of the problem of drainage and flooding. A substantial portion of this area had to be artificially built up with ashes and boiler grit and the river course straightened.[116] These extra works go some way to explaining why the costs of the first 50 cottages were so high.[117]

To understand the significance of the position which New Earswick holds in the history of the housing movement, it is necessary to realize, as Parker pointed out in a lecture, that 'when it was established, housing was almost an undisputed realm of the speculative builder',[118] whom the partners blamed for the worst abuses in house building. Parker and Unwin abhorred this kind of development and were confident that they could build better housing than the 'dreary rows of miserable tenements that we see in all our small suburbs'.[119] The partners' 1904 plan (fig. 22) for over 400 cottages plus public buildings, including provision for a further 300 cottages if necessary, was a much more extensive operation than the founder's original intention. Many of the proposed public, recreational and social facilities which were to be lavished on the development were sited near the green. These included churches, chapels, schools, institutes, a library, shops, swimming pool and a gymnasium. The provision of such facilities, indeed their over-provision, in the plan must be attributed to the partners' enthusiasm rather than the philanthropy of the Trust. The inspiration for the partners was the commonsense application of essential principles such as 'light, sweetness and health'[120] both in the layout of estates and the design of cottages.

Above all else, the layout of the estate is interesting because of its carefully considered informality. The gently curving road pattern, which was to become a common feature in all the partners' later work, with its grass-verged and tree-lined roads east of the Haxby Road, echoes the curve of the river. The slightly more formal road pattern west of Haxby Road reflects the straightness of the estate's western boundary. The offsetting of the terraces at various angles to and at various distances from the road provides an almost unlimited variety of sequential street pictures and additionally numerous glimpses and vistas both into and out of the estate. The partners felt that it was 'important that such glimpses of distance as it is possible to obtain from any of the houses should be contrived to be of the best bits of outlook the site commands.'[121]

The plan was innovatory in the provision of 12 acres for recreation, comprising a linear park, including a children's paddling pool on the banks of the River Foss, a smaller park straddling the stream in the north-west corner of the estate, a children's park at the south-west corner, and provision for children's play areas with sand and other amusements within the safe confines of each section of cottages. Only this last proposal was actually realized, a playground being sited at the junction of Haxby Road and Station Road. Similarly only a handful of public buildings were realised and only the shops were built where originally planned. Successfully implemented, on the other hand, was the network of footpaths complementing the road and building layout. This feature became a characteristic of many of the partners' later designs. It was especially useful because it gave access to the 'backland' areas, allotments and recreation grounds.

One of the major features of both the proposed and the actual layout at New Earswick was the low density of dwellings per acre which, Parker stated, was arrived at through trial, error and experience.[122] The partners were familiar with the Ruskinian idea that a house should not be 'a compartment of a model lodging house, not the number so and so of Paradise Row, but a cottage all of our own, with its garden, its healthy air, its clean kitchen, parlour and bedrooms.'[123] If philosophic and poetic

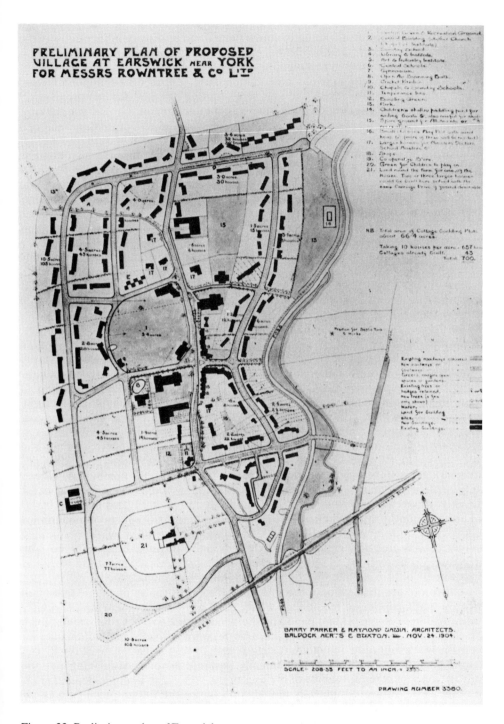

Figure 22. Preliminary plan of Earswick.

justification were not enough, then scientific discoveries of the time were also leading some authorities to think of lower densities. Principally influential was the fact that direct sunlight and health were so strongly connected. It was known that typhoid and tuberculosis germs could live only for a few minutes in direct sunlight but for up to two years in a room which was never exposed to sunlight. In their designs the partners regarded 'sunlight as absolutely essential for healthy lives'.[124] Whilst low-density working-class housing was not uncommon, Unwin was not convinced that the justification for six houses to the acre, as at Bournville, had been established.[125] Indeed, he had argued that the ceiling for such suburban development could be as high as between 20 and 30 houses to the acre including streets. The partners' justification for a density of 10 to 12 dwellings to the acre in terms of economy as well as health and aesthetic criteria did not appear until 1912.[126] The November 1904 plan indicated that the density of dwellings was to be ten to the acre, averaged over the whole estate. The way in which this number was calculated gives an important insight into Parker's statement quoted above. The calculation was based on the average size of garden on the estate, which was 350 square yards – a size determined after careful consideration of 'the amount of land a man could easily and profitably work by spade cultivation in his leisure time'.[127] This, coupled with a dictum that no house should occupy more than one quarter of the site on which it was built, produced an overall density, allowing for recreation areas and roads, of ten dwellings per acre.

The partners also wished to abolish backs, back yards, back alleys and generally, 'the wretched prefix back'.[128] Back projections shaded rooms from sunlight and impeded the circulation of fresh air. Linking Unwin's youthful experience in the quiet cloistered spaces of the colleges at Oxford with their jointly-held socialist belief in co-operation (which in design terms meant the possibility of communal wash-houses, bath houses, kitchens and child-caring facilities), they hoped to solve the layout problem by grouping cottages. 'If, instead of being wasted in stuffy yards and dirty back streets', Unwin pleaded, 'the space which is available for a number of houses were kept together, it would make quite a respectable square or garden. The cottages could then be grouped round such open spaces forming quadrangles opening one into the other, with wide streets at intervals.' By this means, Unwin continued, 'every house could be planned so that there should be a sunny aspect for the chief rooms and a pleasant outlook both front and back.'[129] This more thoughtful arrangement of space gave other benefits. The space in the form of a courtyard could be used for allotments, children's play areas, and gardens, while it provided an increased degree of privacy as overlooking was to a large extent eliminated. The idea was also inspired by the partners' desire to ease the drudgery of the working-class wife by improving her environment both inside and outside the home. It is not too difficult to see the link between this manipulation of space for the benefit of all with the later cul-de-sac techniques which gave not only the benefits previously mentioned but several others, including the saving in the cost of cross streets. Both the quadrangle idea and the chequerboard layout were proposed in the 1904 plan for New Earswick, but only one quadrangle was actually developed, named Ivy Place.

In designing any particular building the partners advocated thinking out the primary functional requirements of the uses of the building in a topological manner. In the case of cottage design they felt that in essence the design problem was the reconciliation of demands for shelter and privacy with those of fresh air and sunlight. The original New Earswick cottages on Western Terrace and Poplar Grove form perhaps the most aesthetically pleasing scheme prepared by the partners throughout their long careers. They are beautifully proportioned and designed, in the idiom of Voysey and Baillie Scott, which was a traditional vernacular style, whitewashed, with gables, barge boards and red tiled roofs. These cottages (blocks 0–42 on Western Terrace and Poplar Grove) were begun in 1902.[130] They were of two types, the workmanship in both of which was of a very high standard,[131] for the partners were insistent that in building, 'work is being done for the future rather than the present'.[132] Those of the first type were non-parlour, through-room cottages mainly in groups of four with a variation in groups of seven and of two. Those of the second type were parlour cottages mainly in groups of four.[133] All conformed to the general Parker-and-Unwin principle that every cottage in the row or group should contain all its rooms and offices under the main roof, and 'present an open and fair surface to sun and air on both its free sides'.[134] A given cubic capacity could also be built more cheaply when it was within the walls under the main roof. The cottages clearly exhibit the partners' design philosophy of 'unity, completeness, comfort and repose'. One interesting feature was the provision in the scullery of a bath with a table top, which the partners considered 'an ideal which some day will surely come to be regarded as an essential'.[135] In later cottages the bath was placed upstairs.

New Earswick was the first substantial opportunity for the partners to turn their theories on low-rent development for the working classes into practical experiment. It was an advance on other philanthropic ventures in that many already well-tried ideas were merged with fundamentally new thoughts in a comprehensive design. The village was planned as a community with the necessary ancillary facilities of school, shops, and open spaces. The cottages were designed with generous space standards, internal toilets and bathrooms, properly ventilated and well orientated, each with its own ample garden. In the early period of development the partners' contribution to site planning at New Earswick may be considered to rest more on their inventiveness in securing improved standards of housing than on major innovations in layout. Nevertheless, layout was handled with a subtlety and sensitivity unusual for the period.

5 Letchworth, first Garden City, 1903–6

'More air and less alcohol' should be the motto of the Garden City Association, Ralph Neville declared starkly whilst presiding over the 1901 Garden City conference at Bournville.[136] The Victorian vision of life expounded by this 'benevolent dictator'[137] reflected part of the ideological legacy of earlier social reformers concerned with the amelioration of the evils of cities. The 1901 conference had been convened to discuss the proposals which Howard set out in his book, *Tomorrow: A Peaceful Path to Real Reform*,[138] and to consider 'the desirability and practicability of a combined movement of manufacturers and co-operators to new areas, so that new towns may be established on land purchased for the community.'[139] Others have described the origins of Howard's ideas,[140] which offered a means of achieving a healthy, natural and economic combination of town and country life, in the form of a garden city – with provision for housing, industry, recreation and rapid transit, and surrounded by agricultural land to produce food to support the city.

Many were critical of the scheme when it first appeared. Osborn remarked that it 'struck the conservative minded as merely fantastic, and the idealists of the political left as disrespectful to their over simplified panaceas and even the reforming Fabian society as futile and impracticable and about as useful as would be arrangements for protection against visits from Mr Wells's Martians.'[141] Howard postulated that the way to solve the over-population of the cities and the depopulation of the country-side was to decentralize and build small compact cities, but he made no mention of what to do with existing cities, redevelopment of housing, renewal of town centres and restructuring of industrial areas. Some sympathizers, including Unwin, thought that this deficiency could be made up by the idea of the development of town suburbs, which with improved municipal town planning powers could offer the slum dwellers a suitable alternative residential area, still within reach of their place of work. Others rejected such 'amelioration' as inimical to the purity of Howard's approach. For all this, there is no denying the impact and influence of Howard's thinking. His ideas, promoted through the Garden City Association, were eventually instrumental in altering government policy in favour of decentralization of population and industry, proper planning controls, higher building standards, green belts, and new towns. In the immediate future, moreover, they led rapidly to the founding, in 1902, of the Garden City Pioneer Company, and the purchase of a large estate in Hertfordshire in the following year.

The estate, of approximately 3,800 acres, 30 miles north of London, was of undulating good agricultural land approximately 300 feet above sea level, overlying chalk with a central valley running north-south, along which flowed the River Ivel. Nearly the whole of the estate was within Hitchin Urban District and comprised the parishes of Letchworth, from which First Garden City took its name, Norton and parts of Willian and Radwell. For 2½ miles of its length the track of the Great Northern Railway Company which ran from London to Cambridge, cut the estate from west to east into two almost equal areas.

Parker and Unwin were invited to take part, with W.R. Lethaby and Halsey Ricardo, in a limited competition to prepare a plan for the estate. This competition, which was sponsored by the Rowntrees, was won by Parker and Unwin, who were then invited to prepare the definitive plan for Letchworth. On being commissioned, Unwin lost no time in moving south, with his wife, son and several assistants, to Baldock, where they took lodgings in March 1904. Parker moved down soon afterwards,[142] but it seems that the first detailed plan was prepared by Unwin and his pupil Robert Bennett, with Parker travelling down to help when possible.[143] C.B. Purdom recalls that during the winter of 1903–4 a contour survey had been made while the architects worked at the plan.[144] The survey, 'which formed a very good basis for the actual planning',[145] was at 5-foot contour intervals and was prepared by Howard Humphreys, who was later to prepare a similar survey at Hampstead Garden Suburb.

As the partners were by now well travelled and fully informed in matters of planning and architecture, with special interests in the classical medieval and renaissance periods, it is not surprising that the plan for first garden city is a mixture of formal spaces and avenues, reflecting continental Renaissance and baroque styles, and informal road and layout patterns reminiscent of medieval England and Germany. Unwin, however, has recorded his regret that he was not familiar with the work of the Austrian architectural historian and theorist, Camillo Sitte, at the time the partners prepared the plan for First Garden City.[146] Nevertheless, their plan was innovatory, being the first significant step in modern British town plan-

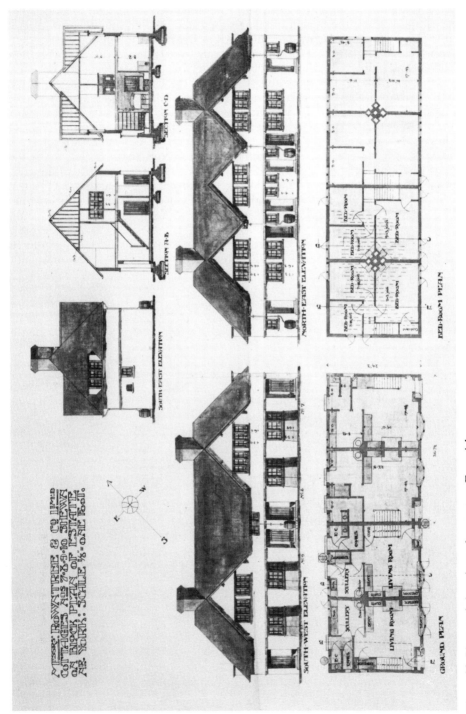

Figure 23. Plans and elevations of cottages at Earswick.

ning. At Letchworth, an entire town was comprehensively planned in advance of construction, without the benefit of planning legislation. This initiative constituted the first major attack on *laissez-faire* methods in British town building.

Unwin recalled in 1930 that 'the plan was made by carrying in the mind a conception of what an industrial town should be and applying and modifying that conception to the natural circumstances and features of the land on which it was to be placed.'[147] That conception had been foreshadowed in Unwin's speech at the Garden City conference of 1901, where he envisaged an 'industrial town' as 'a beautiful city' and a 'community inspired ideal'. The partners claimed that fine city building was an art – 'civic art' as they preferred to call it. Indeed, they referred to themselves as 'civic artists', asserting in Ruskinian terms that: 'If civic art is the expression of the life and ideals of the citizen, we may define the duty of the civic artist as "the well doing of what needs doing".'[148] Unwin suggested that the Garden City should aim at sufficient variety in design to enhance the natural features of the

Figure 24. Plan of Letchworth, 1904.

176

site and to show how 'a factory may form a fitting centre for an area of modern dwellings, the broad space round it [the factory] affording outlook and air space, while serving to isolate any noise, dust or unpleasant odour that may be inseparable from its processes.'[149]

Grouping houses around a factory was, of course, the basic principle at Saltaire, Bournville and elsewhere. Applied rigorously in a town, the principle would have produced a number of local neighbourhoods based on factories. In this respect, Parker and Unwin anticipated the 'neighbourhood unit' of the 1920s, though this American innovation was, of course, based on the focal point of the elementary school rather than the place of work. In the event, Parker and Unwin did not divide Letchworth into factory-dominated districts, but the idea of planned neighbourhoods occupied them nevertheless. Much later, in 1938, Parker referred explicitly to the prophetic character of the planning at Letchworth: 'the principle of the neighbourhood unit has been observed, each unit having its own school and its subsidiary shopping centre, social and sports facilities within easy reach.[150] His assertion is partly borne out, for the plan certainly shows four clear units, each with its own centre of public buildings, schools and shops arranged around an open space or 'green', with the industrial area kept quite separate.

The partners were clear in their minds on how to approach the planning of First Garden City.[151] The road plan came first, responding to the natural advantages of the site. Next, because it was such an important pedestrian and traffic generator, the position of the railway station had to be decided. This determined the position of the municipal centre, because it had to be placed near the railway station, yet clear of its noise and bustle. All these decisions had to take account of the need for an educational centre, recreation grounds and processional ways. The factory sites had to be placed to the east of the town since the prevailing wind was from the west. Vistas of buildings and open country had to be planned and preserved. Finally, the costs of roads needed to be carefully kept in mind and a due relation maintained between them and the arrangement of the building areas.

The partners set aside 1,300 acres for the site of the city, the remainder being devoted to an agricultural belt, smallholdings, open spaces and commons. The total population provided for in the plan was 35,000, of which one-seventh was to be housed in the agricultural belt.[152] This allocation of land reflects a crucial early planning decision as to zone uses. Parker claimed later that at that time this technique was 'almost unheard of'.[153] Unwin also remembered the task: 'about a week was spent tramping over the land and adapting the first conception of the town to the conditions of the site, allocating the industrial area, the commercial, administrative and cultural centres, the residential districts and the recreation parks.[154] If, as Parker's comment implies, the technique of zoning was not entirely original, its application at Letchworth certainly publicized its advantages and for this the partners must be given credit.

Unwin was satisfied that the centre was on much the best site available. 'A high plateau of nearly level ground affords an unbroken site on which the compact centre of the town can economically be erected. This area was entirely free of trees ... except three old oak trees, which stand in the central square ... they proved very helpful in precisely fixing the line of the main avenue [Broadway].'[155] Unwin claimed that the necessity for good road provision, in view of the coming motor age, was foreseen even in 1904, but that the rapid increase in car ownership, and traffic speeds, was not envisaged.[156] Existing roads were preserved as country lanes, including the ancient Icknield Way north of the railway, and the partners success-fully opposed suggestions to divert the Great North Road to run through Letch-worth. They saw that this would have been a second divisive feature, freely admitting that the railway 'has the effect of detaching the two halves of the scheme ... in a way that weakens the general symmetry and ... unity of the plan.'[157]

The south-western sector, which contains the town centre, is almost entirely formal in its layout and neo-Georgian in architectural style, giving impressive vistas both north up to Norton Common and south along Broadway, although the excess-ive tree planting mars some views. Prudent forethought was shown by the partners in allowing a great deal of space for the civic centre, although even today it contains only the town hall, library, museum and art gallery, and the cinema. The area may appear to have too many roads, but it must be remembered that it contains the main shopping zone which required adequate frontages and provision for servicing. Two roundabouts appear on the plan north of the railway in the north-western sector. The partners knew them as 'gyrator-junctions' and borrowed this device for easing traffic flow from work done in France by Eugène Hénard.[158] The south-western sector contains most of the large detached houses and it is obvious from the plan that this result was deliberately sought. Nowhere in the town, however, were there to be more than 12 dwellings to the acre.[159] Culs-de-sac appear for the first time in the partners' work. This method of layout was to become a hallmark of their planning and was a logical progression from their work at New Earswick with its emphasis on communal land, courtyards and enclosed greens. But culs-de-sac were never devel-oped fully at Letchworth. Hampstead Garden Suburb was the place where the part-ners first made full use of this device, in 1906.

The south-eastern sector, divided from the south-western sector by North Road and the linear Howard Park, contains the industrial area and the bulk of the planned working-class cottage development. On the plan the area is mostly informal in layout, as at New Earswick; but part is arranged in the chequerboard pattern employed in the partners' contribution to the exhibition of the Northern Art Workers' Guild in Manchester in 1903.

Proposals for the north-western and north-eastern sectors are not fully developed on the plan and are clearly more tentative. Divided by Norton Common, both areas have sub-centres on a village green. The cattle market is also situated north of the railway in an area of slightly more formal layout on the axial line of Broadway.

Planning the town was one task, building it quite another. As Purdom tells us, there were many difficulties.[160] As the share subscriptions were coming in slowly, money had to be borrowed to complete the contracts for the land. There were no roads on the estate except the Hitchin–Baldock road, the Wilbury–Norton road and the lane from Letchworth corner to Willian. There were no services of any kind; no public transport, no water, drainage, gas or electricity, only a few houses, the farm lands and the 20 acres of Norton Common. During the first summer the construction of Spring Road, Acacia Avenue, Station Road and Norton Way was begun. A drainage scheme was started and the first six cottages were built. Purdom tells us that the cottages were no better in standard, 'except for a little hand from Unwin'[161] than cottages elsewhere and visitors expecting something new in architecture were more than a little disappointed. This led Adams to get in touch with J. St Loe Stra-chey,[162] the editor of the *Spectator*. Strachey had begun a campaign in October 1904 with a series of articles published in the *Country Gentleman and Land and Water* under the general title of 'The search for £150 cottage' to encourage the building of cheap cottages in rural areas to keep workers on the land. Together Adams and Strachey organised the Cheap Cottages Exhibition at Letchworth in the summer of 1905, which brought 50,000 people to the estate. The exhibition stimulated both interest and building in Letchworth. Many entries were attracted, built in concrete, stone, bricks and wood, to a variety of designs. The site for the exhibition was on Wilbury Road, north of Norton Common, where some of the entries can still be seen. The exhibition, which was held from July onwards, was opened by the Duke of Devonshire, who had sold the Track Ring in Buxton to Robert Parker in order that Robert's son, Barry, might start in architectural practice. The judges were distinguished, being Octavia Hill, W.R. Lethaby, J.C. McCowan, Robert Weir Schultz, Thackeray Turner, G. Simms Woodhead and Harriet Yorke.[163] The first prize for cottages costing not more than £150 went to Percy Houfton. The second prize in that class went to Robert Bennett and Wilson Bidwell, one-time assistants of Parker and Unwin who had set up in joint practice in the town.

The partners, however, were concerned about the emphasis on the 'cheap' cottage. They considered that the question should not be 'how good a cottage can we build for £150?' but 'how cheaply can we build a good cottage?'[164] Unwin openly criticized some of the prizewinners from the Cheap Cottages Exhibition.[165] No cottage, the partners asserted, can be said to be good which will not be a 'healthy, comfortable and comely home' for the family.[166] This concern was symptomatic of the partners' constant battles against false economies in both site planning and cottage design. Unwin argued that 'we spend our thousand pounds on some improvement; and for the lack of that small margin which would have made it into guineas we lose at least half of the value we might have had.'[167] In terms of site layout they reiterated their arguments from earlier papers for the grouping of cottages around greens and for their proper orientation; 'where land is expensive', states Unwin, 'one would not expect to find difficulty in arranging for wide grass margins and other simple delights. But people are not accustomed to the common enjoyment of such margins, they look suspiciously on even the very small cost of that, and wish to enclose them in their own gardens.'[168]

Grouping of cottages was first tried out fully by the partners at Letchworth, in their capacity as consultant architects to Henry Vivian's Garden City Tenants Society for their schemes at Bird's Hill (1905), Eastholme (1905) and Westholme (1906). The seven-acre Bird's Hill estate was within easy reach of the factory sites. On this striking site 71 cottages were built facing south and west. The layout is varied in form and includes terraced cottages grouped around a cul-de-sac, the first to be built at Letchworth; and other cottages located around a green (fig. 25). Eastholme and Westholme took the form of cottages arranged around a 'village green'.[169] The partners were also advocating at this time the building of other types of houses for persons with special needs, the old, the single or the childless families. However, it was at Hampstead, not Letchworth, that they were first able to put these ideas into effect.

In contrast to the layouts produced for the co-partnership societies, control of private development was more troublesome. As consultant architects to First Garden City Ltd the partners were in a difficult position. First Garden City Ltd wished to encourage the speculative builder and the private client with his own architect, but at the same time they wished to exercise a certain amount of control. Almost inevitably this compromise produced an incoherent pattern of private development in the early years, which was much regretted by Unwin.[170] The company had published its requirements earlier.[171] This statement, clearly bearing the mark of the partners, read: 'The Directors of First Garden City Limited are convinced that a high standard of beauty, which they desire to attain in Garden City, can only result from simple, straightforward building from good and harmonious materials. They desire as far as possible to discourage useless ornamentation, and to secure that buildings shall be suitably designed for their purpose and position.' The vagueness and generality of the statement reflects the dilemma already mentioned. In general it can be considered unfortunate that the good intentions of the directors in setting the conditions of development were never fully realized. The financial need to encourage almost any type of development proved to be more influential than the desire to achieve high aesthetic standards for the town as a whole.

When, in July 1906, Unwin left for Hampstead, Parker assumed total responsibility for overseeing the development at Letchworth. The partners set up separate offices; nevertheless the closest consultations continued, with frequent exchange visits.[172] Unwin's removal to Hampstead was seen in some quarters as a desertion of the cause of garden cities, especially by those who regarded the garden suburb as a much inferior concept, but Unwin, as past events had shown, relished new experiences and approached his new assignment with great enthusiasm.

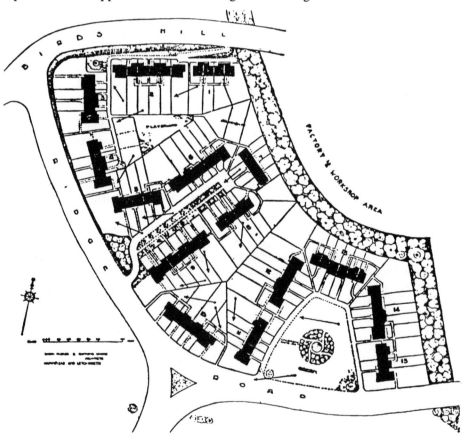

Figure 25. Bird's Hill, Letchworth.

Letchworth's place in the history of modern town planning is of paramount importance whether one agrees with the principles on which it was designed or not. It was a notable step for a group of private individuals to instigate and eventually implement the planning and development of a complete new town. The project was the model for Welwyn and the later government-sponsored post-1945 new towns. Its standards influenced later government legislation on housing standards and decentralization of population. The town also influenced the course of town planning movements in all parts of the world, although not always for the better. Unwin was fond of relating the story of his complete dismay when he accompanied Japan's chief planner around Letchworth. The Japanese official explained that he had been so impressed with Letchworth that he had copied it in every particular throughout Korea, especially in the matter of building on both sides of the railway![173]

In planning terms the partners' contribution to this widespread influence was substantial. Parker and Unwin established the principle of developing a settlement along the lines of a previously agreed plan, based on a sound survey. They established the principle of zoning uses and organizing a proper pedestrian and vehicular circulation pattern. They pioneered an attempt to instigate proper development control. They created working precedents for the proper housing of the working classes on a large scale. They established, on the grounds of health and welfare, the principle of a universal right to a well-designed house and ample private garden space with associated communal open areas and parks. These principles provided a substantial foundation for successive governments' post-1918 planning and housing policies.

6   Hampstead Garden Suburb, 1905–14

Henrietta Barnett, the founder of Hampstead Garden Suburb, conceived the idea of an estate to provide the conditions for all classes to live together in neighbourliness, shortly after she had married Canon Samuel A. Barnett in 1873. The couple lived in Whitechapel, East London, where Canon Barnett founded Toynbee Hall to accommodate fellow social service workers in his struggle to educate and reform the slum dwellers of that area.

Henrietta Barnett had earlier come under the influence of Octavia Hill, the leader of the housing management movement for rehousing slum dwellers. Like her husband and Octavia Hill, Henrietta Barnett believed that decent housing was the first requisite of a better life. The opportunity to realize her ambition did not arise, and then only as a secondary idea, until 1896 when the scheme to extend the northern tube line out of Golders Green was mooted, thus threatening the fine open country around Hampstead Heath with a creeping suburban carpet.

In order to protect the Heath, Henrietta Barnett asserted that 'it became imperative to enlarge it.'[174] In 1900, with the help of Lord Eversley and Sir Robert Hunter, who with Octavia Hill in 1895 had founded the National Trust, Henrietta Barnett formed a committee whose object was to add 80 acres of open space, at North End, Hampstead, to the historic Heath. In June 1903, the Hampstead Heath Extension Council was formed and by early 1905, after a long and hard struggle, the council's object had been achieved and the area was handed over to the London County Council as public open space for all time. Meanwhile, in the light of the difficulty the campaign experienced in raising the necessary funds to purchase the Heath Extension, the Eton College Trust suggested that if a margin of building land were reserved by the college around the 80 acres, and the shape of the extension modified, the enhanced value of the land having a frontage to this open space would enable the college to reduce the price of the land.[175] However, this concession had created a danger that the amenities of the Health extension might be marred by overlooking inferior development. Henrietta Barnett therefore concluded that the only way to protect the Heath extension was to build her own well-planned suburb around it, thus realizing both her goals.

By February 1905, Mrs Barnett had gathered around her a formidable group of backers led by Lord Crewe. Other members of the Garden Suburb Trust, as it was known, included Earl Grey, the garden city enthusiast, Sir Robert Hunter of the National Trust, Herbert Marnham, Walter Hazell and the Bishop of London. In an article in the *Contemporary Review* in February 1905, Mrs Barnett first published the idea of her proposed development. It was to be a scheme in which the classes would not be estranged, 'the estate ... planned ... the dwellings ... attractive, the air pure with the recreational and social amenities a community needs.'[176] By this time, Parker and Unwin had already prepared the first tentative plan for the suburb (fig. 26) and Mrs Barnett's description certainly reflects the plan's composition.

Mrs Barnett always took great care to be well informed and she avidly read everything available pertaining to her suburb scheme. She had read, in September 1904, a paper by Unwin and immediately determined that Unwin was 'the man for my beautiful green and golden scheme.'[177] A few weeks later Lord Brassey introduced Unwin to Mrs Barnett. Unwin reminded her that he had been among her and her husband's social service followers in Oxford. Mrs Barnett describes how, upon once being reminded of the fact, the Canon and herself recalled Unwin with pleasure.[178] A further link with the Barnetts was through Unwin's brother, William, who, as curate at Crosthwaite, Keswick, kept the minutes at the vicarage meetings of the embryonic National Trust for its creators, Octavia Hill, Sir Robert Hunter and Canon Rawnsley.[179]

In July 1905, having a plan, copies of which were attached to the Garden Suburb Trust's prospectus, upon which money could be invested, the Trust decided to form the Hampstead Garden Suburb Trust Ltd.[180] Duly on 6 March 1906, with £76,000 promised, the Trust was registered under the chairmanship of Earl Crewe.[181] The trustees included George Cadbury and W.H. Lever and the directors included Henry Vivian of Co-Partnership Tenants, whose company was to play such an important part in the success of the scheme. The Trust's objects were fourfold. First, to do something to meet the housing problem; second, to lay out the estate as a whole according to an orderly plan; third, to promote a better understanding between members of the various classes; and fourth, to preserve the estate's natural beauty.[182]

The 240-acre site varied in height between 170 feet and 360 feet and covered one of the highest areas in Metropolitan London. The shape of the site was irregular. Adjoining the northern tip of Hampstead Heath in the south, the long and narrow site extended for about 1½ miles in a north-westerly direction from Golders Green towards Finchley. Near the centre of the estate was a high plateau of ground. Immediately to the west of this the land fell steeply away. As at Letchworth, whilst preparing the initial sketch plan in February 1905, the partners commissioned Howard Humphreys of Westminster to carry out a contour survey of the site at

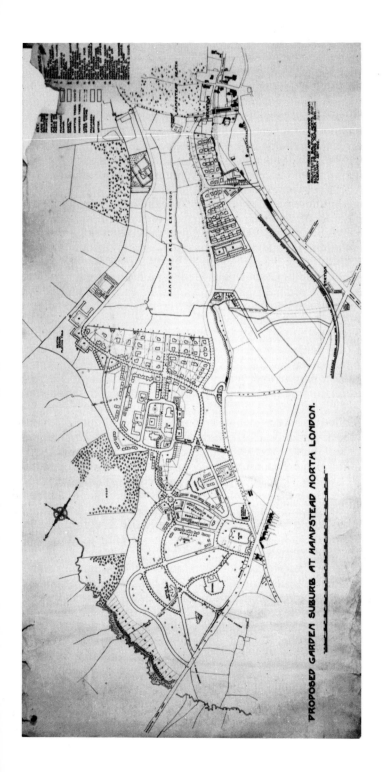

Figure 26. Plan of Hapstead Garden Suburb, 1905.

5-foot intervals. The survey carefully plotted the position of existing trees and approximate spread of their branches.[183] It was their intention that in the execution of the final plan not one tree should be removed.[184]

The detailed planning was influenced by a number of general considerations. In the location and layout of the residential areas, easy access to the Finchley Road and to Golders Green railway station was of prime importance. Secondly, it was also desirable to capitalize on the potential views to the south across the open space of the Heath extension to the well-wooded heights of Hampstead Heath and Golders Hill. Thirdly, Unwin considered it important to provide an effective centre for the estate which, it was intended, should be developed as a community having a unity of social character. In Unwin's view, the physical centre could contribute to the achievement of this social objective.

It was in the planning of the residential areas that Unwin encountered his most serious difficulties. The strip of land surrounding the Heath extension was very narrow, and to exploit it the cul-de-sac device, first introduced on the Letchworth plan, was the obvious solution. The 1905 plan shows very clearly the intended disposition of the expensively leased residential buildings. All overlook the Heath extension, and are carefully sited to give views of the Heath, even from the deepest cul-de-sac, in order to exploit the full financial potential of each plot. However, whereas in rural Hertfordshire the partners had had free rein, in Hampstead they had to reckon with the building bye-laws of suburban London.

Upon his appointment as the architect to the Trust, Unwin immediately advised that if his ideas were to be carried out, then the local bye-laws would need to be changed. This could only be achieved by a special Act of Parliament.[185] Later, Parker amplified the point: 'when we were planning the Hampstead Garden Suburb experience of the degrading influences, the unhealthiness, airlessness and squalor of "blind alleys" and closes had resulted in the existence of legislation forbidding the use of the cul-de-sac and stipulated that all roads must be through roads.' Parker went on: 'we proposed there should be . . . the maximum possible number of houses from which views over the "Heath Extension" were enjoyed. This we proposed to secure by surrounding the "Heath Extension" by open ended culs-de-sac . . . abutting the Heath.'[186] Parker pointed out that it was characteristic of Unwin 'that he could not rest content that existing legislation should thwart us in this.'[187] This also indicates that Unwin probably believed that in the modern cul-de-sac the partners had developed a very useful device in residential layout design, incorporating benefits of safety, quietness, privacy, low density, aspect, vistas, large gardens, and economy in road and service provision.

There being no general act on the statute book enabling local authorities to suspend the operation of their bye-laws in relation to land which was being developed on modern lines, the trustees, with the prompting of Unwin, set about promoting the Hampstead Garden Suburb Act, designed to give them the necessary powers. The bill was introduced into parliament by Henry Vivian, MP, who was chairman of Co-Partnership Tenants Ltd and a director of the Hampstead Garden Suburb Trust. It received the warm support of John Burns, president of the Local Government Board, and passed into law on 4 August 1906. The passage of the Act had important and far-reaching implications. It gave legal form to two new principles: the limitation of the number of houses which could be built to the acre, and the relaxation of bye-laws in order to secure the best form of development. Although Unwin wished the density stipulation to be 12, the Act stipulated that it should be no more than eight, but some leeway was given by the phrase 'throughout a greater proportion of houses'. Power was given to make 'accommodation roads' quite narrow, 20 feet in width including footpaths, provided that such roads did not exceed 500 feet in length. Any other road should not be less than 40 feet wide and if of a greater width the excess should consist of grass margins or grounds planted with trees or laid out in gardens. But whatever the width of the road, the space between the building lines on each side of the road should not be less than 50 feet. Other provisions included common use of recreation grounds and a limit of 5 per cent *per annum* on the dividend payable to shareholders.[188]

The Act was the first piece of modern planning legislation in Britain. Conferring powers on the Trust 'to develop and lay out lands as garden suburbs',[189] it provided a model for parts of the draft town planning bill prepared by the Association of Municipal Corporations.[190] But, more importantly, it stimulated other legislation and many of its provisions were incorporated into John Burns's Housing and Town Planning Act of 1909, the first general Town Planning Act to be placed on the statute book. Indeed, Atkinson maintains that Unwin helped prepare the 1909 Act.[191]

Returning to the 1905 plan, the other main features included a community centre, the focal point of the community's common life, and an essential requisite in the minds of Mrs Barnett and the partners. The emphasis in the provision of facilities was on encouraging participation on the part of the working classes in the life of the suburb. Co-operation 'would enable economy to be practised without undue effort.'[192] Another aim was to provide facilities which would be beyond the means of the inhabitants to own individually. Therefore, apart from amenities to cater for the community's spiritual and social life including churches, library, schools, lecture hall, art gallery, museum and club house, there were facilities to cater for the community's physical well-being. These included ample provision of shops, bath and wash-houses, refreshment rooms, arbours, allotments with communal implements and tools, playgrounds, resting places and seats for the elderly, wooded areas with walks, recreational pools, tennis courts, and hostels for single men, women, the old and infirm. Other features included a 'pleasure walk' at the northern end of the estate along Mutton Brook, linking the footpath system and the woodland areas. The use of courtyards and quadrangles for the hostels is a feature the partners had long advocated,[193] and one which they were able to implement successfully at the suburb. Great care was taken when siting buildings to preserve vistas and in some cases, as with views along roads, to enhance them with some terminal feature – the formal view from the Heath extension to the proposed community centre is an example. This emphasis on composition of street pictures was one of the main characteristics of the suburb and marked a definite progression in the partners' work from the more informal proposals for New Earswick and Letchworth, reflecting the continental, especially German, influence on the partners' work at the time. Apart from his fact-finding trips abroad,[194] Unwin was aware of modern planning methods in Germany through the work of his friend and one-time associate in the Ancoats Brotherhood in Manchester, T.C. Horsfall. Unwin's paper to the International Congress of Architects in London (1906)[195] showed him to be fully acquainted with German planning and the work of Camillo Sitte on which he was to rely so heavily in his book, *Town Planning in Practice* (1909), which remained perhaps the most influential British town planning manual down to the Second World War. Triggs considered the 1906 congress to be one of a series of international meetings, culminating with the RIBA conference in 1910, jointly organized by Unwin, which formed the turning point in the acceptance of modern town planning methods in Britain.[196] It also seems to have been the first occasion when the term 'town planning' was generally used in public discussion.

Building began at Hampstead on 5 June 1907, with the ceremonial laying of the first 100 bricks for one pair of cottages, at the junction of Hampstead Way and Asmuns Hill, by shareholders of the Hampstead Tenants Society, a subsidiary company of Henry Vivian's Co-Partnership Tenants Ltd. The Hampstead Tenants Society had been formed on 18 March 1907, and was one of five societies which leased land from the Hampstead Garden Suburb Trust, to build houses and cottages. The Trust itself was not involved in building operations in any substantial way, although it did build ten cottages on Cotman Close for its own employees, several flats on Corringway and two homes for the elderly, designed by Unwin and known as Homes Field.[197] The Trust, however, retained a development control function through the Hampstead Garden Suburb Development Company. In part this accounts for the homogeneity of the first 240 acres of development, before the estate was extended in 1911.

The policy of the Trust was to create building leases and not to dispose of the freeholds of sites. This enabled the Trust, through its architects, to maintain planning and architectural control of the estate, to direct development according to their development plan, and to preserve the amenities of the estate. Unwin recognized the need for high standards of both planning and architecture in order to give a lead in promoting the necessary co-operation. 'The town planner may', he wrote, 'lay out on the best lines the main thoroughfares and places of the town. The site planner may follow and design the best schemes for arranging the plots, the building lines and the positions of buildings, but the aim of both is almost sure to be frustrated by the work of those to follow ... the designs may be good, but for want of any co-ordination, the result will be little more than an inharmonious jumble.'[198] However, Unwin went on to argue that a company like the Hampstead Garden Suburb Development Company heralded a new departure in estate development, the forerunner in fact of positive development control in town planning rather than negative byelaws. The company would co-operate with the site planner and the client and there was a good chance that they might produce 'special groups of buildings essential for the realisation of the total effect aimed at.'[199]

Unlike at Letchworth, the partners designed many of the cottages and other buildings on the estate, amongst which were 270 cottages for the Hampstead Tenants Society at 12 dwellings to the acre in Asmuns Place, Asmuns Hill and Hampstead Way. Together with E.L. Lutyens, Unwin was also responsible for the design of the central square. As completed, the square seems empty and isolated and is foreign to the rest of the suburb in architectural style. Unwin's original plan for the square was modified several times and a more formal plan was eventually adopted to suit 'Mr Lutyens's finer renaissance scheme of treatment'.[200] In contrast, in the northern and western portions of the original estate can be found the partners' 'ways' and 'closes' which provide a succession of charmingly picturesque views.

Hampstead Garden Suburb was once remarkably described as an 'un-suburban suburb'.[201] The journalist was probably trying to indicate the suburb's exceptional character, being unlike the bye-law suburbs of the late nineteenth century and possibly more like a garden city. There was much confusion at the time concerning the terms 'garden city' and 'garden suburb'. Many garden city enthusiasts disdained the 'garden suburb' and looked upon it as a bastardized version of their dream, whilst the 'garden suburb' enthusiasts felt that the benefits of open development were being brought right into the town. 'Open development' was the keynote. Many speculative builders built small, low-density estates which were not socially balanced communities and were without social facilities, but to make them attractive called them 'garden' suburbs, thus allowing the concept to be tarnished. However, the idea that the growing demand for urban accommodation during the Edwardian period could have been met by pure garden cities is clearly unrealistic. It was virtually inevitable that the expansion should take the form of suburban accretions on the edges of existing towns. Unwin was one who recognized this. He did not abandon, as some thought, the garden city movement when he left Letchworth for Hampstead. Indeed, Osborn believes that the garden city movement would not have got far without him.[202] A simple and personal reason for Unwin's removal to Hampstead was that the partners, having completed the development plan for Letchworth, found that the remaining task as consultants was not big enough to keep both of them fully occupied.[203] But probably the chief reason for Unwin's move was that he saw the danger of massive ill-planned suburban expansion and recognized the need for a lead to be given. On the other hand, Osborn feels that Unwin did not fight strongly enough against the unplanned suburban sprawl which he deplored, nor hard enough for garden cities.[204] Further, Mumford claims that if Unwin did make a serious error, it was that of 'sliding into the policy of expediency in furthering town expansions, rather than balancing communities.'[205]

Unwin's own explanation was contained in his pamphlet, written for the Garden City Association in 1912, entitled *Nothing Gained by Overcrowding! How the Garden City Type of Development May Benefit Both Owner and Occupier*. The pamphlet is tractarian in character. It strongly reflects garden city principles and the 1909 Town Planning Act, but was equally directed at the developers of traditional suburban estates. In earlier papers Unwin had stressed health, sunlight, co-operation, amenity and aesthetic quality; he now moved on to an area that the building trade and other agencies could understand, economics. Unwin used small-scale site planning examples in the pamphlet to demonstrate false economies in a cost-benefit analysis, and using the principles derived therefrom, moved on to large scale metropolitan examples. He asserted that 'much the same economic principles which determined the possibility of limiting the proportion of the individual buildings to the surrounding space, also influenced the limitation of the proportion of urban areas to surrounding country.'[206] He observed that it was generally assumed that the more houses that were built on each acre of land, the more economical was the use made of the land and the less would each householder have to pay for it. Further, it was generally assumed that though it was necessary to put a limit to the number of houses that might be crowded upon an acre, this limit should be fixed as high as possible and that any limitation must necessarily constitute a serious tax on the community. But, maintained Unwin, this view was very far from correct; indeed, generally the contrary was true. 'The greater number of houses crowded upon the land, the higher the rate which each occupier must pay for every yard of it which his plot contains, the smaller will be the total return to the owners of the land in increment value, and, indeed, the less will be the real economy in the use of land.'[207]

Unwin used as his examples ten-acre layouts of bye-law streets, which he contrasted with a hypothetical superblock form, and complemented by statistical tables. Assuming that both developments were in two-storey form, and the land cost the same in both cases, then the road service costs for the low-density superblock were

50 per cent less per square yard than the high density bye-law layout, but the ground rents per house were half as much again. For the ground rent to be equal in both cases, the cost of the land had to be half as much in the low-density example as compared with the high-density example. This was the one weakness in the argument, for to achieve the same aggregate rate of return in low-density as in high-density development, the landowner had to release more land. Any logical weaknesses in the economic argument, however, were outweighed by the improvements in the quality of the residential environment that adherence to the low-density design principles produced.

Unwin's density theories, especially when developed in practice by Parker, were lasting and influential, particularly in the inter-war municipal estates. As for their overseas influence, Mumford considers that *Nothing Gained by Overcrowding* had a decisive impact on Stein and Wright, the planners of Sunnyside Gardens, New York, and Radburn, New Jersey. 'Unwin's economic demonstration, plus their visit to Letchworth in 1923 [to see Parker][208] were the foundation stones for their work.'[209] Even more significantly, Unwin had actually worked on the Radburn scheme as a consultant.[210] It was at Sunnyside Gardens and later at Radburn that the Americans developed the superblock and the neighbourhood unit foreshadowed in Unwin's diagrams and thesis.

Hampstead's importance in design terms can be attributed, then, to several factors. The partners introduced the cul-de-sac into modern design, a device of great utility in allowing for the fullest possible development of a total site area by opening up 'back land'. To secure these opportunities they promoted legislation which in turn stimulated others to introduce further and even more significant planning legislation. The development company idea, which was to become so effective as a positive instrument of both land development and development control, was a great advance over the methods of control used at Letchworth. It encouraged professional acceptance of the idea of development control. Indeed, Hampstead Garden Suburb became a model for many estates, by improving on the standards set at New Earswick and Letchworth. These improved standards were eventually to be incorporated into several influential government reports – not least the Tudor Walters report (1918). The partners' work at Hampstead also provided an important focus for the development of the embryonic planning profession. Assistants who came to learn and work in Unwin's office at Wyldes included Herbert Welsh, who was later at the Ministry of Health, Charles Wade, who illustrated *Town Planning in Practice*, A.J. Penty, Alwyn Lloyd, Allen, and Mottram, all of whom designed many residential areas, and Ernst May, later to become the most celebrated of all German planners.

Finally, in retrospect, we might ask whether the Trust had achieved all its objectives at Hampstead. It was unfortunate that the suburb went only part of the way towards demonstrating how to resolve London's housing problem. The rehousing of the working classes was the most pressing problem. The relatively few low-rent dwellings built, plus the potentially high cost of longer journeys to work, meant that few, if any, of the really needy removed to Hampstead. But the Trust progressively pioneered housing provision for single working men and women and the disabled. No evidence exists to gauge whether or not the estate promoted better understanding between the classes, partly perhaps because the spectrum of classes was not in accordance with the Trust's aspirations. Up to 1914 the estate was laid out to an orderly plan, although the coherence of the plan suffered because of the poor location of the central square and its unsympathetic design in relation to the rest of the development. The Trust was clearly successful, however, in its aim to preserve the natural beauty of the area. The Heath extension was and is protected from development, and clearly enhanced and still enhances the amenity of the suburb.

7   Unwin's work for the government and its influence

Upon being made an honorary member of the RIBA in 1910, Unwin achieved formal recognition of his services to town planning; indeed it was an acknowledgment of his pioneering leadership in the field. He had not sought this honour, but he realized its significance. It gave him new opportunities and opened new avenues for the achievement of his long-held aims.

Within a year he was the first lecturer in town planning at the University of Birmingham, his course sponsored by the Bournville Trust. From 1913 onwards he served on several influential committees including the departmental committees of the Board of Agticulture and Fisheries on buildings and smallholdings and on labourers' cottages, and the departmental committee of the Local Government Board on building bye-laws. He also advised the Admiralty on their massive dockyard development at Rosyth, Scotland.

Herbert Samuel became president of the Local Government Board in February 1914, and in the following December appointed Unwin as the Board's chief town planning inspector, the most important technical town planning post in the Civil Service, in succession to Thomas Adams. Thus began Unwin's most influential period as a town planner. Before his retirement under the age limit rule in 1928, Unwin, amongst other things had founded the building research station, had been made the second president of the Town Planning Institute (1915–16), had worked during 1917 on the housing panel of the Ministry of Reconstruction, and had been appointed soon afterwards to the Sir Tudor Walters Committee which was to investigate post-war housing needs and future standards of layout and construction.[211] Also at this time he became chairman of the research committee at the new Department of Scientific and Industrial Research.[212] After his retirement he became adviser to the Greater London Regional Planning Committee and continued to serve the government in an advisory capacity on the Crown lands advisory committee and the central housing advisory committee of the Ministry of Health.

The partnership between Parker and Unwin was officially dissolved upon Unwin's appointment to the Local Government Board in 1914. Parker continued in practice, specializing in housing developments, and was in an ideal position to put into practice the official housing standards and legislation in the elaboration of which Unwin had been instrumental. During the inter-war period, following some work abroad, Parker was responsible for the design and layout of many thousands of new houses on behalf of several local authorities, the most notable scheme being perhaps that at Wythenshawe near Manchester.

With the outbreak of war, Unwin was loaned in July 1915 to the explosives department of the Ministry of Munitions, to take charge of the planning of munitions settlements. It is interesting to note that the war caused Unwin great distress, as did his own part in it, for that year he published a short book, entitled *The War and What After*, in which he made it clear that he deplored all wars and advocated an international body to mediate between potential belligerents.[213] Unwin reorganized the housing branch of the Ministry and was instrumental in preparing the layout plans of various estates to house munitions workers, including the cordite factories at Gretna and Eastriggs in Dumfries. Initially accommodation in the Gretna township was of a temporary nature, but later permanent dwellings and other amenities, including shops, churches, a school, institute, public hall, cinema, hospital and recreation areas were provided.

In his work at the Ministry of Munitions Unwin's experience in organizing and implementing such large-scale schemes as Letchworth and Hampstead must have been invaluable. Each development had the partners' hallmark of sympathetic layout and was remarkably human in concept, marking a considerable advance both physically and socially over the standards achieved in previous government installations. What was fundamentally important was that the housing effort of the Ministry of Munitions made it easier for post-war governments to accept responsibility for public housing. It is also important to note that the developments attracted considerable technical attention and proved to have an interesting impact in the USA.

Unwin's work became the centre-piece of a campaign in the USA which advocated the development of policies and designs on similar lines, in the hope of encouraging the US government to assist in solving America's housing problems. Charles Whitacker, the editor of the *Journal of the American Institute of Architects*, played a leading part in this campaign.[214] In 1917, Unwin's designs and publications were described in several articles.[215] In 1918, Congress appropriated funds for State-aided housing for war industry workers, to be built by the United States Housing Corporation and the housing division of the Emergency Fleet Corporation. Amongst the initial schemes were Yorkship village, New Jersey, designed by E.D. Litchfield; Hilton, Virginia, designed by J.D. Leland and Henry Hubbard; and Atlantic Heights, New Hampshire, designed by Kilman and Hopkins. Childs suggests that Yorkship was designed on 'the lines of Letchworth'.[216] The use of both formal and informal road patterns, and low-density terraced cottages with both front road and rear footpath access, are all reminiscent of Letchworth. However, Ackerman, who had been Whitacker's special correspondent in Britain during the war, suggested much later that the campaign fully realized its aims only after the Tennessee Valley Authority scheme prompted the government to implement large-scale public housing programmes.[217]

Perhaps Unwin's most widely influential contribution to the development of housing and site planning may be considered to be in the report drawn up by the committee on housing of which Sir Tudor Walters was chairman. This report, a milestone in housing and town planning history, led to fundamental improvements in housing standards. Previously rigid bye-laws had restricted imaginative and progressive residential development. The recommendations were not superseded for 25 years, when the Dudley report (1944) was published, and indeed were not fundamentally altered until the Parker Morris report, *Homes for Today and Tomorrow* (1961). This lack of revision, through no fault of the Tudor Walters Committee, was to be disadvantageous, as will be seen later. Unwin's contribution to the report is clear, especially in the sections on site planning and housing standards which recommended many features that Unwin and his partner had been advocating for at least ten years. Indeed, the report carries many illustrations from Unwin's pamphlet, *Nothing Gained by Overcrowding*. Unwin had already gained official acceptance for many of these standards in 1913 when he had served on the Board of Agriculture and Fisheries committee on buildings and smallholdings.

Between 1914 and 1919 building operations in the housing sector had all but ceased, save for the few munitions settlements. No repairs had been made and therefore the normal wastage of buildings had been increased. After studying the house production figures from 1905, the committee found that, even with the expected decreasing rate of population increase, there was a backlog of 500,000 houses to be made up in addition to the expected annual demand of 100,000 houses for all sectors of the working classes. The committee also recognized that by raising standards more houses would, by definition, become unfit and hence an increased number would need to be built to replace them. Even with substantial government aid to local authorities, the private sector of the building industry was expected to bear the brunt of this development. The committee did recognize, however, that there were likely to be shortages of materials and that upon demobilization the building industry would take time to reorganize itself. The committee strongly insisted that the housing problem could not be adequately dealt with unless the housing department of the Local Government Board (later to become the Ministry of Health) was able to bring within its scope the entire housing requirements of the community and was vested with the power to supervise and co-ordinate the housing work of both local authorities and private enterprise.[218] In order to perform this function the committee recommended the appointment of a strong central housing commission with regional commissioners to administer a simplified housing and town planning act which should incorporate less rigid bye-law provisions and give increased powers of compulsory purchase to local authorities. Decentralization of population was also advocated, not in the form of garden cities, but in the form of suburbs on the edges of large towns with good connecting transit facilities.

The main recommendations dealing with sites, layout and development, accommodation and economy in its provision are Unwin-inspired. Although they were not all Parker and Unwin innovations, the practices recommended in the report had all formed an integral part of the partners' layout and housing schemes from New Earswick and Letchworth onwards. It is the unification of all these techniques into a comprehensive and sensible code that makes this report so significant. For example, the committee recommended that the density of dwellings in working-class development should not exceed 12 houses to the acre in urban areas and eight houses to the acre in rural areas;[219] that sites for development should be properly surveyed and selected with a view to their links with industry and amenities and that full advantage should be taken of all the opportunities which the site afforded including provision for the social, economic, educational and recreational needs of the population;[220] that aesthetic and artistic considerations in layout were essential to true economy;[221] that the cul-de-sac, courtyard and the green in conjunction with open spaces, allotments and playgrounds, were all necessary elements of proper layout;[222] that proper orientation of houses was also vitally important;[223] that proper assessment of road needs and road widths according to use was necessary and that good access to the rear of houses was essential;[224] that space standards in the home should be generous[225] and that bathrooms should be on the first floor;[226] and that either parlour or non-parlour houses were acceptable, the committee considering that there were good arguments for both.[227]

In June 1919 Unwin, having been chiefly responsible for the high standards of Britain's war-time housing, was appointed as chief architect and ultimately chief technical officer for building and town planning at the newly created Ministry of Health under Christopher Addison, a position which he held until his retirement in

1928. Thus for a decade Unwin was ultimately responsible for the evaluation of all the country's housing projects during the first phase of Britain's inter-war housing drive. To assess his particular contribution in each individual case would, therefore, be impossible. The Housing and Town Planning Act (1919) (the 'Addison Act') had introduced the principle of compulsory town planning, requiring that the councils of every borough or urban district with a population of 20,000 or more should submit to the Ministry of Health for approval a planning scheme for the development of all or part of their area by January 1926. The Town Planning Act (1925) consolidated these powers and other planning law. Between January 1919 and April 1932 over 1,800,000 houses, 19 per cent of the total stock in 1932, were erected by public and private agencies under the supervision and control of the Ministry of Health. Whilst subsequent Housing Acts reduced standards in terms of both size and cost of dwellings, because of the poor state of the national economy, nevertheless, 1,000,000 houses were built for the working classes and both in quality and quantity they constitute perhaps the largest public achievement of any country between the wars.

To many critics, including Mumford and Sharp,[228] house building during the inter-war period is synonymous with 'urban sprawl' and 'open development', ironically the very features Unwin had protested against in his 'dreary suburb' speech of 1901.[229] Each successive government was politically committed to building houses through the subsidy system and, as Edwards points out, 'this period was a very important one as far as housing policy was concerned as it marked the introduction of the so-called "open development" and its codification as a government sponsored bureaucratic system enforced by law.'[230] The inflexibility of the various governments, once they had accepted 'open development' in principle, prevented the countenancing of any other type of local-authority development.

What was more unfortunate was that although propaganda by Unwin and others in the garden city movement was mainly responsible for encouraging the acceptance of this dogma, nowhere in Unwin's writings will be found examples typical of the estates built in the 1920s and 1930s that we see today. The environment which resulted was one of endless anonymous estates of semi-detached dwellings at regulation intervals. What was worse was that no standards were set for the provision of community buildings, shops, schools, halls, etc., and so few were ever built. As *Nothing Gained by Overcrowding* shows, Unwin had always advocated the grouping of buildings to ensure that adequate communal space could be provided and that provision of associated community facilities was ensured.

The paramount difficulty was to encourage individual authorities to use their imagination. Edwards states that Unwin had 'the impossible task of reducing "open development" to a number of simple rules capable of being understood by agents and functionaries of average intellectual ability.'[231] Unwin and his staff could not hope to ensure first-class designs in every case. Mumford points out that because of this factor, in the estates built during this period, there was 'no active dramatization of the new forces and possibilities of modern life'; even the superblock, he claims, was 'merely a step further both in economics and amenities'.[232] In this sense the 1920s and 1930s can be considered the low point in modern urban design in this country. But that of course is not the only criterion by which the period can be judged. The essential achievement was that government had been persuaded irrevocably to take on the responsibility of subsidizing housing on a massive scale. Houses were built – nearly two million of them. The internal standards were much higher than anything to which the working classes had been accustomed – the Tudor

Walters report ensured that. The general environment was improved. Families had their own large garden – an extension of the house in which children could play in safety. It was to be regretted, however, that there had been no attractive physical demonstration to lead the way as Letchworth had done in the garden city context. It was unfortunate, for example, that Wythenshawe, designed by Parker, was not commenced in 1918 when it was first mooted, instead of ten years later. Much of Parker's inter-war municipal housing work for various local authorities was of a notably higher quality of environmental design than the norm, but it was on too small a scale and too scattered geographically to catch the professional and public imagination.

8. Postscript

Unwin, the one-time socialist agitator, friend of Morris, Carpenter, Glasier and Hardie, and himself among the founders of the British Labour Party,[233] became a seeming Establishment figure, a high-ranking civil servant who was knighted and honoured. But he did not seek honours, they were bestowed upon him. He never compromised his life-long social or artistic beliefs. His move to the Civil Service, as he believed, was an opportunity to gain lasting and fundamental improvements in living conditions for the mass of the people. It was the 'service of man'.

Parker, too, although leading a more retiring public life and content to take part only in local affairs, was at pains not to compromise his artistic or political principles. This is not to say that Parker and Unwin were inflexible in their thinking, but 'their views were essentially simple and basic.' They were pioneering and radical in their approach and as such it took a long time for their ideas to become generally accepted. They were thus credible professionals throughout their own time. Even towards the end of their careers they were both considered by the 'Establishment' to be rather 'long-haired'.[234]

Official and obituary tributes to Parker and Unwin follow a consistent pattern. It is said that Unwin had singleness of purpose, selflessness, the absence of personal ambition, hopefulness, buoyancy and courage. Parker had wisdom, charm, tolerance and a regard for his fellow men. Parker and Unwin's long record of constructive ability and sincere idealism, always consistently directed to improve and enrich the lives of the people, remains impressive today. Their social idealism, tempered as it was by a scientific approach to every problem, gave immense authority to their leadership in shaping the course of the early modern town planning movement at home and abroad.

NOTES

1 Sir Frederic J. Osborn, typescript, Centenary Address (November 1963), Parker Collection.
2 C.A. Perry, 'The neighbourhood unit – a scheme of arranging for the family-life community', *Regional Survey of New York and its Environs*, VII (1929), 26.
3 *Ibid.*, 75.
4 R. Unwin, 'The planning of towns and suburbs', *JRIBA* (March 1910), 365.

5 *People and Planning; Report of the Committee on Public Participation in Planning* (1969).
6 Speech delivered by R. Unwin at the Dublin Town Planning Competition, November 1916, reported in *TPR*, vii (1917), 105.
7 R. Unwin, 'Presidential inaugural address', *JRIBA*, xxix (1931), 5.
8 *Ibid.*
9 Osborn, *op. cit.*
10 Letter to the author from Carl Feiss, June 1971.
11 B. Parker, 'Sir Raymond Unwin', *JRIBA*, (July 1940), 209.
12 R. Unwin, 'Urban development, pattern and background', *Planners J.* (January 1936), 21. Unwin, with his father, had attended the first meeting of Russell Wallace's Land Nationalization Society in 1882.
13 R. Unwin, 'Presidential inaugural address', 5.
14 S.P. Adshead, *Town Planning Inst. Discussion Papers*, vii (1920–1), 46.
15 Interview with Mrs R.B. Parker, May 1971. Unwin corresponded regularly with Geddes on planning matters and both he and Parker regularly visited Geddes in Edinburgh.
16 H.S. Woodham, 'Interview with Sir Raymond Unwin', *Daily Independent*, 5 December 1932.
17 *Ibid.*
18 G. Beith (ed.), *Edward Carpenter in Appreciation* (1931), 234.
19 R. Unwin, MS note for a speech on the occasion of the presentation of prizes at Magdalen College School, June 1933, Unwin Papers, University of Manchester, File UN 1.7.
20 Letter from R. Unwin to E. Parker, August 1891, HC. (The material referred to as the Hitchcock Collection was the private collection of papers, letters and photographs, held by Mrs Curtis Hitchcock, daughter of Raymond Unwin, at the time the present author was researching this subject.) Ethel Parker, Barry Parker's sister, was half-cousin to Raymond Unwin whom she was later to marry.
21 G. Beith, *op. cit.*, 234.
22 *Ibid.*, 234.
23 Unwin, MS, UN 1.7 Collected Papers, RIBA.
24 Letter from R. Unwin to E. Parker, November 1885, HC.
25 Letter from R. Unwin to E. Parker, May 1883, HC.
26 Interview with Mrs Curtice Hitchcock, Sir Raymond Unwin's daughter, May 1972.
27 Beith, *op. cit.*, 234.
28 Letter from R. Unwin to E. Parker, May 1885, HC.
29 Letter from R. Unwin to E. Parker, October 1885, HC.
30 Woodham, *op. cit.*
31 R. Unwin, Presentation of Memorial to R. Unwin, *JRIBA*, xli (February 1934), 398.
32 R. Unwin, *JRIBA*, xlii (December 1934), 159.
33 W. Morris, 'Art and socialism', Lecture to the Secular Society of Leicester, 23 January 1884, *Collected Works*, xxiii (1915), 209.
34 W. Morris, 'The revival of architecture', *Fortnightly Review* (May 1888), 327.
35 Woodham, *op. cit.*
36 Letter from R. Unwin to E. Parker, November 1885, HC.
37 Letter from R. Unwin to E. Parker, April 1885, HC.
38 Letter from R. Unwin to E. Parker, May 1885, HC.
39 *Commonweal*, August 1885, 72.
40 *MG*, 28 September 1885, 7.
41 Parker, 'Sir Raymond Unwin', 209.
42 Letter to the author from M.W.H. Schreuder, Librarian, The International Institute of Social History, Amsterdam, April 1972.
43 R. Unwin, 'The axe is laid unto the root', *Commonweal*, n.d.
44 R. Unwin, 'Social experiments', *Commonweal*, 5 March 1887.

45 *Ibid.*
46 R. Unwin, 'Socialism and progress', *Commonweal*, 7 April 1888.
47 Letter from R. Unwin to E. Parker, April 1891, HC.
48 Woodham, *op. cit.*
49 Unwin, 'Socialism and progress'.
50 Letter from R. Unwin to E. Parker, 4 November 1885, HC.
51 Letter from R. Unwin to E. Parker, undated, c.1888, HC.
52 Letter from R. Unwin to E. Parker, 9 January 1891, HC.
53 Letter from R. Unwin to E. Parker, undated, c. 1888, HC.
54 J. Murray, *Handbook for Travellers in Derby, Notts., Leicester and Stafford* (3rd edn, 1892), 24.
55 S. Berresford, 'Some notes on the history of the Staveley Coal and Iron Co. Ltd', *Staveley Company's Magazine* (1927).
56 Staveley Coal and Iron Co., Minutes, 155 and 332.
57 R.B. Parker, 'The life and work of Sir Raymond Unwin', *TPIJ*, xxvi (July/August 1940), 160.
58 J.E. Williams, *The Derbyshire Miners: a study in industrial and social history* (1962), 451.
59 Staveley Coal and Iron Co., Minutes, 251.
60 R.B. Parker, in the *Craftsman*, xvii (January 1910), 416.
61 Notebook, May 1888, Parker Collection.
62 Parker, *Craftsman*, 416.
63 W. Tomlinson, *The Pictorial Record of the Royal Jubilee Exhibition in Manchester 1887* (1888), 67.
64 W.L. Creese, *The Search for Environment – The Garden City: Before and After* (1965), 247.
65 Tomlinson, *op. cit.*, 67.
66 R. Unwin, Diary, 1887, Town and Country Planning Dept, Manchester University.
67 Parker, *Craftsman*, 416.
68 Interview with Mrs R.B. Parker, May 1971.
69 N. Pevsner, *The Buildings of England: Herefordshire* (1963), 91.
70 Interview with Mrs R.B. Parker, May 1971.
71 Parker, 'Sir Raymond Unwin', 209.
72 Staveley Coal and Iron Co., Minutes, 231.
73 N. Pevsner, *The Buildings of England: Derbyshire* (1953), 57.
74 Staveley Coal and Iron Co., Minutes, 193.
75 R.B. Parker, 'Presentation of the Royal Gold Medal to Sir Raymond Unwin', *JRIBA*, xliv (April 1937), 582.
76 Parker, 'Sir Raymond Unwin', 161.
77 Parker, 'Presentation of the Royal Gold Medal to Sir Raymond Unwin', 582.
78 Interview with Mrs R.B. Parker, May 1971.
79 Letter from R. Unwin to E. Parker, August 1891, HC.
80 R. Unwin, *JRIBA*, xli (February 1934), 398.
81 Parker, 'Sir Raymond Unwin', 209.
82 *Ibid.*, 209.
83 R.B. Parker and R. Unwin, 'Cottages near a town', *Exhibition Catalogue of the Northern Art Workers' Guild, Manchester* (1903), 34–43. Parker and Unwin had been members of the Guild since at least 1901 and were both members of its council by 1903.
84 L. Thompson, *The Enthusiasts* (1971), 135.
85 R.B. Parker, 'Some principles underlying domestic architecture', *BA*, xxxxiii (March 1895), 181.
86 R.B. Parker, 'The artist', *Letchworth Magazine*, June 1907, 69.
87 R.B. Parker and R. Unwin, *The Art of Building a Home* (1901), 38.

88 R.B. Parker, 'Our homes', *BN*, 19 July 1895, 103.
89 R.B. Parker, 'Materials', *Letchworth Magazine*, September 1907, 30.
90 R.B. Parker, 'The planning of a small house', *City*, I (1909), 142.
91 Parker, 'Materials', 30.
92 Parker and Unwin, *The Art of Building a Home*, 86.
93 Parker, 'Materials', 31.
94 Parker, 'Our homes', 98.
95 Interview with Mrs R.B. Parker, May 1971.
96 Creese, *op. cit.*, 247.
97 Parker, 'Our homes', 108.
98 Parker and Unwin, 'The art of designing small houses and cottages', *ACR*, 8 February 1901, 98.
99 Parker, 'Our homes', 96.
100 *Ibid.*, 105.
101 Interview with Captain M.B. Glasier, November 1971.
102 Interview with Mrs R.B. Parker, May 1971.
103 Parker, 'Some principles underlying domestic architecture', 181.
104 Parker and Unwin, *The Art of Building a Home*, 92.
105 *Ibid.*, 97.
106 *Ibid.*, 83.
107 *Ibid.*, 97.
108 Joseph Rowntree Village Trust, Minutes, December 1904. At the time of its foundation the assets of the Joseph Rowntree Village Trust were estimated to be £62,165.
109 G.B. Brown, 'The Joseph Rowntree Village Trust', *GC*, n.s.I (1906), 169. G.B. Brown was clerk of works to the Joseph Rowntree Village Trust until his resignation in December 1910.
110 'New Earswick, York', *Handbook of the Joseph Rowntree Village Trust* (July 1913), 3.
111 R.B. Parker, 'Earswick, Yorks.' (6 October 1923), offprint, Parker Collection, 3.
112 Interview with Rendel Ridges, resident and past editor of the 'New Earswick Village Bulletin'.
113 'New Earswick, York', 4.
114 L.E. Waddilove (ed.), *One Man's Vision; the story of the Joseph Rowntree Village Trust* (1954), 12. In fact the prefix 'New' did not appear in the Joseph Rowntree Village Trust minutes until 1910.
115 Parker, 'Earswick, Yorks', 3.
116 Joseph Rowntree Village Trust, Minutes, November 1907.
117 Costs per cottage were up to and over £300.
118 Parker, 'Earswick, Yorks', 3.
119 R. Unwin, 'Speech moving the first resolution at the Garden Cities Conference, Bournville', *Report of Proceedings* (2nd edn., 1901), 14.
120 R. Unwin, 'Cottage plans and common sense' (Fabian Tract no. 109, 1902), 3.
121 Parker and Unwin, 'Cottages near a town', 36.
122 Parker, 'Sir Raymond Unwin', 161.
123 Unwin, 'Cottage plans and commonsense', 4.
124 Parker and Unwin, 'Cottages near a town', 36.
125 Unwin, 'Cottage plans and common sense', 4.
126 Unwin, *Nothing Gained by Overcrowding*.
127 G.B. Brown, 'The Joseph Rowntree Village Trust', *GC*, n.s.I (1906), 197.
128 Unwin, 'Cottage plans and common sense', 4.
129 *Ibid.*, 4.
130 By the first meeting of the Joseph Rowntree Village Trust in December 1904, 31 cottages had been completed and occupied.
131 Interview with Mr Graham, clerk of works, New Earswick (1971).

132 Unwin, 'Cottage plans and common sense', 2.
133 Although these cottages were designed during this period the first were not built until 1906.
134 Unwin, 'Cottage plans and common sense', 6.
135 *Ibid.*, 14.
136 Garden City Conference, Bournville, *Report of Proceedings* (2nd edn, 1901), 11. This was the first conference of the Association. Speeches were made by Earl Grey, Ralph Neville, George Cadbury, Ebenezer Howard, George Bernard Shaw and Raymond Unwin. Others attending included Seebohm Rowntree and Walter Crane.
137 N. Macfadyen, 'The fight for the Garden City', *Town and Country Planning* (September 1953), 407.
138 Reprinted as *Garden Cities of Tomorrow* (1970).
139 Garden City Conference, Bournville, *Report of Proceedings* (2nd edn, 1901), 11.
140 See W.A. Eden, 'Ebenezer Howard and the Garden City Movement', *TPR*, xix (1947), 123–43; D. Macfadyen, *Sir Ebenezer Howard and the Town Planning Movement* (1933); W.L. Creese, *The Search for Environment – The Garden City: Before and After* (1966); W. Petersen, The ideological origins of British New Towns', *American Inst. of Planners J.*, (May 1968), 160–70.
141 F.J. Osborn, preface to *Garden Cities of Tomorrow* (1970), 11.
142 Interview with Mrs R.B. Parker, May 1971.
143 Parker, 'Sir Raymond Unwin', 209.
144 C.B. Purdom, 'At the inception of Letchworth', *Town and Country Planning* (September 1953), 429.
145 R. Unwin, 'Making the plan of Letchworth', *Garden Cities and Town Planning*, xx (June/July 1930), 156.
146 Unwin, *Town Planning in Practice*, 225.
147 Unwin, 'Letchworth', 156.
148 R. Unwin, 'The improvement of towns', paper to the National Union of Women Workers of Great Britain and Ireland, November 1904, 1.
149 R. Unwin, 'On building of houses in the Garden City', Garden City Conference, *Report of Proceedings* (2nd edn, 1901), 73.
150 R.B. Parker, 'Re Letchworth plan, 1904', typescript Memorandum (1938), Parker Collection.
151 Unwin, 'The improvement of towns', 4.
152 T. Adams (ed.), *Guide to Garden City* (1906), 10.
153 Parker, 'Re Letchworth plan, 1904'.
154 Unwin, 'Letchworth', 156.
155 *Ibid.*
156 *Ibid.*
157 *Ibid.*
158 Unwin, *Town Planning in Practice*, 240, and P.M. Wolf, *Eugène Hénard and the Beginning of Urbanism in Paris* (1968).
159 Ebenezer Howard, reprint of an article of August 1906, *Town and Country Planning* (October 1954), 527. See also R. Unwin, 'Cottage planning', *Catalogue of the Urban Cottage and Rural Homesteads Exhibition, Letchworth* (1907), 103.
160 Purdom, 'At the inception of Letchworth', 427.
161 *Ibid.*, 429.
162 Thomas Adams (ed.), 'How the Exhibition came about', *Catalogue of the Cheap Cottages Exhibition* (1905), 11.
163 *Ibid.*, 17.
164 R.B. Parker and R. Unwin, 'The cheap cottage: what is really needed', *GC*, o.s.i (1905), 55.
165 R. Unwin, 'Cottage planning', 104.

166 Parker and Unwin, 'The cheap cottage: what is really needed', 104.
167 Unwin, 'The improvement of towns', 2.
168 *Ibid.*, 3.
169 Henry Vivian, MP, 'The Garden City tenants scheme', *Catalogue of the Urban Cottages and Rural Homesteads Exhibition, Letchworth* (1907), 57.
170 Unwin, 'Making the plan for Letchworth', 156.
171 'First Garden City Ltd, suggestions and instructions regarding building other than factories on the Garden City Estate, June 1904', First Garden City and Corporation File C13, Letchworth Museum and Art Gallery.
172 Interview with Mrs R.B. Parker, May 1971.
173 Freda White, typescript 'Memoir of Raymond Unwin', Parker Collection.
174 H. Barnett, *The Story of the Growth of the Hampstead Garden Suburb 1907–1928* (1928), 5.
175 R. Unwin, 'Town planning at Hampstead', *Garden City and Town Planning*, I (1911), 6.
176 S.A. and H. Barnett, *Towards Social Reform* (1909), 339.
177 Barnett, *op. cit.*, 7.
178 *Ibid.*, 7.
179 Interview with Mrs E. Unwin, the widow of Sir Raymond Unwin's son, Edward, November 1971.
180 S.A. and H. Barnett, *op. cit.*, 345.
181 The Hampstead Garden Suburb Trust Ltd, *The Story of the Garden Suburb at Hampstead* (1908), 23.
182 *Ibid.*, 24.
183 R. Unwin, 'Hampstead Garden Suburb', *RIBA Town Planning Conference, Members' Handbook* (1910), 70.
184 G. Stickley, 'The growth of the Garden City Movement', *Craftsman*, XVII (December 1909), 308.
185 W.A. Eden, 'Hampstead Garden Suburb 1907–1957', *JRIBA* (1957), 494.
186 Parker, 'Sir Raymond Unwin', 161.
187 *Ibid.*, 161.
188 The Hampstead Garden Suburb Act, 1906.
189 *Ibid.*, 1.
190 Hampstead Garden Suburb Trust Ltd, *The Hampstead Garden Suburb, Its Achievements and Significance* (1928).
191 G. Atkinson, 'Raymond Unwin: founding father of Building Research Station', *JRIBA*, (October 1971), 446.
192 Unwin, 'Hampstead Garden Suburb', 70.
193 Parker and Unwin, *The Art of Building a Home*.
194 Interview with Mrs R.B. Parker, May 1971.
195 R. Unwin, 'The planning of residential districts of towns', *Trans. 7th International Congress of Architects* (RIBA, 1906).
196 H. Inigo Triggs, *Town Planning, Past, Present and Possible* (1909).
197 Barnett, *op. cit.*, 20.
198 R. Unwin, Preface to *Town Planning and Modern Architecture in the Hampstead Garden Suburb* (1908).
199 *Ibid.*
200 Unwin, 'Hampstead Garden Suburb', 70.
201 'Progress at Hampstead', *Garden City and Town Planning*, n.s. III (1908), 80.
202 M.R. Hughes (ed.), *The Letters of Lewis Mumford and Frederic J. Osborn: A Transatlantic Dialogue 1938–70* (1971), 58.
203 Interview with Mrs Curtice Hitchcock, May 1972.
204 Hughes, *op. cit.*, 59.
205 *Ibid.*, 134.

206 Unwin, *Nothing Gained by Overcrowding*, 5.
207 *Ibid.*, 7.
208 Interview with Mrs R.B. Parker, May 1971.
209 Hughes, *op. cit.*, 102.
210 Letter to the author from Charles Ascher, July 1971. Ascher had been the attorney for the Radburn development.
211 *Report of the committee to consider questions of building construction in connection with the provision of dwellings for the working classes in England and Wales and Scotland, and report upon methods of securing economy and despatch in the provision of such dwellings*, Cd.9191 (HMSO, 1918).
212 Atkinson, *op. cit.*, 446.
213 R. Unwin, *The War and What After* (1915). Unwin was an active member of the League of Nations Union, a pressure group which saw its work come to fruition with the founding of the League of Nations in 1920.
214 C.S. Stein, 'Housing and reconstruction', *J. American Inst. Architects*, VI (1918), 469.
215 C. Whitacker, 'Eastriggs – an industrial town built by the British government', *J. American Inst. Architects*, V (1917), 499, and F.L. Ackerman, 'The significance of England's programme of building workmen's houses', *J. American Inst. Architects*, V (1917), 539.
216 R.S. Childs, 'Yorkship Village', *J. American Inst. Architects*, VI (1918), 249.
217 F.L. Ackerman, 'An appraisal of war housing', *Pencil Points*, September 1940, 535–45.
218 This recommendation was partly implemented in the Housing and Town Planning Act, 1919.
219 This idea was first put forward by Unwin in 'Cottage planning', 103.
220 Unwin, 'The improvement of towns', 4–5.
221 *Ibid.*, 2–3.
222 These ideas appear in Unwin's 'Cottage plans and common sense', and in *Nothing Gained by Overcrowding*.
223 This idea is stressed in Parker and Unwin's 'Cottages near a town'.
224 Unwin, *Town Planning in Practice*, 289–318.
225 Similar standards to those incorporated into the report were first publicized by Parker and Unwin in 'The cheap cottage: what is really needed' and Unwin's 'Cottage building in the Garden City', *GC*, n.s. I, (1906).
226 This was first shown in plan form in Unwin's 'Cottage plans and common sense', 9.
227 The advantages of both had been reiterated in the writings of the partners since 1902.
228 See especially the criticisms of T. Sharp in *Town and Countryside* (1937).
229 R. Unwin, 'First Resolution to the Garden City Conference at Bournville, 1901', *Report of Proceedings* (2nd edn, 1901), 14.
230 Letter to the author from Trystan Edwards, November 1971 (Trystan Edwards was a member of Unwin's staff at the Ministry of Health, 1919–25).
231 *Ibid.*
232 L. Mumford. 'England's two million houses, new', *Fortune*, VI (1932), 84.
233 Freda White, Unwin's cousin, TS biographical note, September 1962, Parker Collection.
234 Interview with Mrs Curtice Hitchcock, May 1972.

BIBLIOGRAPHY

Adams, M.B., *Modern Cottage Architecture* (2nd edn, 1912)

Adams, T., *Recent Advances in Town Planning* (1932)

Aldridge, H., *The Case for Town Planning: a practical manual for the use of councillors, officers and others engaged in the preparation of town planning schemes* (1915)

Armytage, W.H.G., *Heavens Below: utopian experiments in England 1560–1960* (1961)

Ashton, T.S., *Economic and Social Investigation in Manchester 1833–1933* (1934)

Ashworth, W.A., *The Genesis of Modern British Town Planning* (1954)

Barnett, H., *Canon Barnett: his life, work and friends* (1921)

Barnett, H., *The Story of the Growth of Hampstead Garden Suburb, 1907–1928* (1928)

Barnett, S.A. and H., *Towards Social Reform* (1909)

Beith, G. (ed.), *Edward Carpenter in Appreciation* (1931)

Boardman, P., *Patrick Geddes: maker of the future* (1944)

Boardman, P., *The Worlds of Patrick Geddes: biologist, town planner, re-educator, peace-warrior* (1978)

Bonham-Carter, E., 'Planning and development of Letchworth Garden City', *TPR*, xxi (1950), 362–76

Bournville Village Trust, *The Bournville Village Trust, 1900–1955* (1955)

Briggs, A., *Social Thought and Social Action: a study of the work of Seebohm Rowntree, 1871–1954* (1961)

Cadbury, G. Jun., *Town Planning With Special Reference to the Birmingham Schemes* (1915)

Cherry, G., *The Evolution of British Town Planning* (1974)

Cherry, G.E., 'The town planning movement and the late Victorian city', *Inst. British Geographers Trans.*, n.s.iv (1979), 306–19

Cockrill, J., 'The position of town planning in Great Britain, 1916', *J. Inst. Municipal and County Engineers*, xlii (1916), 453–87

Collins, G.R. and C.C., *Camillo Sitte and the Birth of Modern City Planning* (1965)

Creese, W.L., *The Legacy of Raymond Unwin: a human pattern for planning* (1967)

Creese, W.L., *The Search for Environment: the garden city, before and after* (1966)

Culpin, E.G., *The Garden City Movement Up-To-Date* (1913)

Darley, G., *Villages of Vision* (1975)

Day, M.G., and Garstang, K., 'Socialist theories and Sir Raymond Unwin', *Town and Country Planning*, xliii (1975), 346–9

Dewsnup, E.R., *The Housing Problem in England: its statistics, legislation and policy* (1907)

Fishman, R., *Urban Utopias in the Twentieth Century: Ebenezer Howard, Frank Lloyd Wright, and Le Corbusier* (1977)

(Garden City Association), *The Practical Application of Town Planning Powers: Report of National Town Planning Conference* (1909)

(Garden City Association), *Town Planning in Theory and Practice* (1908)

Gardiner, A.G., *Life of George Cadbury* (1923)

Gaskell, S.M., 'Sheffield City Council and the development of suburban areas prior to World War I', in S. Pollard and C. Holmes (eds), *Essays in the Economic and Social History of South Yorkshire* (1976), 174–86

Geddes, P., *Cities in Evolution: an introduction to the town planning movement and to the study of civics* (1915)

Geddes, P., *City Development: a study of parks, gardens and culture-institutes* (1904)

George, W.L., *Labour and Housing at Port Sunlight* (1909)

Gibbs, E.M., *The Future Extension of the Suburbs of Sheffield: a lecture delivered to the Sheffield Society of Architects and Surveyors* (1911)

Gotch, J.A., (ed.), *The Growth and Work of the Royal Institute of British Architects 1834–1934* (1934)

Grafton Green, B., *Hampstead Garden Suburb, 1907–1977* (1977)

Hampstead Tenants Ltd, *Cottages with Gardens for Londoners* (1907)

Hardy, D., *Alternative Communities in Nineteenth Century England* (1979)

Harris, G.M., *The Garden City Movement* (1905)

Harrison, M., 'Burnage garden village: an ideal for life in Manchester', *TPR*, XLVII (1976), 256–68

Hawkes, D., 'The architectural partnership of Barry Parker and Raymond Unwin, 1896–1914', *AR*, CLXII (1978), 327–32

Henderson, P., *William Morris: life, work and friends* (1967)

Higgs, M., *Glimpses into the Abyss* (1902)

Horsfall, T.C., 'An address on the planning and control of town extensions in Germany', *Procs. Inc. Ass. Municipal and County Engineers*, XXXIII (1906–7), 70–82

Horsfall, T.C., *The Improvement of the Dwellings and Surroundings of the People: the example of Germany* (1904)

Horsfall, T.C., *The Relation of Town Planning to National Life* (1908)

Howard, E., *Garden Cities of Tomorrow* (ed. F.J. Osborn, 1946)

Howkins, F., *An Introduction to the Development of Private Building Estates and Town Planning* (1926)

Hughes, M.R. (ed.), *The Letters of Lewis Mumford and Frederic J. Osborn: a transatlantic dialogue 1938–70* (1971)

Jenkins, F., *Architect and Patron* (1961)

Johnson, P.B., *Land Fit for Heroes: the planning of British Reconstruction 1916–19* (1968)

Kaye, B., *The Development of the Architectural Profession in Britain* (1960)

Kitchen, P., *A Most Unsettling Person: an introduction to the ideas and life of Patrick Geddes* (1975)

Land Enquiry Committee, *The Land: The Report of the Land Enquiry Committee*, vol. II: *Urban* (1914)

Lever, W.H., *The Buildings Erected at Port Sunlight and Thornton Hough* (1902)

Macfadyen, D., *Sir Ebenezer Howard and the Town Planning Movement* (1933)

Mairet, P., *Pioneer of Sociology: the life and letters of Patrick Geddes* (1957)

Masterman, C.F.G., *The Condition of England* (1909)

Masterman, C.F.G. (ed.), *The Heart of the Empire: discussions of problems of modern city life in England, with an essay on imperialism* (1901)

Mawson, T.H., *Civic Art Studies in Town Planning, Parks, Boulevards and Open Spaces* (1911)

Mawson, T.H., *The Life and Work of an English Landscape Architect* (1927)

Mawson, T.H., *Scheme for Pittencrieff Park Glen and City Improvements* (1904)

Meakin, B., *Model Factories and Villages: ideal conditions of labour and housing* (1905)

Meller, H.E., 'Patrick Geddes: an analysis of his theory of civics, 1880–1904', *Victorian Studies*, XVI (1973), 291–316

National Housing and Town Planning Council, *1900–1910: A Record of Ten Years Work for Housing and Town Planning Reform* (n.d. [1910?])

Nettlefold, J.S., *Practical Housing* (1908)

Nettlefold, J.S., *Practical Town Planning* (1914)

Osborn, F.J., *Green Belt Cities: the British contribution* (1946, 1969)

Parker, R.B. and Unwin, R., *The Art of Building a Home* (1901)

Parsons, J., *Housing by Voluntary Enterprise* (1903)

Purdom, C.B., *The Building of Satellite Towns: a contribution to the study of town development and regional planning* (1925)

Purdom, C.B., *The Garden City: a study in the development of the modern town* (1913)

Purdom, C.B., *The Letchworth Achievement* (1963)

Purdom, C.B. (ed.), *Town Theory and Practice* (1921)

Reynolds, J.P., 'The model village of Port Sunlight', *Architects' J.*, cvii (1948), 492–6

Reynolds, J.P., 'Thomas Coglan Horsfall and the town planning movement in England', *TPR*, xxiii (1952), 52–60

Royal Institute of British Architects, *Town Planning Conference; London, 10–15 October 1910: Transactions* (1911)

Scott, M.H. Baillie (ed.), *Garden Suburbs, Town Planning and Modern Architecture* (2nd edn, 1910)

Searle, G.R., *The Quest for National Efficiency* (1971)

Sennet, A.R., *Garden Cities in Theory and Practice* (2 vols, 1905)

Sidebotham, E.W., *Burnage* (1925)

Tarn, J.N., *Five Per Cent Philanthropy: An Account of Housing in Urban Areas Between 1840 and 1914* (1973)

Thompson, F.L., *Site Planning in Practice* (1923)

Thompson, F.M.L., *Chartered Surveyors: the growth of a profession* (1968)

Thompson, F.M.L., *Hampstead: building a borough, 1650–1964* (1976)

Thompson, L., *The Enthusiasts* (1971)

Thompson, W., *The Housing Handbook Up-to-Date* (1907)

Triggs, H. Inigo, *Town Planning: past, present and possible* (1909)

Unwin, R., *Cottage Plans and Common Sense* (1902)

Unwin, R., *Nothing Gained by Overcrowding! How the Garden City Type of Development May Benefit Both the Owner and the Occupier* (1912)

Unwin, R., *Town Planning in Practice: an introduction to the art of designing cities and suburbs* (1909)

Unwin, R., and Scott, M. Baillie, *Town Planning and Modern Architecture at the Hampstead Garden Suburb* (1909)

Vivian, H., *Co-Partnership in Housing in its Health Relationship* (1908)

Waddilove, L. E. (ed.), *One Man's Vision: the story of the Joseph Rowntree Village Trust* (1954)

Walters, J. Tudor, *The Building of Twelve Thousand Houses* (1927)

Waterhouse, P. and Unwin, R., *Old Towns and New Needs: also The Town Extension Plan: being the Warburton Lectures for 1912* (1912)

Weaver, L., *The Country Life Book of Cottages* (2nd edn, 1919)

Wike, C.F., *Description of Town Planning and Housing in Sheffield: Paper Read at a Conference . . . of the Institute of Municipal and County Engineers* (1913)

Yerbury, J.E., *A Short History of the Pioneer Society in Co-operative Housing* (1913)

INDEX

Abercrombie, P., 11, 47–8, 95–6, 114, 126
Adams, M., 29
Adams, T., 11, 79–80, 87; departure from
    Letchworth 9, 83; early career 81;
    foundation of Town Planning Institute,
    10, 66, 92–4, 96–7, 99; garden suburb
    plans, 84, 90–1; Letchworth work,
    178–9; Local Government Board work,
    92–3, 189; secretary of Garden City
    Association, 81–3; studies of, 6
Addison, C., 191
Adshead, S., 28, 95–7, 100, 158
Agate, C., 126–7
Aintree, 89
Alderdale, 118
Aldridge, H., 116
Alkrington, 42–3, 84, 86, 116, 128–9
Allotments and Smallholdings Association,
    25
Anchor Tenants Estate, 52
Ancoats, 109–14, 117
Ancoats Brotherhood, 161
Ancoats Healthy Homes Society, 112
Ancoats Recreation Movement, 118
Angel Meadow, 112
Archer, J., 138
architectural profession, 65–6, 71–5, 84
Ardwick and Longsight, 112
Arkwright Town, 162
Armitage, G., 163
Arts and Crafts movement, 156
Ashton, M., 124
Ashworth, W., 5–8, 18, 20, 39, 44, 145
Association for Improving the Condition of
    the People, 25
Association of Municipal Corporations, 185
Association of Municipal Engineers, 68, 76

Baillie-Scott, C., 118
Bainbridge, E., 162
Baker, H., 111
Bannerman, H. C., 41
Barlborough, 162
Barnett, H.
    and Hampstead Garden Suburb, 67–9,
        181–2, 185; influence on Unwin, 9;
        interest in Unwin, 82
Barnett, S., 9, 160, 181
Barrow, 75
Barrow Hill, 162
Beautiful Oldham Society, 36

Belcher, J., 72
Bennett, R., 174, 179
Bidwell, W., 179
Birkett, J., 97
Birmingham, 2–3, 47, 77, 123; bye-law
    housing, 23; Nettlefold's work in, 18
Birmingham University, 94, 158, 189
Blackburn, 91
Blackley, 43, 47, 118–23
Blatchford, R., 112
Blomfield, R., 95
Blow, D., 84
Boer War, 113, 144
Bolsover, 162
Bolton, 91
Bond, G., 162
Booth, C., 110
Bournville, 39; architecture, 23; conference
    at, 83, 169; influence of, 68, 115, 123,
    133, 137; rents, 26; road widths, 26
Bournville Village Trust, 189
Bradford, 45
Bristol, 84
British Architect, 122
British Association for the Advancement of
    Science, 122
Brown, F., 161
Brown, H., 81
Buder, S., 83
Builder, 73, 79
Building Research Station, 189
building societies, 29–30
building bye-laws, 26–9, 43–5, 184
Burnage, 34, 37, 123–32, 137
Burns, J.
    parliamentary speeches, 19, 41; relations
        with architectural profession, 74;
        support for Hampstead Garden Suburb
        Act, 184; and Town Planning Act, 19,
        41–2, 65, 185; and Town Planning
        Institute; 98; views on garden suburbs,
        145

Cadbury, G., 23, 46–7, 67–9, 83, 89, 169, 182
Camberwell, 31
Canada, 89, 93
Carlyle, T., 80
Carnegie, A., 91
Carnegie Trust, 82
Carpenter, E., 9, 80, 156, 159–60
Chadwick, E., 67–8, 70–1

205

Index